Lightweight Cycle Components
Volume I

Steve Griffith

The John Pinkerton Memorial Publishing Fund
Following the untimely death of John Pinkerton in 2002, a proposal was made to set up a fund in his memory.

The objective of the Fund is to continue the publishing activities initiated by John Pinkerton, that is to publish historical material on the development of the cycle of all types and related activities. This will include reprints of significant cycling journal articles, manufacturers' technical information including catalogues, parts lists, drawings and other technical information.

Published by the John Pinkerton Memorial Publishing Fund, (a part of the Veteran-Cycle Club. www.v-cc.org.uk)
© John Pinkerton Memorial Publishing Fund 2013
Reprinted with minor additions **October 2013**
Design and layout by Brian Hayward JPMPF
Thanks to Stephen Trott, Clive Foreman and Cyril Hancock for final proofing
Printed by Quorum Print Ltd, Cheltenham, England
ISBN 978-0-9566337-9-8

JPMPF Publication List:-

- *Lightweight Cycle Catalogue Volume 1*: (2005)
- *An Encyclopaedia of Cycle Manufacturers* - compiled by Ray Miller: (2006)
- *Frederick H Pratt and Sons* - Complete Cycle Engineers - Alvin J E Smith: (2006)
- *The Electric-Powered Bicycle Lamp 1888-1948* - Peter W Card: (2006)
- *The Pedersen Hub Gear* - Cyril J Hancock: (2007)
- *It wasn't that Easy. The Tommy Godwin Story* - Tommy Godwin: (2007)
- *The End to End & 1000 Miles Records* - Willie Welsh: (2007)
- *Lightweight Cycle Catalogue Vol II*: (2007)
- *Origins of Bicycle Racing in England* - Andrew Ritchie: (2007)
- *Here Are Wings* - Maurice Leblanc (Translation by Scotford Lawrence): (2008)
- *The Origins of the Bicycle* - Andrew Ritchie: (2009)
- *Lightweight Cycle Catalogue Vol III*: (2009)
- *East Anglian Rides* - Charles Staniland, Edited by Gerry Moore; (2009)
- *The Stanley Show, Review* 1878 to 1889 & Catalogue 1890: (2009)
- *Flying Yankee* - The International Career of Arthur Augustus Zimmerman - Andrew Ritchie: (2009)
- *An Encyclopaedia of Cycle Manufacturers* - 2nd Edition- compiled by Ray Miller: (2009)
- *Cycle History 19*- Proceedings of the 19th ICHC, Saint-Etienne, France, 2008: (2010)
- *Cycle History 20* - Proceedings of the 20th ICHC, Freehold, New Jersey, USA 2009: (2010)
- *Boneshaker Reprints Vol 5, Issues 41-50*: (2010)
- *The Veteran-Cycle Club 1955-2005* - compiled by Cyril Hancock: (2010)
- *A History of the Tricycle* - Roger Alma, Cyril J Hancock and Derek Roberts (2011)
- *Marque Album No. 1 Centaur* - Alvin Smith & Lionel Ferris (2011)
- *Cycling History No. 1, Malvern Cycling Club 1883-1912* - Roger Alma (2011)
- *Marque Album No. 2, Ivel* - Ray Miller & Lee Irvine (2011)
- *Dan Albone, Cyclist, Inventor & Manufacturer.* - Ray Miller & Lee Irvine (2011)
- *Cycling History No. 2 - Rough Stuff, Charly Chadwick Story.* David Warner (2012)
- *Marque Album No. 3 - Rensch - PARIS* - Alvin Smith at al (2012)
- *Cycling History No 3 - Vernon Blake 1875 - 1930* - Steve Griffith (2012)
- *Cycling History No. 4 - Charlie Davey* - Christine Watts (2012)
- *Cycling History No. 5 - Herne Hill,* John Watts (2013)

All publications are available through the Veteran-Cycle Club Sale Officer.
www.v-cc.org.uk

Back cover from Ron Kitching's 1960 catalogue *Everything Cycling* from which some of the illustrations in this book have been taken

CONTENTS

Image from Resilion leaflet c. 1947

FORWORD

Steve is a publisher's dream, contact him close to publication for some additional copy and it will be on your desktop within hours. Alternatively discuss some obscure item or event and again within a couple of days something will arrive ready for uploading.

He sometimes delves into the subjects that may be considered a bit below the radar and has produced article after article on the components regarded as less than the 'cream' by many collectors, yet which had to be used by cyclists of the classic period due to financial constraints. Surely everyone would have liked the blue-chip specification of Chater, Harden/ Airlite with Conloy, top-of-the range Campag and Brooks, on the best frame on the market but in reality, for many, the cheaper components were the only option, a fact recognised by Holdsworth and Kitching who produced their own-brand selection of more-affordable parts. It is an ironic fact that most collectors these day only fit the very best parts as they can afford them now, making up for the premium components they couldn't have in their youth. Assuming of course that they were around in that period.

Having said that, Steve has also produced masterpieces on companies such as Harden and Constrictor and his interests cover many of the Continental makes not so well known on these shores. Like myself, Steve likes to follow the fortunes of these manufacturers beyond what is loosely defined as the classic era and to study the way they developed - or didn't - and how new markets were created by incoming manufacturers such as those from the Far East

PETER UNDERWOOD

Front cover from Ron Kitching 's 1960 catalogue

INTRODUCTION

When I started writing about components my original intention was to provide a time line and sort of family tree showing development and changes against this. I was unable to create a satisfactory format so I resorted to writing up a manufacturer's history adding in a bit of technical information and trying to place this in a wider social context. For example many European manufacturers failed to understand the growth of the Mountain Bicycle in the 1980's and Far East Asian competition which effectively leads to the decline and in some cases end of their business

I originally wrote about personal favourites for example Mafac and Lucifer. Then I decided to concentrate on often ignored companies who I felt deserved to be recorded for posterity, for example Bayliss Wiley.

In the V-CC many members are naturally very interested in the different products and what is period correct. Hopefully this volume will enable readers to understand this although of course over time many machines if they were used at all would have been upgraded with newer components as things worn out .

The majority of the articles originally appeared in V-CC publications; however one of the benefits is that after publication new information comes to light this is one of the real strengths of the V-CC. Thus this book is an opportunity to revise and correct many of the original articles. I have added catalogue extracts as a means of providing further information an option I would not have with magazine publication due to lack of space

Reading through I am struck by the similarities e.g. many British companies declined in the 50s and similarly many European ones in the late 80s early 90's. The causes were similar; an unwillingness to change, inability to understand the changing market and not able to compete with a superior often Japanese product. For example TA cranks (a design dating back to the 1930s) were simply not compatible with the new more effective design of front mech which required a much bigger clearance between crank arm and outer chainring.

For each manufacturer I have sought to provide a comprehensive account not just focusing on the most popular or more successful products. I was surprised just how many products Weinmann for example made, chainsets, wingnuts, stems yet they are really only known for brakes and rims.

Steve Griffith

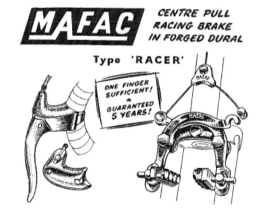

The classic and very distinctive centre-pull design made with minor changes 1951 to the mid 1980s

INDEX FOR STEVE GRIFFITH V-CC ARTICLES
The Boneshaker

News and Views

Articles in **BOLD type** are reproduced with updates in this publication

News and Views continued

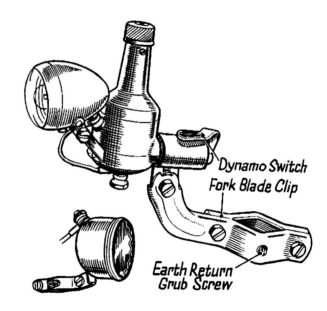

Lucifer Sports Baby 800 (1949-1965) with seat stay fitting rear light

A Guide to Dating Components

Probably one of the first questions we ask about any bike or component is; how old is it? Apart from the frame number there are a number of components that have their own date code which may be an aid to dating.

Of course this assumes that the parts are original, so be careful. Well known and useful guides to dating (components which were widely used and made over a long period of time):

Sturmey Archer

All hubs from the early 30s has the last digit of the year of manufacture e.g. a 7 is 1937. Post-WW2 they have the year and month e.g. 52 6 is June 1952; this carried on right up to the end of the 1980s.

Fig. 1 Sturmey Archer hub dating: a 1936 TC hub. Pre-war hubs had the last letter of the year, later hubs have the 2 digits of the year and the month

Williams Cranks and Chainrings

Williams featured a letter date code from 1913 right up to their demise in the early 70s (see Williams article in this book). The letters are usually found on the inside of the crank arm near the cotter end and below the Williams sword logo. It is not uncommon to find chainrings with a later date than cranks so check both.

Campagnolo Record and Tipo hubs

Year of manufacture is on the inner side of the locknut; the earliest I have seen is 56 and the latest 83. Campag hubs were made by FB in the '50s and their hubs have the same system marked eg FB 51. Other Campag components also have dates, Nuovo Record rear mechs have the year on the upper body. Cranks have the last digit of the year inside a shape, a diamond for the 70s and a circle for the 80s.

Weinmann Brakes

Starting in the early 70s sidepulls and centre pulls have the year and in some case the month on one of the inner arms. Many Dia Compe brakes also use the same system. Some Weinmann brakes have the year in the middle of a ring of numbers with a line pointing to the month. Some Weinmann rims have in the well a letter followed by two numbers which is the year eg S81 = 1981 Another indication of age is if the Weinmann rim or brake is marked 'Made in Belgium' it is a later product, probably 1980s.

Normandy, Maillard, Atom and Le Tour hubs

This is an extended French family of seemingly interchangeable names. Pre- 1970 these hubs have no dates but in the 70s and 80s on the hub barrel is the year and month. So if it hasn't got a date it's older. A couple of other useful ways to date these very widely used hubs: if the cut outs on the large flanges are round its older that the later ones that were slotted. Older Atom hubs have the name in script rather than stamped.

Lucifer Dynamos

All Lucifer dynamos have a six figure serial number. With the introduction of the Baby series at the end of WW2 a letter prefix indicating year was introduced. The most common is D which was 49/50 and the series ends at Y, 1969/70. The first generation 700 series without a badge is 1940 to 1946, the 800 was introduced in 1949 and the 900 series in 1966. Lucifer dynamos without the letter prefix are 1940. Amazing to think that every dynamo was given an individual serial number!

Brooks' Saddles

Any saddle with an oval badge is pre-mid '50s. From the late '50s Brooks started putting the year on the cantle plate at the side. Often this needs some cleaning up to find. Many Brooks' saddles have a single letter, two digit code eg 9K9; unfortunately the code book to decipher this has been lost.

Fig. 2 Lucifer badged by the Dutch importers showing the D prefix indicating 49/50

Lucas

Most Lucas bells, milometers, lamps and dynamos have the two digits of the year. On bells this can be difficult to find sometimes being on the clip body or even on the inner workings.

Shimano

Shimano use a letter system (still current) which is alphabetical to indicate year and month .This started in 1976 with A the second letter is the month with A being January; thus BD is April 1977. As they exhausted the alphabet with Z being 2001 A is also 2002. For gears the code is usually found on the inner front cage or rear of the rear mech body. Be careful to ensure you find the actual date code. Shimano part numbers begin FD then a series of numbers, so if you are not careful everything is dated as April 1981.

Shimano Year Code

A	B	C	D	E	F	G	H	I	J	K	L	M
1976	1977	1978	1979	1980	1981	1982	1983	1984	1985	1986	1987	1988
2002	2003	2004	2005	2006	2007							

N	O	P	Q	R	S	T	U	V	W	X	Y	Z
1989	1990	1991	1992	1993	1994	1995	1996	1997	1998	1999	2000	2001

Shimano Month Code

A	B	C	D	E	F	G	H	I	J	K	L
Jan	Feb	Mar	Apr	May	Jun	Jul	Aug	Sep	Oct	Nov	Dec

Suntour

Suntour also used a two letter system the month being the same as Shimano. The year started with N in 1972 which means A is 1984! This ran until 1992 when the company went bankrupt. MA is Jan 1973.

Carradice Bags

Many bags have remained in production with only cosmetic changes over 50 years, this is particularly true of the Camper and the Nelson. The best way to date older bags is by the address on the oblong label. This was always in Nelson, Lancs.
- Pre-World War II 16 Bedford Street From mid-'40s to 1960
- Leeds Road 1961 to 1979
- North Street 1980 to 1983
- Brook Street 1984 to present:
- St Mary's Works Westmoreland St. (A former weaving mill.)

NB The post-1983 bags just have Carradice of Nelson without any address.

Components with more limited use with regard to dating

GB bars and stems, starting in the late '60s some bars and stems are stamped with the year. Unfortunately given this is a very widely used item the use of this is not consistent.

Maes Kint handlebars and stem have the year on the vertical part of the stem and underside of the central portions of the bars.

Mafac 2000 and Competition brakes of the '70s '80s like Weinmann have the date and month on one of the inner arms. The Competition and Raid (long arm) were introduced in 1970 and the 2000 in 1973.

SR seatpins and stems. Some have the year and month below the limit line e.g. 849 September 1984.

Huret, Mavic and Simplex dated some of their '70s and '80s components but this is somewhat inconsistent and is only on a minority of gears in the form of month and year e.g. 1081.

Post-World War Two Standard Cyclos made in Birmingham have the year stamped on the plate by the top jockey wheel bolt. These seem to range from 1947 to 1954.

The record for the item made over the longest period of time must go to the Williams five pin chainwheel and cranks (B100). Made from 1914 to the mid '60s over 50 years, can this be beaten?

So happy dating but remember machines were often upgraded or even retro fitted.

Acknowledgement: the *www.vintage.trek* website was extremely useful in researching this article

for Roadmen . . . Trackmen . . . Tandemists . . . and Tourists.

The RESILION STORY
A Real Engineering Job

Resilion is a name synonymous with one product – cantilever brakes.

Throughout the 1930s they were one of the hallmarks of a quality lightweight. As this article will show, they produced not just one of the more innovative and efficient brake designs, but also other brake and cycle components. Although all subsequent brake design developed along completely different principles it is interesting to note that when, in the 1990s, Shimano introduced their direct pull (V) brakes they copied the Resilion idea of long brake blocks, curved to follow the rim. Indeed some Shimano V brakes pads will fit Resilion brake shoes, This design has now replaced cantilevers as the standard fitting on all but racing bikes and the cheapest mountain bikes.

The Origins Of Resilion

The Resilion Company was founded in 1927 for the manufacture of a saddle top made from sponge rubber, and it was this product that gave the company its name. Originally employing just two people, the design was an immediate success. Mentioned in glowing terms in the *CTC Gazette's* review of the 1928 Olympia show[1], it was recommended as a cure for saddle sores and general saddle discomfort[2]. By the early 1930s the company produced a variety of models designed to fit all standard saddles (Fig 1). At the end of 1931,the

---

1 *CTC Gazette* November 1928 p414.
2 *CTC Gazette* July 1928 p288.

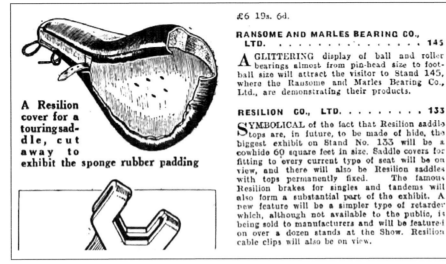

Fig. 1 Olympia Show forecast *Cycling* 27 November 1931

outer cover was changed to cowhide, publicised by featuring a 60 square feet cowhide on their stand at Olympia. In 1933 prices ranged from 14s 6d to 18s 6d. In addition to separate saddle tops, the company also produced a range of complete saddles, all with the tops sewn in.

The Cantilever

The Resilion Cantilever was introduced in 1929 and launched at the show of that year. Instantly acclaimed as a huge advance in braking , I would go so far to say it was a revolution in braking, as until then many cyclists relied upon the application of reverse pressure on fixed wheel drive, or crude and ineffective plunger type brakes to stop.

The Cantilever was awarded the CTC plaque that year for the greatest advance in cycle design[3], and in contemporary reports it is described as 'a sound or real engineering job'. It is interesting to note that there was no award the previous year as the CTC felt there had been nothing of sufficient merit. Writing in *Cycling* on 25 April 1930 in an article entitled 'The Plaque Test of Progress', that elder statesman of the pastime, and father of time trialling, FT Bidlake stated the success of Resilion was due to:

...the development which gives each brake block its own separate fixing and own mechanism of application gets away from the calliper as well as the horseshoe....

Added length of brake block increases the contact area.. and the brake design is the subject of the CTC award. Bolting the stirrup to the frame was the common way of attaching a calliper brake at this time. The use of a centre bolt had started in France in the mid 1920s but was still the exception. The Resilion Cantilever was extremely popular with both touring and racing club cyclists. Unlike the later generation of cantilevers (Mafac and

---

3 *CTC Gazette* October 1930 p443.

successors) it did not require any braze on fitting to the forks or seat stays. Although this may seem like an advantage in that it could be fitted to any frame, in practice the number of different fittings required contributed to the high cost of manufacturing and complexity of attachment. However, it is a measure of its effectiveness that it became the de-facto standard for tandems and tricycles. On the latter, when fitted to the front wheel, it meant the second brake could also be fitted without the need for braze-on fittings. Higgins fitted Resilion as standard equipment on many of their trikes well after WWII. Until post war advances in brake design it reigned supreme as the quality brake for lightweights.

The Resilion Cantilever was invented by Mr L T Marr, who later became managing director. A keen cyclist and member of the Bath Road Club, he died in 1936[4]. Marr was just 52, the same age as both his father and brother, though in his case a contributory factor may have been that he was gassed during WW1. Marr's father had run a plating business in Clerkenwell and also did some light engineering. One of Marr's sales techniques was to bicycle around Europe dressed in a Norfolk jacket and deerstalker demonstrating Resilion brakes. He lived in Hornsey, North London, which was quite a select area at the time, and his main non-cycling interest was collecting Persian carpets. He left quite a substantial fortune to his nephew Harold, who unfortunately had a weakness for slow horses and fast women and thus it was quickly squandered.

Marr was not just a gifted inventor but also extremely good at marketing, as evidenced by his achievement in getting the lightweight trade to adopt his brakes, in spite of their complexity and the amount of fittings a dealer would need to hold for different sizes and shapes of forks and stays. Resilion became, in a very short space of time, a byword for good braking and many of the smaller lightweight builders fitted them as standard, including Maclean, Selbach and Claud Butler, into the immediate post war years. Early Thanets were fitted with a braze-on modification for the Cantilette. The range was available in chrome or black enamel, at a slightly lower cost. Early 1930s models can be identified by having a differently shaped cut-out in the sides of the arm.

At a number of shows during the 1930s Resilion demonstrated the effectiveness of their brake by attaching a 6 lb weight to a lever and challenged the public to try and move the bike forward[5]. According to the CTC Show reports the bike was immovable.

From a poetic advertisement in Cycling, 14 September 1934 p 17: Fit a cantilever/Live life's allotted span/Stop just where you want to/And not just when you can … …Resilion brakes are better than insurance policies they ensure you remain alive.

The brakes were expensive and Marr realised they were out of the reach of many cyclists in the impoverished 1930s. His response was to manufacture a cheaper simplified version, the Cantilette, also known as the 'B', which was about 30% cheaper. It was introduced in 1931, though only supplied to cycle manufacturers for the first two years. The sheet metal stampings of the Cantilever were replaced by lightweight malleable castings; the brake blocks were also somewhat shorter.

By the mid 1930s Resilion employed over 200. However, the success of the company was very much linked to L T Marr – he was clearly the driving force. After his death there was no real innovation and in this regard there are some parallels with Constrictor and the direction that company took after the death of Leon Meredith. There were no brake design changes until 1948 when a part alloy version was introduced[6].

The Cantilever was somewhat complex but very well designed. The lever fulcrum was such as to maximise mechanical advantage and cable breakage was usually at the lever end. The cable was in three parts, soldered into a small flat brass block that slid within its casing when the lever was pulled. At the working end the cables were attached to the brake side plate for extra rigidity. The long brake blocks (twice as long as a normal block) dramatically improved performance. It had a reputation for being difficult to set up and maintain, and this was something the company sought to counter by stating it could be fitted within five minutes. When fitting attention had to be paid to the following:

1. Size of frame: larger frames required a longer cable for the rear brake.
2. Fitting to forks and seat stays was specific to their design – round, D section, oval etc. This meant the brakes were not interchangeable. It was essential that anything fitted to the forks would not come loose as this could cause a serious accident.
3. Different clearances between stays/ forks and wheel rim required Resilion to offer proprietary brake blocks in three thicknesses to achieve the correct setting.

4 *Cycling* 25 July 1936 p96

5 CTC *Gazette* November 1937 p367.

6 *Cycling* 17 November 1948 p421.

Another problem was with wheel removal when fitted with wider tyres as there was no quick release facility. One innovative option was to modify the brake block and shoe to enable swift removal of the brake shoe, and this was done by J J Cooper, a small East London builder of frames under 'The Upton' marque. A headless screw was fitted to the open end of the brake shoe and then a knurled nut that could be unscrewed so that the brake block would slide out.

Resilion produced a multi purpose tool about 6 cm long for fitting the brakes. They also provided dealers with a wooden box approx 12cm by 10cm by 4cm which had two levels of compartments to hold the specialist fittings required (Fig 2). Supplied with the brakes were steel cable clips for attaching the rear brake cable to the frame.

The action of the brake was extremely smooth,

Fig. 2 The parts list on the inside of a dealer's brake spares box cover.Supplied by Ray Miller

and quite different in feel to the later Mafac cantilever. The levers also work well with other brakes and are one way of improving the effectiveness of pre war brakes. Of course, neither the fork crown nor the seat stay bridge had to be drilled and frames built for Resilion brakes often have the bridge undrilled, utilising a clip to attach the mudguard. In the 1949 Holdsworth 'Aids' it was claimed that Resilion brakes 'will stop a bus'. Special versions were available for tandems (an extra 2s 6d). A reminder of the complexity issue is provided by the following note: 'When ordering Resilion brakes specify whether the front is required for D, oval or round fork blades and if rear is for ½" or 5/8" diameter seat stays.'

A major problem with the brakes was that there was no method of adjustment to compensate for an out of true rim. Adjustment to compensate for brake block wear was also quite complex. Furthermore the position of the brake, lower than normal on the stays, means it receives the maximum amount of road debris causing wear especially to the pivots

Handlebar Grips

During the 1930s Resilion manufactured a handlebar grip, like the saddle top, from a combination of leather and rubber (Fig 3).

Dynamic Coupling

In 1932 Resilion introduced a means of activating two brakes with one lever, the brakes being linked by a Bowden cable. This innovation became very popular with tandem riders as it enabled three or even four brakes to be fitted (often combined hub and rim brakes). It became the subject of correspondence in the *CTC Gazette*,

Fig. 3 Advert for Resilion handle bar grips from the 1934 catalogue.

and the overwhelming view was that it was a great step forward, though with the proviso that it was not for the novice – the system was too powerful! According to the December 1932 *CTC Gazette* the coupling worked as follows:

In its commonest and perhaps best form it consists of two hub brakes. The hand lever is only applied to the front brake and the arm of that brake instead of being anchored to the front fork is connected by cable to the rear brake. Thus the operation of the front brake converts the front wheel into a lever that operates the rear brake, the bicycles speed being the power, and if that speed is high the power is great and the retarding force is accordingly very powerful and effective. It is certainly the fiercest 'stopper' we have tried.

The Anchor Brake

The advert in *Cycling*, 4 December 1935 shows the prices for the Cantilever, aimed at the top end, and the Model B, or Cantilette, aimed at the middle ground (Fig 4). It also lists the new, and cheaper, Anchor brake 'for popular priced bicycles', aimed at 'the younger generation of Cyclists whose means are limited.' Brake blocks were conventional and the brake arm was clamped to the stays/forks, but in operation it was more like a centre pull than a cantilever (Fig. 5).

According to a review in the December 1935 *CTC Gazette* (p453) it was, 'a complete departure from calliper action and has great advantage over this type in that it is anchored at its working parts and cannot yield to the thrust of the wheel.' At 4s 11d each it was less than half the price of the Cantilever but was a far less efficient brake.

Post War Developments

During 1948 Resilion started to use alloy parts in both brakes and levers and offered red brake blocks designed for alloy rims. The alloy version of the Cantilever was 7s 5d more expensive than the all steel one and, according to *Cycling*[7], the alloy lever had 'the moving parts in the brake lever reinforced by the insertion of steel bushes in the pivot holes, thereby providing a happy compromise with the wearing propensities of steel and the weight saving of alloy…Two types of lever are available: straight lever pattern and the curved C type.'

7 *Cycling* 14 July 1948 p28.

Fig. 4 Advert for the full Resilion brake range *Cycling* 4th December, 1935

Resilion reassured riders that any part that took strain was still made from steel. This reflected the widespread suspicion of the time that alloy was not really strong enough for such a critical component as a brake.

The company was clearly losing market share as more and more cyclists opted for the simpler post-war brakes offered by GB, Burlite, Stratalite etc. In the December 1951 *CTC Gazette* they advertised a reduction in price of the alloy cantilevers from 32s 6d to 22s 6d. The reason given was a shortage of steel but I suspect by then the brakes were viewed as too complex and old fashioned by most riders and were not selling.

One innovative idea in 1948 was a lever with a lock that allowed the brake to be applied and locked in that position, making it 'impossible to ride or wheel the machine away' (Fig 6).

Hubs and Derailleurs – the Final Products

From the mid 1950s to the early 1960s Resilion marketed large flange solid three piece all steel hubs, though it is unclear whether they were made in house of bought in. They were fitted as original equipment to many medium to low price sports bicycles.

There were two Resilion derailleurs, the first a 3 speed, 1/8" model introduced in 1954. This was a chainstay mounted device using the same braze on fitting as a Standard Cyclo. It was made by Phillips and fitted as original equipment on a number of

Fig. 5 The new Resilion Anchor brake *CTC Gazette* December 1935

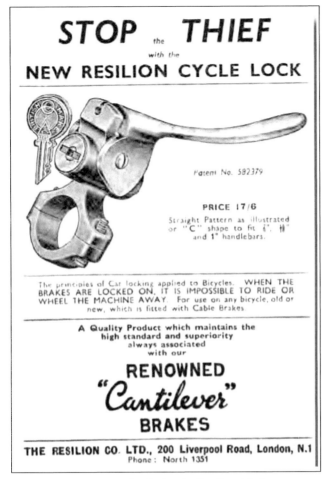

Fig. 6 New Resilion Cycle Lock *Cycling* 12 January 1949

Phillips cycles; see p169 of *The Dancing Chain*, second edition. The second was the 1958 Crimson Star (Fig 7) with very distinctive red pulleys and very similar to Cyclo's Mk7 Benelux. It was cheap and robust and had the benefit of being suitable for 3, 4, and 5 speed freewheels and both 3/32" and 1/8" chains. The only drawback with the design was that the pulleys were unshielded, leaving the metal bushing exposed in the centre. This omission caused rapid wear in contrast to the shielded design used by Simplex.

Some time in the mid 1950s the company relocated from Islington, North London to Birmingham. After 1952 it ceased to exhibit at the annual cycle shows. It is not yet clear exactly when Resilion ceased trading but the name disappeared around 1961. In the mid 1950s they were taken over by Phillips, based on the 1955 General Fitting Company catalogue, which refers to the Cantilevers as 'Phillips Resilion'. Also the last version of Resilion brakes came with levers stamped 'Phillips'.

Without doubt Resilion's heyday was during

Fig. 7 Crimson Star 1958 to c1961 (photo by Peter Brueggeman)

the 1930s. Following its introduction in 1929, and within a very short space of time, the Cantilever defined the standard for lightweight cycle braking. Failure to innovate after the death of L T Marr meant the company was left behind, and experienced an ever declining market share post war. The brakes were seen as just too complicated and inflexible. For example, a key requirement for many racing cyclists was, and still is, a quick release to enable a swift wheel change in the event of a puncture. With the GB this required the flick of a lever on the stirrup, or on a Mafac the unhooking of the straddle cable, whereas with the Cantilever it was just not possible without partial disassembly. The derailleur gears and hubs were very much copies of other products so ultimately it is one product that Resilion should be remembered for – the Cantilever Brake.

Other Sources

Frank Berto: *The Dancing Chain* 2nd Edition 2005 pp167- 69 and 179 . Details of Resilion Gears.
1950s *Brown Brothers catalogues* for Resilion hubs and gears.
1949 Holdsworth *Aids to Happy Cycling* p3.
The cycles in the National Cycle Museum at Llandrindod Wells fitted with Resilion Cantilevers and Cantilettes.
The *General Fittings Company Catalogue* c1955

Acknowledgements

Alexander von Tutschek for source material. Peter Brueggeman for the Crimson Star photograph.

David Higman at the National Cycle Museum, Llandrindod Wells, for allowing me to mess around with their Resilion equipped cycles in the collections.

Ray Miller for a copy of the 1934 Resilion catalogue in the V-CC library and images of the Resilion spares box.

RESILION
CATALOGUE
1934

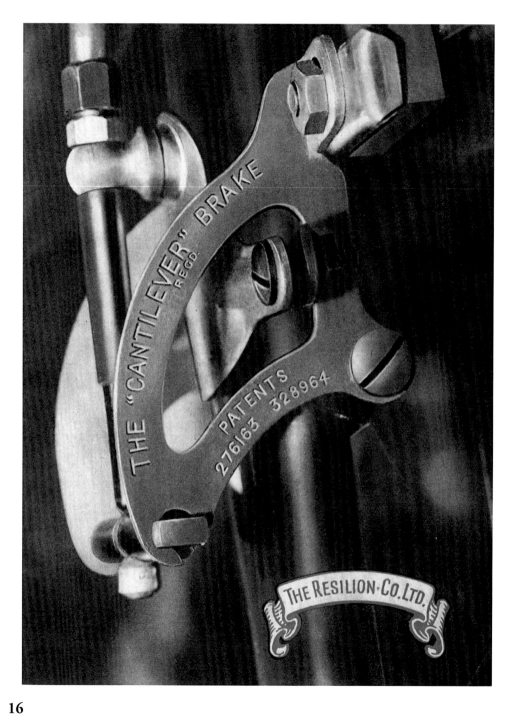

"*The 'Cantilever' Brake is a striking illustration of the truism that* 100% *efficiency always goes hand in hand with beauty in a shapely well-balanced design.*"

RESILION "CANTILEVER" BRAKES

MANUFACTURED IN ENGLAND
WHOLLY FROM BRITISH MATERIALS

WHAT ACTUAL USERS OF
RESILION CANTILEVER BRAKES SAY . . . .

" . . . . . I suppose it is really unnecessary for me to add that your brake is the most efficient I have ever used, and exceeded my expectations, in efficiency, in wet weather."

* * *

"I am perfectly delighted with the brakes which you fitted to my Sunbeam Special."

* * *

ON ALPINE ROADS—"The Resilion brakes I fitted to my tandem have been a revelation to me. I have never felt such security on bad hills before.

In course of a tour of 500 miles, including some long and steep Alpine roads, I was always in full control of the machine.

I have cycled in the Alpine districts for more than twenty years and used often to dismount to relieve the strain of holding on my brakes, but this is now no longer necessary ; the Cantilever puts no strain worth mentioning on the hands, even on the steepest grades."

* * *

"I decided to specify your brakes on a new machine I was ordering, and thought my observations after a six weeks' test might interest you.

The first thing that was most noticeable was the evenness of the braking under all conditions of use, whether applied gently, or suddenly for an emergency, there was just that steadiness that was lacking in the brake I had been using previously, and I have nothing but admiration and praise for them. Another feature was the action of the brakes in wet weather, the same firm action on wet rims, due, I surmise, to the extra length of the brake blocks."

* * *

"I must say that the Resilion Cantilever Brake is the best Brake I have fitted since I have been in the Trade, which is over 25 years."

RESILION "CANTILEVER" BRAKES

THE RESILION COMPANY'S CANTILEVER BRAKES were first introduced in 1929, and quickly secured the approval of the leading Cycling Authorities and the award of the C.T.C. Silver Plaque for the greatest improvement in cycle or equipment design. They have since been adopted as standard equipment by most of the famous makers of bicycles whose names, far too numerous to mention here, are household words, and many of these are using Cantilever Brakes on their complete range of Lightweight Models. They have consequently become so widely known that it is needless to give anything beyond a general description as a guide to new comers, concerning the finest and most reliable cycle brake on the market at the present time, but we would like just to repeat the considered opinions of the late Mr. F. T. Bidlake, which were published in "Cycling," *i.e.*, "The Cantilever Brake is in the true line of evolution of a real improvement." After two years he wrote again : "Happily for the multitude this brake is not cornered, and has fastened itself on the forks, and in the affections, of a host of folk since the day, some two years or more ago, when the original specimen was marketed. I enjoyed the feel of it then at first acquaintance, and I retain the impression, after prolonged use, that it is admirable as an adaptation of the scientific use of leverage, and of materials to secure strength and lightness. What I like in it is, there always seems to be a bit more, even when you have all you want, and a reserve in a brake is sometimes even more useful than a reserve in a bank.

ANYONE WHO EXAMINES the construction of CANTILEVER BRAKES will be impressed with the originality and engineering skill with which all the many difficulties attendant on brake design have been met to make Resilion Cantilever brakes adaptable alike for Endrick, Westwood, or wood rims, or any section or size of tubes. The design and construction were carried out entirely by the Resilion Company, and the illustrations show that new principles in cycle brake work were applied in practically every detail, and all the inherent faults of calliper brakes have been eliminated.

THE BRAKE MEMBERS, pivoted on brackets, are anchored to stays or forks by means of screw clamping shields, the latter being designed, also to carry the cable stops and adjusters. Each side is independently adjustable to the rim with the greatest nicety, and the absence of any bridge work makes a useful saving in weight and a surprisingly neat, attractive appearance and in fact conveys the impression that the brakes are an integral part of the design of the bicycle, instead of a "heavy chunk

RESILION "CANTILEVER" REGD. FRONT BRAKE

The Brake Members—continued

of ironmongery clapped on as an afterthought." The quadrants passing each side of the forks or stays, are stamped from sheet steel and held parallel at six points by cross members, forming a rigid box-like construction of great strength which cannot weaken with use and is always positive in action ; while the off-set springs enclosed in telescopic tubes are of the pressure type which cannot fail to act through breakage nor choke with dirt. All parts, including the wire casing, are grease packed and readily lubricated.

THE LEVER has been specially designed, so that the brake members respond instantly to very light pressure of the fingers. The motion exerts a parallel and direct pull on the cable, the design rendering it impossible for the cable nipple to jolt out of place.

STOPPING POWER. Certified tests prove that one brake with only 6 lbs. pressure on the lever will stop an 11½ stone rider on a steep slope travelling at 16 miles an hour in 20 yards, against 334 yards in similar tests of other types of brakes.

THE CABLES operating the brake comprise a main lead from lever to a junction box, fitted with an adjuster. From this point twin cables are led which, in the case of the rear brake, pass each side of the seat pillar, each one operating an independent brake member, the cables passing through spring guides to a pull-bar at the extreme lower edge as seen in the photographs.

STRENGTH OF JOINTS AND CABLES

Sets of inner wires, taken haphazard from stock bundles, are submitted periodically to the National Physical Laboratory for test. The certificates show that it requires 730 lbs. to fracture the central joints when tested on a two-ton Vertical Avery Testing Machine. This is many times more than the strain it would be needful to exert under the most abnormal conditions of cycling. British made cable only is used which has a mean breaking test of 1,100 lbs. for the main single wire and 630 lbs. for the twin wires, each of which does only "half duty" compared with ordinary calliper or hub brakes. The certified holding strength of the nipple solderings is 739 lbs. at the forward end, and it has so far been found impossible to pull off a back end nipple without fracturing the wire. The elongation or "Stretch" of the wire used is only 0.05" per foot or slightly over one-quarter of an inch on a full rear cable unit under a load of 300 lbs.—twice the weight of an average man.

THE "CANTILEVER" BRAKE may be seen as a permanent exhibit of modern cycle improvements at THE SCIENCE MUSEUM, SOUTH KENSINGTON.

THE
RESILION "CANTILEVER" REGD.
REAR BRAKE

100% EFFICIENCY goes hand in hand with BEAUTY in a well-balanced symmetrical design.

SIZES, FINISHES AND STOCK NUMBERS

For guidance of Customers in ordering
"CANTILEVER" BRAKES

It is necessary to give only the NUMBER in COLUMN 3 when ordering, unless a non-standard fitting is required as in the case of OVAL, instead of DEE or ROUND, and longer twin wires for FRAMES over 22" high.

•

CRANKED LEVERS FOR RIGHT OR LEFT HAND will be supplied, if ordered, to suit the curves of flat or upturned handle-bars.

•

TWO "CANTILEVER" BRAKES SAVE 3 LBS. OF WEIGHT WHEN COMPARED WITH MOST HUB-BRAKES AND OVER 1 LB. AGAINST NEARLY ALL CALLIPERS, WHILE THEY ARE AT LEAST TWICE AS EFFICIENT AS ANY OTHER TYPE OF BRAKE.

•

SEE PAGE 12 FOR MODEL "B CANTILEVER" BRAKES

SIZES Measurements are the widths of forks or diameters of stays.	FINISH	STOCK NUMBER Clip fixing	PARTICULARS required when not Standard sizes	RETAIL PRICE EACH
CANTILEVER REAR BRAKES			Always give frame height if over 22 inch.	s. d.
GENT'S SINGLE				
½ inch	Black Enamel	1	Made for Round tubes only	10 6
,,	Nickel Plated	3		10 6
,,	Chrome ,, ...	5		12 6
⅝ inch	Black Enamel	7	Made for Oval or Round tubes. Round sent if not otherwise stated. The ⅝ in. or ¾ in. round clamping shields are unsuitable for Oval or Dee tubes.	10 6
,,	Nickel Plated	9		10 6
,,	Chrome ,, ...	11		12 6
¾ inch	Black Enamel	13		10 6
,,	Nickel Plated	15		10 6
,,	Chrome ,, ...	17		12 6
CANTILEVER FRONT BRAKES				
SUIT LADY'S OR GENT'S				
⅞ inch	Black Enamel	19	Occasionally these sizes are required as REAR brakes and will be made up to order. Please state the stock number "mounted as a rear brake." When Front brakes are required for the new Accles & Pollock or Reynolds resilient forks state "A. & P." or "Reynolds" after Number.	11 6
,,	Nickel Plated	21		11 6
,,	Chrome ,, ...	23		13 6
1 inch	Black Enamel	25		11 6
,,	Nickel Plated	27		11 6
,,	Chrome ,, ...	29		13 6
1⅛ inch	Black Enamel	32		11 6
,,	Nickel Plated	34		11 6
,,	Chrome ,, ...	36		13 6
TANDEM REAR BRAKES				
DOUBLE GENT'S				
⅝ inch	Black Enamel	38	D.G. Tandem cable lengths 9½ in. for twin wires, 4 ft. 7½ in. forward wire. Overall length with junction box 5 ft. 8 in.	12 6
,,	Nickel Plated	40		12 6
,,	Chrome ,, ...	42		14 6
¾ inch	Black Enamel	44		12 6
,,	Nickel Plated	46		12 6
,,	Chrome ,, ...	48		14 6
TANDEM REAR BRAKES				
LADY BACK				
⅝ inch	Black Enamel	50	L.B. Tandem cable lengths, 11½ ins., for twin wires, 5 ft. 6 in. forward wire. Overall length with junction box 6 ft. 8½ in. Front or Rear Tandem brakes made specially to operate from rear handle-bar if required.	12 6
,,	Nickel Plated	52		12 6
,,	Chrome ,, ...	54		14 6
¾ inch	Black Enamel	56		12 6
,,	Nickel Plated	58		12 6
,,	Chrome ,, ...	60		14 6
LADY'S SINGLE REAR BRAKES				
LOOP OR SPORTS FRAME				
⅝ inch	Black Enamel	62	Oval or Dee should be stated when required, or round will be sent.	10 6
,,	Nickel Plated	64		10 6
,,	Chrome ,, ...	66		12 6
¾ inch	Black Enamel	68		10 6
,,	Nickel Plated	70		10 6
,,	Chrome ,, ...	72		12 6
TANDEM FRONT BRAKES				
SUIT ALL TYPES				
1¼ inch	Black Enamel	74	Dee always sent unless stated. Note, Dee shields are unsuitable for Oval blades.	12 6
,,	Nickel Plated	76		12 6
,,	Chrome ,, ...	78		14 6

The Resilion "Cantilever"

QUADRANT BRACKETS

(State size between upright sides)

Front Pattern (Clip fixing) — 1/- each

Rear Pattern (Clip fixing) — 1/- each

BRAKE BLOCK SHOE

Showing projectors for use with wide clearance.

As shown, per pair .. 2/-
Chrome   ,, .. 2/4

(Blocks extra) **7d.** pair

CLAMPING SCREW
1/3 per doz.

QUADRANT PIVOT BOLT
(State overall length)
7d. per pair

CABLE BAR
(State overall length)
1/- per pair

BRAKE BLOCK SHOE AND NUTS
(State size between stud centres)
1/- pair ; Chrome, 1/4 pair
(Blocks extra) **7d.** pair
For Model "B" **1/-** pair
(Blocks extra) **5d.** pair
Nuts, 1/- dozen ; Chrome, 1/3

LEVER CLIP AND LINER
8d. each
Chrome, **10d.** each

LEVER BOLT NUT AND CLAMP BLOCK
8d. per set
Chrome **10d.** per set

Back and Front Cable Nipples
1/- dozen

FITS ALL NUTS AND SCREWS ON RESILION CANTILEVER BRAKES

Price **6d.** each

CABLE UNITS COMPLETE

Front, 3/10 ; Rear, 4/6 ; Tandem, 5/6. All units, Tandem or Single, including Model "B," are exchangeable for new ones at 2/6 each by any Appointed Service Agent throughout Great Britain. Addresses on application.

Handsome Cabinets containing useful quantities of spare parts are available for Agents—Price on application.

---

brake... Spare Parts List

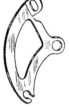

CLAMPING SHIELDS
Clip fixing
(State size between hole centres)
6d. each ; Chrome, 8d. each

QUADRANT PLATES
REAR   FRONT
(State left or right)
6d. each ; Chrome, 8d. each

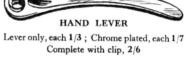

HAND LEVER
Lever only, each 1/3 ; Chrome plated, each 1/7
Complete with clip, 2/6
Chrome plated, complete with clip, 3/-

CASING CLIPS
3 sizes : $\frac{7}{8}$", 1", $1\frac{1}{8}$"
The finest spring clip made.
2d. each
Cards of 5, 10d.

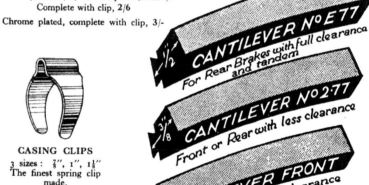

CANTILEVER No E77
For Rear Brakes with full clearance and tandem

CANTILEVER No 2.77
Front or Rear with less clearance

CANTILEVER FRONT
Shallow for small clearance

Guarantee
is not sustained if other makes of brake-blocks are substituted for replacements.
Insist on genuine Resilion Co.'s blocks.

SPECIAL ANTI-SQUEAK COMPOUND. HOLDS WELL IN WET and DRY WEATHER.

Blocks for Model "A", 3" long, all sizes, 7d. per pair
Also packed in cartons, 1 doz pairs assorted, 7/-

Blocks for Model "B", $2\frac{1}{4}$" long, all sizes, 5d. per pair
Also packed in cartons, 1 doz assorted pairs, 5/-

The Model B "Cantilever" Brake
REGD.

—for Popular Priced Bicycles

THE Model "B" Cantilever was designed in response to pressing requests by several large Manufacturers for a really efficient brake of sound design for use on their popular priced cycles. These firms stated that they were experiencing an increasing demand for the Cantilever Brake, but they found it impossible to utilise it on machines costing less than £7, however much they would like to do so.

After a considerable amount of experimental work, we were successful in producing a modified design in which all the essential principles of the best Cantilever Brakes were embodied, and the same action and leverage obtained, but in which the quadrant members could be made in one piece, and by the use of pivoting rivets dispense with the more costly shouldered pivot bolts and nuts, and the intricate work on the cable bars and quadrant brackets which give fine action in the "Senior" Cantilever Brakes, but which make them costly to produce. The cable units themselves are the same high standard of quality and only the best material obtainable is used for all brakes.

A further reduction in cost was effected by using shorter brake blocks, and we were eventually able to arrive at the necessary economies in production to bring a "Cantilever" Brake within the reach of Manufacturers for any but the very cheapest grade of cycles, without departing, to any extent, from the essentials in the original design.

The Model "B" Brakes were increasingly used for about two years but, until 1933, were reserved to Manufacturers. Their performance has, however, come under the eye of the Great Cycling Public, and there were insistent demands for supplies through the usual trade channels, for this very efficient brake for use in replacement of the quickly failing cheap callipers hitherto fitted on the popular priced machines. Model "B" Cantilever Brakes were in response to this demand released for Retail Sales at Olympia Show, 1933, and sales are expected to run into six figures by the end of 1934. They are used by nearly 100 Manufacturers for equipment purposes, and stocks are carried by all leading Factoring Houses as well as by nearly all good Cycle Agents throughout the British Isles.

Model "B" Brakes are available in two sizes only, i.e., ⅝" Rear for Round seat stays and 1⅛" D for front forks, but a second fitting to suit Accles & Pollock or Reynolds H.M. tapering Resilient Front forks (D Section only), will be carried in stock for special orders. There will be one finish generally for all Model "B" Brakes, i.e., best bright stoved Black Enamel but, if required, any brake will be supplied with Chrome-plated hand-lever at an extra cost of 6d.

A considerable number of minor improvements have been made in Model "B" Cantilevers in recent months. A new design nipple has been introduced which entirely prevents the chafing of cables at the lever end, and so strongly does this new nipple hold that, with four sets sent to the National Physical Laboratory it was certified as impossible to pull off these nipples without fracturing the wire, which in itself has a tensile strength of 750 lbs, when tested in an Avery two-ton testing machine.

AFTER SALES SERVICE.—The cable units are made with the best quality waterproof covered casing, and the Company's Service Scheme for exchange of worn-out cable units, at a charge of 2/6 each, will be applicable to Model "B" as well as the best Cantilevers. In fact all Cantilever brake cable units are interchangeable for one of the same type under this Scheme, which works admirably and greatly simplifies the question of repairs and replacements when needed.

Only first-class workmanship and the best material, consistent with the price, are being employed on Model "B" Brakes. They are a thoroughly sound effective brake which can be fully relied upon, at a price which will suit the pockets of most cyclists who care for their own safety.

PRICE LIST

Model "B" Cantilever Brakes.

FRONT BRAKES (weight only 14 oz.) suitable for 1⅛" D. forks. Best Bright Black Enamel throughout. **7/6** each

If required for A. & P. or Reynolds H.M. forks give necessary details when ordering. **7/6** each

REAR BRAKES (weight only 15 oz.) suitable for ⅝" or ½" Round **7/6** each

Chrome Plated Lever with any Brake, 6d. each extra.

CRANKED LEVERS (right or left) for flat or up-turned Bars will be fitted if ordered.

Page 12

Page 13

22

Ideal Saddles for Long-distance Riding and Road Racing

"RESILION" CYCLE SADDLE TOP
— REG D. —

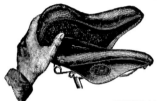 

Models and Fittings for the guidance of customers when ordering the Resilion Saddle Top. Stocks are carried of all the numbers and fittings given.

STANDARD LIGHT-WEIGHT PATTERNS

MODEL	FITTINGS FOR :—	SIZE	WEIGHT	PRICE
A3	B.10, B.18, B.66, B.75, B.90, and average standard touring saddles ..	10" × 8" to 11" × 8¼"	7½ oz.	9/-
A4	Ladies' Saddles of similar numbers to above	9" × 8" to 10" × 8¼"	7¼ oz.	9/-
A5	Large touring Saddles as B.90/2, and others	11½" × 9"	9 oz.	9/-
A6	The most popular Racing Model. Hundreds of prominent records and road events have been won on this since it was introduced. B.17, B.17/N, B.17 Sprinter, M.38, M.38/N, M.42 Sprinter; Lycett L.9 and 99, B.18, B.66 and B.10, Champions; Dunlop F.8, etc. ..	11" × 4½" to 12" × 6"	5½ oz.	9/-
A7	The "End-to-End" Model, used by Mr. Jack Rossiter and Mr. Tom Hughes in breaking the Land's End to John o' Groats and 1,000 miles Records on Bicycle and Tricycle. B.19 ; Dunlop H.39, etc.	13" × 7"	6½ oz.	9/6
A8	B.90/3, and all the largest touring Saddles	12½" × 9½"	9 oz.	9/6
	Any Saddle, including the spring top types, can be fitted with the Resilion top to order. (If the Saddle is sent to us it will be returned without delay) ..			12/6

Fitting Directions are enclosed in every carton.   *Postage 6d., all Models*

15/6

Model A5/41
THE CLUBMAN'S FAST TOURING MODEL

is a good shape with well rounded curves and light springing. *Length* 11 ins. *Width* 9 ins. *Weight* 2 lbs. 2 ozs.

16/-

Model A4/2 (Lady's)
companion model to "The Clubman's Fast." *Length* 10 ins. *Width* 8 ins. *Weight* 1 lb. 11 ozs.

15/-

Model A6/6
THE STANDARD MODEL FOR ROAD RACING—

on which most of the popular events and records have been won. *Length* 11½ ins. *Width* 6 ins. *Weight* 1 lb. 11 ozs.

Model A4/75

A well-made three-coil spring saddle of highest grade leather. Is suitable for ladies and gentlemen who prefer a well-sprung narrow type.

Length 10½ ins.   *Width* 6½ ins.
Weight 2 lbs. 3 ozs.

Price **18/6**

Model A5/41 (size 2)

is a perfect saddle for ROBUST or ELDERLY RIDERS

Length 11½ ins.   *Width* 9½ ins.
Weight 2 lbs. 8 ozs.

Price **18/6**

Model A3/48
THE GENERAL-PURPOSE MODEL

Suitable for ladies' or gentlemen's roadster machines about town or on rough roads.

Length 10½ ins.   *Width* 8 ins.
Weight 2 lbs.

Price **15/-**

MODEL A7/91   IDEAL FOR LONG-DISTANCE WORK

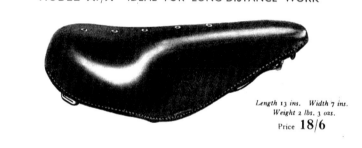

Length 13 ins.   *Width* 7 ins.
Weight 2 lbs. 3 ozs.

Price **18/6**

Model A6/17

Ideal for PATH and GRASS TRACK RACING.

Length 11½ ins.   *Width* 4½ ins.
Weight 25 ozs.

Price **14/6**

All Saddles have the "Resilion" Top SEWN-ON
REG D.

1934/35

RESILION HANDLE BAR GRIPS

Made like the Resilion top in leather and Cellular Rubber.

PRICE 4/6 per pair

THE PERFECT GRIP

Designed Patented & Manufactured only by

"RESILION" CO. LTD.

200 LIVERPOOL ROAD, LONDON, N.1

Telephone: NORTH 1351   Telegrams: "RESILIONCO, NORDO, LONDON"
Cables: "RESILIONCO, LONDON"   Codes: BENTLEY'S & PRIVATE

EAST LONDON RUBBER Co., LTD.

THE PROMPTEST FACTORS

Cycle and Motor Accessories and Equipment

29/33 Great Eastern Street, LONDON, E.C.2.

Telephone : Bishopsgate 4321 (25 lines)   Telegrams : " Akerene, Phone London"
Branches at : SHEFFIELD, BRIGHTON, IPSWICH, LEICESTER, CROYDON

*Clarke & Sherwell Ltd.
Northampton and London*

THE *New* "Resilion" Cycle Lock

Patent No. 447379

A MODERN SAFEGUARD FOR BICYCLES

THE new RESILION LOCKING LEVER is undoubtedly the accessory most urgently required by Cyclists at the present time. It is an efficient, yet simple and clean Locking Device which can be fitted not only on to new bicycles, but also on to old machines.

The LOCK is of the Yale type and is incorporated in the Lever which can be fitted to ANY Cable Brake. It is operated by putting on the Brake which becomes fixed on turning the key. A simple device ensures that the Pivot Bolt cannot be withdrawn when the Lock is engaged, and consequently it becomes impossible to detach the Lever from the Bracket while the Lock is in operation. To allow for various rim clearances of the Brake Blocks, three different locking positions are provided, but to ensure perfect working of the lock, it is IMPORTANT that the Cable should be adjusted to give a narrow clearance between the face of the block and the rim of the wheel.

WHEN THE BRAKES ARE LOCKED ON, IT IS IMPOSSIBLE TO RIDE OR WHEEL THE MACHINE AWAY. To free the Machine, the key is merely turned in the reverse direction thereby releasing the Brake and freeing the Lever for normal use.

The LOCK is simple to operate and does not soil the hands. It is an integral part of the Brake and remains a permanent fixture, ready for use at any moment, and the inconvenience of carrying a separate article, fixing and dismantling to secure or free the bicycle is avoided.

The complete assembly which is highly polished, is not over bulky and is shapely in design. The Lever and Brackets are manufactured only from High Quality Light Alloy of suitable strength and endurance and of High Corrosive Resistance. As with our other Alloy Products, the parts which are subject to the greatest wear are given the WEARING PROPERTIES OF STEEL to ensure MAXIMUM LENGTH OF SERVICE. STEEL BUSHES are inserted in both Pivot Holes. The Locking Pin, which is made of SILVER STEEL, locks into a STEEL Plate ingeniously fixed on the inner face of the Lever.

Our special Ball Nipple will be supplied with all levers so that they can be used with ANY Cable Brake. Locks are available with Straight (as illustrated) or "C" shape levers, and are provided with two keys. The Lever Brackets, which are made to fit 1″ handlebars, will be supplied with liners to fit either ⅞″ or 1⅛″ handlebars. Unless otherwise requested Orders will be executed with Straight Levers and liners for ⅞″ handlebars. The extra cost when compared with our ordinary Alloy Lever is only 7/-.

It is well known that the loss to the Cycling Community, due to thieving, runs into thousands of pounds every year, and we are confident that the use of our new Locking Device will reduce the losses from this cause to an absolute minimum.

RETAIL PRICE **17/6**

"Cantilever" BRAKES

SAFETY FIRST   Second Thoughts are Lost Too

Designed Patented & Manufactured only by

"RESILION" CO. LTD.

200 LIVERPOOL ROAD, LONDON, N.1

Phone: North 1351   Cables: "Resilionco, London"
Grams: "Resilionco, Nordo, London"   Codes: Bentley's & Private

LUCIFER DYNAMOS
The Devil has the Best Lights

'Whatever happened to Lucifer dynamos? They were far superior to any modern offering being efficient, lightweight and reliable'

Letter to the CTC magazine *Cycletouring* c1975

"the first class way to better lightning".

(advertising strap line 50s /60s)

From the 1930s Lucifer was a byword for quality in lighting for many cyclists until quite recent times. The history of this Swiss company is far older than than that as this article will show.

First the name: Lucifer is obviously chosen because of the connotation with the burning fires of hell. However the name was based upon a wordplay involving the Latin 'lux ferre' which rough translates as 'bring light ahead'.

The company Magneto Lucifer was founded in 1910 in Geneva and still exists today as part of a multinational electronics group. The first dynamo appears to have been patented in 1911. This dynamo was manufactured until at least 1932. (fig 1).

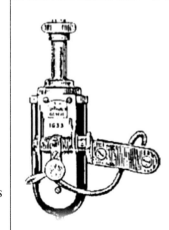

Fig. 1 First version of the Pedlite

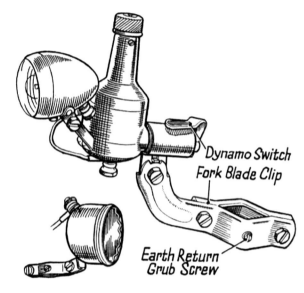

Fig. 2 The Baby Lucifer Combi model was adored by British cyclists for many good reasons, but appears to be shunned by the French. From R J Way *The Complete Cyclist* 1952

The first reference I have found to Lucifer in Britain is a report of the annual Cycle Show in Cycling 25th November 1920. It is marketed as the Pedlite and was imported by Dekla of Birmingham (see fig 1). In the Netherlands it was sold as the VT after the initials of the importer, Van Tertholen.

Dynamos do not seem to have been marketed in Britain under the Lucifer trademark until the early 1930s. I have found a reference in a 1931 Cycling with a two year guarantee and being imported by Sowerby of Goswell Street, London EC1. In the 1930s a 12-pole

Fig. 3 Lucifer dynamo from around 1930 – note that even these early ones were serial numbered and became known as the *flat type* and in the 1930's as the *standard type*

dynamo was introduced which was made until 1940

The Baby Lucifer made its appearance in 1939.

Lucifer Dynamos very quickly found favour because:

1 Their efficiency. Even at walking speed a good light output was produced.

2 They were very durable; most dynamos I have seen at cycle jumbles are still usable.

3 The drag was far lighter than most of the competition, comparable to some of the dynamos developed in the 1990s eg the Axa and Nordlicht.

4 The grip was excellent and they only slipped in very poor conditions eg very greasy or icy. Grip could be improved by not using the rubber pulley

cap, but this did have the disadvantage of making them noisier.

5 The lenses of the front lights were very well designed to provide a light you could safely ride by.

6 Front bulb changing could be done without the need for any tools; something quite important in the dark.

The only product that did not find favour was the rear light. This was because it was first designed for mudguard fitting and therefore vulnerable to damage also it could be difficult to tell if it was on. Later they supplied a bracket that enabled it to be stay mounted.

These ceased to be legal with the lighting regulation changes of November 1969. From the early 1960s Miller produced a badged rear light for Lucifer. Most British club cyclists preferred a rear light mounted on the seat stay or rear carrier

Pre-WWII they offered a front light with a focusing system, which enabled the rider to adjust the beam as desired whilst riding. In the early 1950s they introduced a new light, the 822A with adjustable focusing and this was made until about 1965.

Fig. 4 The Lucifer rear light was initially designed for mudguard mounting – here it is seen with a Lucifer bracket for stay mounting

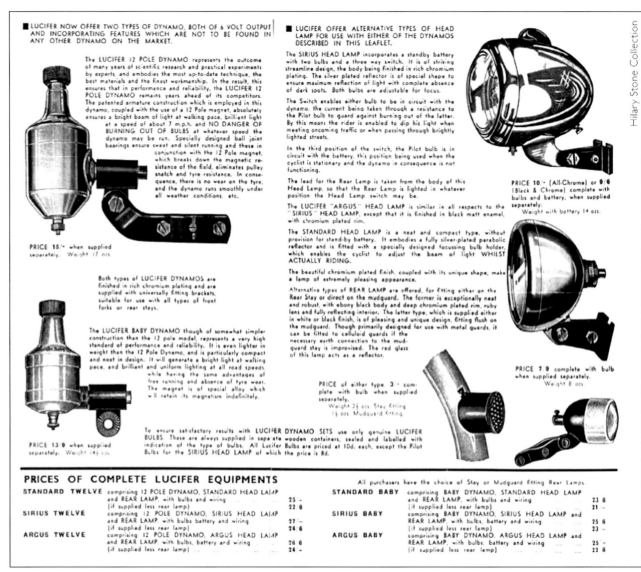

Fig. 5 Page from 1939 Lucifer catalogue The 12-pole dynamo shown top left has almost no friction but is lower powered that the Baby series. The headlight middle right is easily adjustable for focus – the bulb holder can be pushed forward or pulled back to get the optimum beam. Also bottom right is a special rear light for stay mounting, these did not feature in post-war catalogues. The Baby Lucifer, bottom left was a new introduction for 1939.

The Develpment of the Baby Lucifer

The smaller diameter model was available in three different models from 1939 until the end of the 1960s. The first version was the 700 series. All Lucifer's had individual numbering. This was a letter followed by a six figure number e.g. B288678. This attention to detail has always appealed to me and I can't think of any other cycle component, which has an individual number. These letters and numbers would seem to run sequentially, eg I have a couple of 700s, a B and F and the former is clearly the earlier model. My research leads me to the conclusion that post-WWII the letter prefix began.

In terms of dates this means:

700	1939–1952	A–F
800	1949–1967	D–T
900	1967–1971	T–V

NB the overlap, I assume the two models were available concurrently

These dates are not exact but correspond with known dates of purchase and information in period adverts about when models were new.

The early version 700s were not polished. They have the number rather crudely stamped on the side. Engraved on the upward facing surface was Baby 700 Lucifer Made in Switzerland.

The later 700s and subsequent models had a 30mm wide riveted plate on the side, which identifi ed the model and advised on the bulb combina- tions, which could be used. The 700 was rated at 6v 0.4a, the 800 and 900 were rated at 6v 0.5a but this could be split a number of ways between the front and rear lights. Also printed was 'model déposé' .

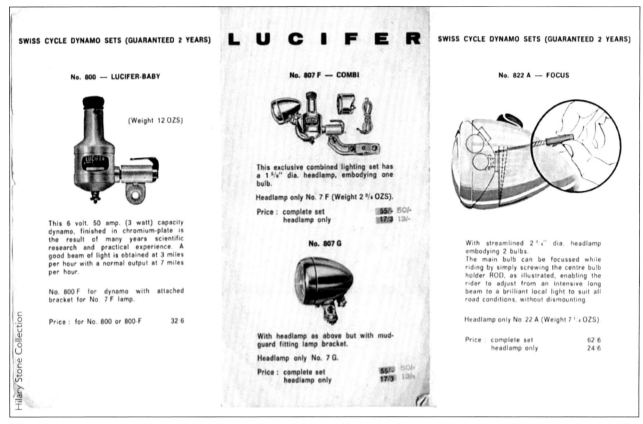

Fig. 6 Three pages from an early 1950s Lucifer catalogue. Far left is the newly introduced 800 model, centre is the Combi version of the 800 with headlamp and right is the special focusing headlight, model 822A

A late 1940s catalogue produced by Walter Flory refers to the changes in model design saying that pre- WWII dynamos have to be returned to Switzerland for servicing.

The next model introduced about 1948 was the series 800. Like the 700 it had a small screw just below the pulley cap which was for oiling – a tea- spoon of fine sewing machine oil twice a year was the advice. This amount of oil seems a bit excessive!

Fig 7 (p40) from a 1956 Brown Bros catalogue shows the available range. Note the different model with adjusting focus headlight and the Combi, which as it was continental was designed to mount on the left fork. Lucifer never made a right fork dynamo for the British market so all their dynamos were left handed fitting. Fig 7 shows the range from the 1962 Holdsworthy Aids catalogue. In terms of price they were always more expensive than Lucas or Miller, the home grown competition.

LUCIFER DYNAMO SETS

A two years' guarantee is an indication of the quality of these famous sets. We only stock Lucifer as we have found them to be without equal for finish and performance. All sets incorporate the No. 800 'baby' 6v. 0.5 amp. dyno, which produces a good light at three miles per hour and full output at seven m.p.h. Swiss made, range as follows:

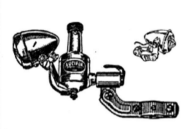

No. 807F Combi. As illustrated. Fits to left fork blade with headlamp on bracket from dyno. Neat rear lamp that meets British legal requirements **45/-**

No. 807G. As Combi but with lamp fitting to the mudguard **45/-**

No. 820A. "Aero". Streamlined 2⅛" diam. headlamp embodying one bulb **45/-**

No. 816A. "Lux". This set has a long beam headlamp with 2¼" diam., but weighing only 6¼ oz. ... **45/-**

No. 814A. "Aero-Bi". This has a similar headlamp to the 820A but carries two bulbs **50/-**

No. 819A. "Bi-Lux". Headlamp embodies 2 bulbs and two-way switch. Headlamp weighs 7 oz. ... **50/-**

No. 809A. "Battery". Headlamp 3¼" diam. taking stand-by battery embodying 2 bulbs 6v. 0.4 amp. for dynamo 3.5v. 0.2 amp. for battery or dynamo. Special resistance for the pilot bulb for use on dynamo incorporated in four-way switch. **52/6**

No. 822A. "Focus". 2¼" headlamp with 2 bulbs. Main bulb can be focused to adjust from intensive long beam to brilliant local light **55/-**

Fig. 7 From 1962 *Holdsworth Aids Catalogue*

In the early 1960's prices were reduced as the advertisements in *Sporting Cyclist* show. This suggest a falling demand in line with the general decline in cycling

Walter Flory, a Swiss national who also brought in Weinmann, imported Lucifer. He seems to have had excellent connections with the Swiss cycle trade so much so that Ron Kitching in his book *A Wheel in Two Worlds* complains about how difficult

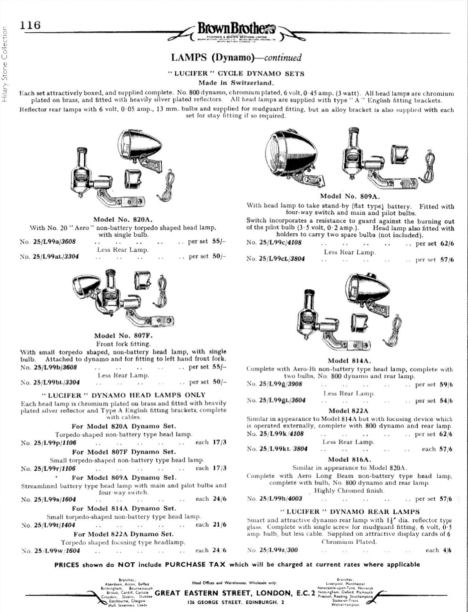

Fig. 8 The Lucifer range of dynamo sets from the 1956 *Brown Bros Wholesale Catalogue*

was for him to get Swiss suppliers![1] Flory stopped importing Lucifer in 1968.[2]

The final model, the 900, had 12 poles which made the dynamo far smoother and also gave an even better output at low speed. The oiler screw was gone and the dynamo described as self oiling.

Dynamo production seems to have stopped in the late 60s. In the early 70s *Cycling* in their annual lighting review were suggesting cyclists could do well to search out remaining stocks. Around this time another Swiss make, Siluma appeared, imported by Ron Kitching. Their headlight, the K2 was exactly the same as the Lucifer Aero, although the dynamo is not a copy. (See fig 10).

Interestingly, Siluma continued the tradition of individual numbering, this now to be found stamped on the inside by the spring casing.

The tradition of Swiss

LUCIFER DYNAMO SETS

All sets incorporate the new improved No. 900 Dynamo with self-lubricating bearings which gives excellent lighting at walking pace.
No. 907F "COMBI". Fits to left fork blade with headlamp on bracket from dynamo 55/-
No. 920A "AERO". Streamlined 2¼" diam. headlamp, embodying one bulb 55/-
No. 909A "BATTERY". Large diameter headlamp with standby battery and two bulbs 55/-
No. 914A "AEROBI". With two bulbs 60/-
No. 900 DYNO only. 6v. 3 Watt complete with bracket ... 35/-
No. 7F & 7D. Headlamp only 15/-
No. 20A AERO. Headlamp only 15/-
No. 9A BATTERY. Headlamp only 15/-
No. 14A AEROBI. Headlamp only 21/6
Pulley Rubbers ... ... 9d.
Bulbs. Use 6v. 0.4 amp. Front with 6v. 0.1 amp. Rear ... 11d.

Fig. 9 From 1966/7 *Holdsworth Aids* the introduction of the 900 series

Fig. 10 Lucifer 900 dynamo – this model introduced around 1966/7 is visually very similar to the earlier 700 and 800s but has a new 12-pole magnet. It is even smoother than the earlier models and produces a strong light from 3mph but cannot be serviced as easily. Also shown here is the Miller made rear light.

dynamo making has continued after Siluma with Nordlicht of Basel producing the model 2000 in the mid 1990s which in 2012 was further improved, it is the best bottle dynamo currently available. This model was very highly regarded by Chris Juden, the CTC technical expert.

Finding and Using

It is a testament to their durability that you will find Lucifers at almost every cycle-jumble, usually the 800 series. It is advisable to check that the spring is working OK (reject any with weak springs) and that the pulley wheels spins and there is not excess play – if there is, then the dynamo will not run silently. Don't worry too much about appearance, most will have lost their plating. Usually by spinning a Combi by hand you can get a light. It is possible to use a Lucifer with a modern halogen bulb, the results are a light safe to use in modern traffic conditions Front lights are rarer but Lucifer used a very thin brass for their light shells – this means that they are a lot lighter than other contemporary lights but it is common to find headlight shells with numerous cracks. Within reason this will not make the light unusable though. You can use a LED bulb but this will need to be done in conjunction with a voltage resister

Baby Lucifers are fitted to left hand fork blade (this does make it very easy to turn the dynamo off and on) but it is essential to ensure the fixing is very secure. Lucifer did make a braze on which the dynamo fitted with two bolts to the frame. Like most dynamos you need to ensure all elements are earthed and the generator is aligned to the centre of the hub and fitted quite high on the tyre.

So full beam ahead and no excuses for not fitting period lighting to that bike.

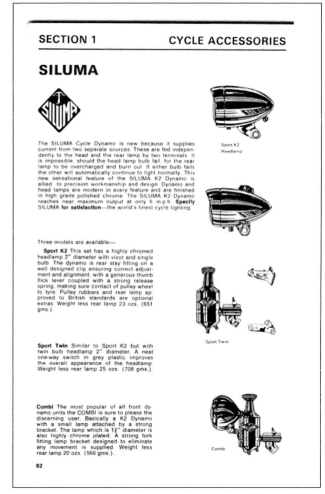

Fig. 11 Siluma Dynamos from the 1970 Ron Kitching *Everything Cycling*. The K2 is identical to the Lucifer Aero light.

Used for Research

Holdsworthy Aids catalogues: throughout the post-WWII period

Lucifer Catalogues produced by Walter Flory

Appendix A: Numbering and Dating

Believe serial number with letter prefix post WW2

Known dynamos: 700 unbadged $, 700", 800*, 900**

A $	N*
B "$	
C "	P*
D*	R*
E*	S*
F* "	T***
G*	
H*	V**
J *	
	X**
L*	Y**
M* **	

700 A to F, 800 D to T, 900 T to Y so overlap
T= 1966   D 1949

Known receipt a D800 bought in FW Evans February1952 (older stock?) D is by far the most common prefix.

Only dynamo that doesn't fit with above is an M900 series of which I have seen two and are likely to be prototypes as one came from a rider who tested components for Ron Kitching, Harry Aspden.

Production ceased 1970/71

Appendix B: Front Lights

Post war lamps are numbered and have the prefix of the series in front when sold as a set eg 807:

7. Combi (also known as the Sport) 41mm diameter

9. Battery/Dynamo (large) with resister to stop battery bulb being blown by dynamo and also wired so rear light stays on when stationary NB no 8 enamelled. Version, 85mm diameter

11 Torpedo   85mm (pre-war design)

Aero Bi   58mm

Bilum   85mm (as 9 but without battery)

Lux (long beam)   68mm

19   Bi Lux with battery   68mm

20 Aero   58mm

22 Two bulb focusing 68mm

Appendix C: References:

Cycling 25th Nov 1920 Pedlite (flat type) illustration but no mention it being Swiss price 40/-
CTC Gazette December 1921 p248 show report Ref to Dekla and the Pedlite cost 45/-
Cycling 30th Nov 1922 Pedlite illustration in show report

Cycling 12th Oct 1923 Pedlite illustration and description as part of the show. Also advertisement. 19th October further review
Cycling 31st October 1924 show review Pedlite illustrated p 394 26s de Luxe, 24s standard
Cycling 7th November 1924 Pedlite mentioned but no illustration p426
CTC Gazette Nov 1924 p340 illustration of the Pedlite imported by Dekla.
Cycling 8th October 1926 illustration and reference to them being imported by Constrictor
Cycling 21st Sept 1928 note saying Sowerby of EC1 now import Lucifer
CTC Gazette Dec 1929 letter by Vernon Blake saying Lucifer made the French Radios dynamos and he prefers the latter.
Cycling 26th Sept 1930 review with illustration of headlight and ad with flat type (Sowerby).
CTC Gazette Nov 1930 p397 letter on using a Lucifer with a resister.
Cycling 1931 23rd Nov p307 lighting review illustration of headlight
Brown Brothers 1933 shows the flat type
CTC Gazette Jan1935 p32 letter Lucifer 4.5v regarded as ideal set.
CTC Gazette Feb 1935 p59 letter saying Lucifer lights not being imported anymore.
CTC Gazette July 1935 p264 letter describing Lucifer as magnificent as and much lighter than English sets.
CTC Gazette Jan 1936 p35 ref to Lucifer front light and request for lightweight front lights.
Brown Brothers 1937 p202 illustration of lights and the two dynamos
The Bicycle 2nd November 1937. Review of show

and W Hills stand mentions the flat and new 12 pole dynamo

CTC Gazette Nov and Dec 1937 Halfords ad. has illustration of the 12 pole

The Bicycle 5th November 1938 review of the show and W.Hills stand

Holdsworth Aids 1938 and 1939 illustration of 12 pole also features standard

CTC Gazette Feb 1938 p52 two letters about how good the twelve pole and flat type are

Brown Brothers supplement Aug 1939 Baby described as new and illustration of the 12 pole and headlight.. Also their 1939 catalogue has two pages on Lucifer

Cycling 2nd November 38 show review introduction of baby series and ref to maximum light output obtained at 8mph

Cycling 25th August 1949 p213 first reference to the 800 series.

The Bicycle 21st Dec 49 Ron Kitching advert: Lucifer Baby sets 52/6

Holdsworth Aids 1951 800 series

Cycling 16th Sept 1954 Lucifer ad and article on winter lighting

Cycling 7th Oct 54 First of a series of Lucifer ads by Buntings of Staples Corner p14 supplement.

1955 *General Fitting Company* catalogue.

1950's *The Complete Cyclist R J Way* p88 illustration of Baby 800 and seat stay rear light.

1957 to 1963 *Sporting Cyclist*, Walter Flory advertisements.

Cycletouring April 1974 letter comparing the poor quality of 70's dynamos with Lucifer.

Cycletouring Oct 1977 Equipment review of lights, feedback from CTC members none of the

modern sets approach Lucifer for quality and reliability.

Cycletouring Feb 1990 letter "Where has Lucifer gone"

Lionel Joseph: The First Century of the Bicycle and its Accessories 1996 has illustrations of the Pedlite & Standard with Pre-war focusing light

News and Views Dec 2009 p31 photos of a Lucifer standard

Importers /Wholesalers

Dekla	1920 to 25?
Constrictor	1926/7
C H Sowerby	1928 to The Bicycle 5/11/1938 review of the show
W Hill	1930s and 40s
Holdsworth	early 30s and to 1970
Walter Flory	1948 to 1970

LUCIFER CATALOGUE
1940s originally printed
for the 700 series but
hand amended with the
introduction of the 800
Thanks to John Harvie for
this item

" LUCIFER "

the oldest manufacturers of Electric
Cycle Lighting Sets maintain their fundamental principle of exclusively manufacturing well-conceived products which
satisfy their customers in every respect.

Just as they led in the field of technical
perfection when Cycle Lighting Sets
were in their very infancy, so they are
still in the vanguard to-day. "Lucifer"
means quality! This is the reason why
"Lucifer" products are so much in the
public favour everywhere. To the dealer
"Lucifer" products ensure handsome
profits.

Many thousands of retailers throughout
the world stock

Lucifer

First in 1910   -   Foremost to-day !

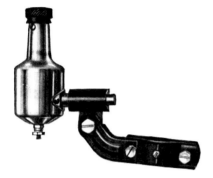

"Lucifer-Baby" Dynamo

No. 800

all chromium finished, 6 Volts — 0,45 Amp.

Weight with bracket, without flex :
14¹/₂ ozs. — 410 grammes.

Although this dynamo is extremely small, its electrical output is that of a much larger dynamo and its shape is very smart. It is one of the most perfect generators which have been manufactured up to date.

Perfect output control

Thanks to a patented shunt of special conception, a perfect output control is ensured with this dynamo. Bulbs will therefore no longer burn out prematurely. A good beam of light is obtained at a speed of 3 miles an hour and the normal output is reached at 7 miles per hour.

Easy replacement of bearings

The special construction of the dynamo permits an extremely easy replacement of worn-out bearings. Any cycle dealer will be able to do the job within less than two minutes!

Easy running

The running of this dynamo is particularly smooth. It works perfectly under any weather conditions and without fatiguing the rider.

No contact brushes

The adoption of the rotary type magnet has enabled us to do away with contact brushes and all their inconveniences, such as rapid wear, bad contacts, etc.

No loss of magnetic power

Thanks to the use of a special magnetic steel, Lucifer magnets will never lose their strength. They are even unaffected by short-circuits.

Minimum wear

Even after several years of steady use, the only replacement likely to be necessary is that of the driving pulley and perhaps of the bearings, which can be changed by any cycle dealer without difficulty in less than two minutes.

Smartness of appearance

The whole mechanism of the "Lucifer-Baby" dynamo is enclosed in a chromium plated waterproof case, which gives the dynamo a smart and attractive appearance of its own.

New hardening process

All steel parts exposed to wear are subject to a modern process of hardening, which gives them an unequalled hardness.

Brackets and cables

All generators are supplied with brackets, but not with flexes. Flexes are attached to the headlamps. Unless otherwise specified, we supply cables for fixing to frontwheel.

Two years guarantee

All "Lucifer" sets are guaranteed for two years against any defect in material or workmanship.

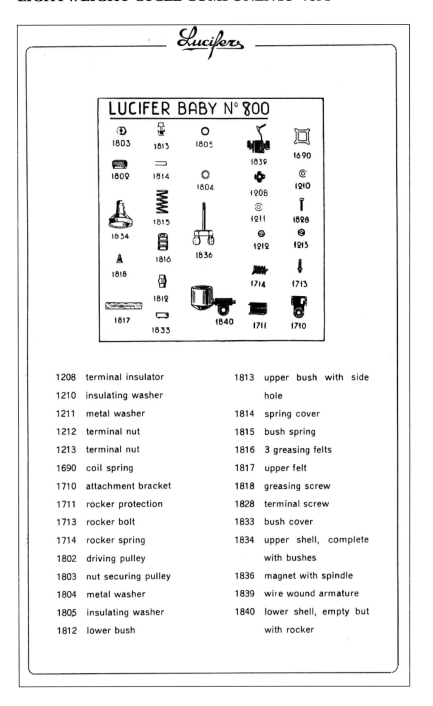

LUCIFER BABY N° 800

1208	terminal insulator	1813	upper bush with side hole
1210	insulating washer		
1211	metal washer	1814	spring cover
1212	terminal nut	1815	bush spring
1213	terminal nut	1816	3 greasing felts
1690	coil spring	1817	upper felt
1710	attachment bracket	1818	greasing screw
1711	rocker protection	1828	terminal screw
1713	rocker bolt	1833	bush cover
1714	rocker spring	1834	upper shell, complete with bushes
1802	driving pulley		
1803	nut securing pulley	1836	magnet with spindle
1804	metal washer	1839	wire wound armature
1805	insulating washer	1840	lower shell, empty but with rocker
1812	lower bush		

How to take to pieces

1. Unscrew upper shell. Use our special wooden pincers; with a lathe the shell may be crushed.
2. Unscrew the oiling screw.
3. Unscrew pulley-nut and pull out the magnet.
4. Unscrew with special screw-driver the bush cover 1833. Bushes and spring will then come out easy.

Repairing: Change bushes, felts, clean and oil. Polish axle if necessary.

Putting together:

1st Operation

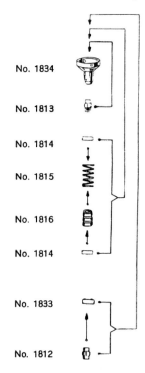

No. 1834	Keep upper shell in indicated position.
No. 1813	Introduce upper bush 1813 lateral opening first.
No. 1814	Put cover on to the spring.
No. 1815	
No. 1816	Introduce 3 felts into the spring.
No. 1814	Shut the spring with cover.
No. 1833	Introduce lower bush 1812 into the bush cover 1833; hold it by the bush and introduce it into the shell. Then tighten with special screw-driver.
No. 1812	

Lucifer

2nd Operation

No. 1805

No. 1804

No. 1836

Introduce first metal washer, insulating washer afterwards.

3rd Operation

Oil axle and bushes with sewing machine oil.

No. 1818

Move the axle in all directions once introduced into the shell in order to obtain the alignment of the bushes.

Oil through hole and put the screw 1818.

4th Operation

No. 1803

No. 1802

1. Lay the nut 1803 into the pulley 1802 and screw both together on the axle.

2. Tighten the pulley **(not the shell)** in a lathe, hold the nut with a screw-driver and turn the shell with the other hand.

3. Loosen and tighten as often as necessary until an easy rotation of the shell is obtained.

4. Screw upper shell on to the lower shell and make sure of easy running.

Could either fitted to the Combi or mounted on the front mudguard

---

Lucifer

"Lucifer-Sport" Headlamp

No. 7

Weight without bracket: $2^1/_3$ ozs. — 65 grammes.
Diameter of front glass: 1.6 ins. — 41 mm.

This miniature-headlamp is of smart design and very carefully executed.

It is fully chromium plated, and provided with an excellent reflector and a special domed glass.

The adjustable bulb holder which is placed in the interior of the lamp is adjustable for focussing purposes and enables a very good lighting effect to be obtained.

The "Lucifer-Sport" headlamp has been especially constructed to be fitted on the mudguard by means of the bracket "G", or directly on the "Lucifer-Baby" dynamo itself. In the latter case it forms one unit with the dynamo under No. 707 F, of which full description will be found on next page.

For brackets see special page.

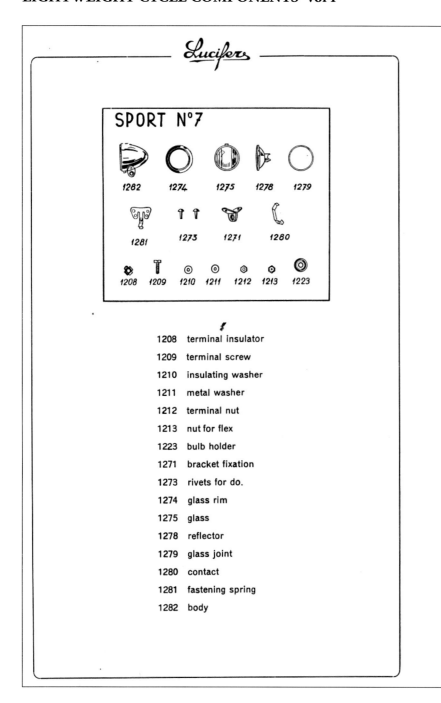

SPORT N°7

1282	1274	1275	1278	1279
1281	1273	1271	1280	
1208	1209	1210	1211	1212	1213	1223

1208 terminal insulator
1209 terminal screw
1210 insulating washer
1211 metal washer
1212 terminal nut
1213 nut for flex
1223 bulb holder
1271 bracket fixation
1273 rivets for do.
1274 glass rim
1275 glass
1278 reflector
1279 glass joint
1280 contact
1281 fastening spring
1282 body

Known as
Combi

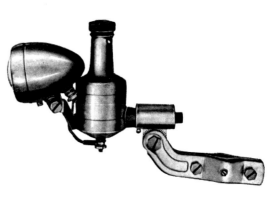

"Lucifer-Sport" Lighting Set
No. 907 F

Weight complete with dynamo and headlamp brackets :
18 ozs. — 510 grammes.

This set consists of the Baby dynamo No. 900 and the Sport headlamp No. 7 as shown on the previous page. Headlamp and dynamo are fully chromium plated. The headlamp is fitted on the dynamo by means of a chromium plated bracket, so that both form one harmonious unit. The combined " Lucifer-Sport " lighting set is supplied only with the " Lucifer-Baby " generator.

This lighting set has been especially designed to be fitted on racing cycles and carrier cycles with front carriers.

Special rubber pulleys : For this " Lucifer-Sport " lighting set and for each of our dynamos to be fitted to racing cycles with sprint tyres, we particularly recommend our special rubber pulleys, which prevent rapid wear of the tyre. This special rubber pulley can be supplied with the " Lucifer Baby " dynamo for a small increase in price.

For brackets see special page.

Lucifer

" Lucifer-Battery " Headlamp

Enamelled **No. 8**

Chromium **No. 9**

Weight without bracket: 10 ²/₃ ozs. — 295 grammes.
Diameter of glass : 3.3 ins. — 85 mm.

This battery headlamp is of a very smart stream-lined design with a special domed glass which still further increases its smartness. It can be supplied with a chromium-plated glass rim and enamelled body, or with an all-chromium plated body. Its reflector is watertight and no dust can penetrate into it to diminish its reflecting power. This battery headlamp has been very carefully studied and may be regarded as the very best solution of the combined dynamo and battery lighting set.

By means of the two bulbs in the interior of the body, the cyclist will have light not only when riding, but also when the cycle is stationary. The main bulb only is fed by the dynamo, but the pilot bulb, an ordinary 3 ¹/₂ Volts pocket-lamp bulb, can be fed by the battery as well as by the dynamo, thus giving a good pilot light which is especially appreciated in heavy traffic and when encountering other vehicles.

Lucifer

Both bulb holders are adjustable; the filament of the bulb can thus be placed exactly in the focussing centre of the reflector, which ensures a really good lighting effect. Any ordinary pocket-lamp battery of 3—4 ¹/₂ volts can be employed and placed quite easily into the battery holder.

There are two new features which deserve to be specially mentioned :

The pilot bulb, an ordinary pocket-lamp bulb, although fed by one of the powerful " Lucifer " dynamos, will not burn out by reason of a resistance which has been built into the circuit.

The rearlamp, which has to be connected to the headlamp, can be fed not only by the dynamo, but also by the battery, thus giving a sufficient protection to the cyclist not only when riding but also when the bicycle is stationary.

The smart and strong switch placed in easy reach on the body of the headlamp operates by means of a mechanism of the finest construction which will give no trouble.

For brackets see special page.

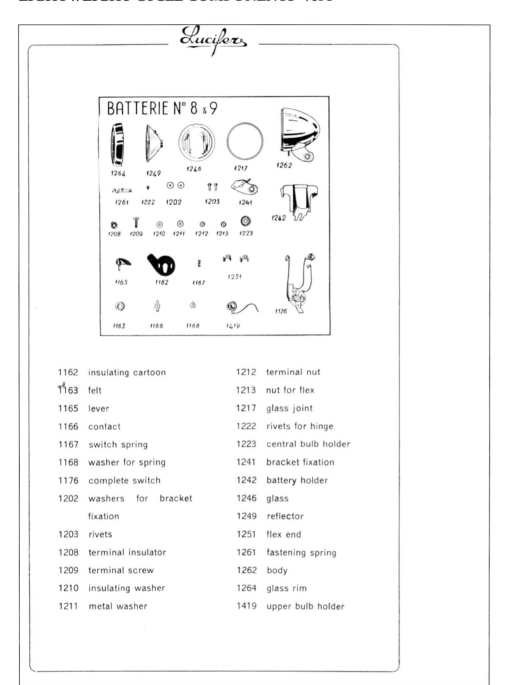

1162	insulating cartoon	1212	terminal nut
1163	felt	1213	nut for flex
1165	lever	1217	glass joint
1166	contact	1222	rivets for hinge
1167	switch spring	1223	central bulb holder
1168	washer for spring	1241	bracket fixation
1176	complete switch	1242	battery holder
1202	washers for bracket fixation	1246	glass
1203	rivets	1249	reflector
1208	terminal insulator	1251	flex end
1209	terminal screw	1261	fastening spring
1210	insulating washer	1262	body
1211	metal washer	1264	glass rim
		1419	upper bulb holder

"Lucifer-Torpedo" headlamp

with 1 bulb

No. 11

Weight without bracket : $6\frac{1}{3}$ ozs. — 180 grammes.
Diameter of glass : 3.3 ins. — 85 mm.

Streamline shaped, all-chromium plated, with one bulb and flat glass.

The bulb holder is placed in the interior of the body and enables perfect adjustment to the focussing centre of the reflector, thus ensuring a very good projection.

The reflector is completely waterproof and especially designed for excellent diffusion of the light.

The "Lucifer-Torpedo" headlamp is the ideal lamp for luxury and tourist cycles.

For headlamp brackets see special page.

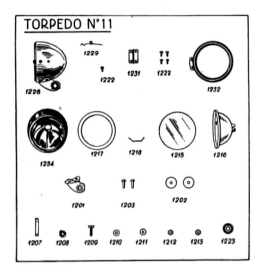

TORPEDO N°11

1201	bracket fixation	1216	reflector
1202	washers	1217	glass joint
1203	rivets	1218	glass spring
1207	contact	1222	rivets
1208	terminal insulator	1223	bulb holder
1209	terminal screw	1228	body
1210	insulating washer	1229	fastening spring
1211	metal washer	1231	hinge
1212	terminal nut	1232	glass rim
1213	nut for flex	1234	reflector with glass rim fitted
1215	glass		

"Lucifer Aero-Bi" Headlamp

With 2 bulbs
No. 14

Weight without bracket : 6 ozs. — 170 grammes.
Diameter of glass: 2.3 ins. — 58 mm.

Streamline designed, all chromium plated, with two bulbs, smart switch on the body and provided with a special optical glass.

The two adjustable bulb holders in the interior of the headlamp permit an exact adjustment of the filament of both bulbs to the focussing centre and thus ensure an excellent projection.

The reflector is watertight and produces a large diffusion of the light with no dark spots.

Changing from the main bulb to the pilot bulb, or the reverse, is effected by means of a switch which is placed on the headlamp body, and can easily be manipulated by the cyclist whilst riding.

The pilot light is especially useful in heavy traffic and when encountering other vehicles.

For headlamp brackets see special page.

Lucifer

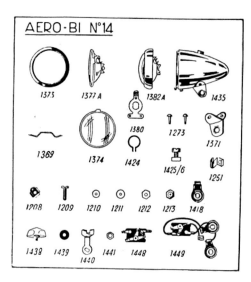

AERO-BI N°14

1208	terminal insulator	1380	fastening spring
1209	terminal screw	1382A	reflector with glassrim
1210	insulating washer	1418	bulb holder
1211	metal washer	1424	bulb holder fastener
1212	terminal nut	1425/6	screw and nut for do.
1213	nut for flex	1435	body
1251	flex end	1438	lever
1273	rivets	1439	washer
1371	bracket fixation	1440	switch contact
1373	glass ring	1441	nut
1374	glass	1448	switch alone
1277A	reflector	1449	switch with flexes and
1369	glass spring		·bulb holders

Lucifer

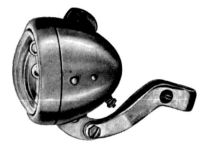

"Lucifer-Bilum" Headlamp

With 2 bulbs

No. 15

Weight without bracket : $8^3/_5$ ozs. — 245 grammes.
Diameter of glass : 3.3 ins. — 85 mm.

Streamline designed, all chromium plated, with two bulbs, smart switch on the body and a special domed glass.

The two adjustable bulb holders in the interior of the headlamp permit an exact adjustment of the filament of both bulbs to the focussing centre, thus ensuring an excellent projection.

The reflector is completely watertight and produces a very large diffusion of the light with no dark spots.

Changing from the main bulb to the pilot bulb, so as to obtain a good pilot light, or the reverse, is effected by means of a switch placed on the headlamp body, wich can easily be manipulated by the cyclist whilst riding.

The light produced by the pilot bulb is an excellent pilot light, which will be particularly useful in heavy traffic and when encountering other vehicles.

For headlamp brackets see special page.

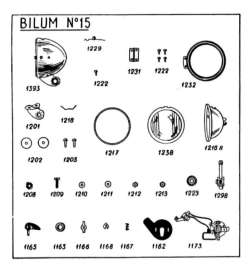

1162	switch insulator	1211	metal washer
1163	felt	1212	terminal nut
1165	switch	1213	nut for flex
1166	switch contact	1216 A	reflector
1167	spring	1217	glass joint
1168	washer	1218	glass spring
1173	switch, interior complete	1222	rivets
1201	bracket fixation	1223	bulb holder
1202	washers	1229	fastening spring
1203	rivets	1231	hinge
1208	terminal insulator	1232	glass rim
1209	terminal screw	1238	glass
1210	insulating washer	1298	contact
		1393	body

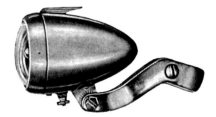

"Lucifer-Aero" Headlamp

No. 20

Weight without bracket: 4¹⁄₂ ozs. — 130 grammes.
Diameter of glass: 2.3 ins. — 58 mm.

All chromium plated, of striking streamlined shape with top external decoration, giving it a smart, modern appearance.

It is provided with a special domed glass. The adjustable bulb holder is placed inside the body and ensures a very bright light due to the possibility of accurate focussing. The whole headlamp is very carefully manufactured, as it is the case with all Lucifer products.

The "Aero" headlamp has been especially constructed for fitting on the frontwheel mudguard by means of the bracket "H". It can, however, also be fitted to the head stem by means of all other brackets except F and G.

This headlamp of medium size will appeal particularly to ladies and clubmen.

For headlamp brackets see special page.

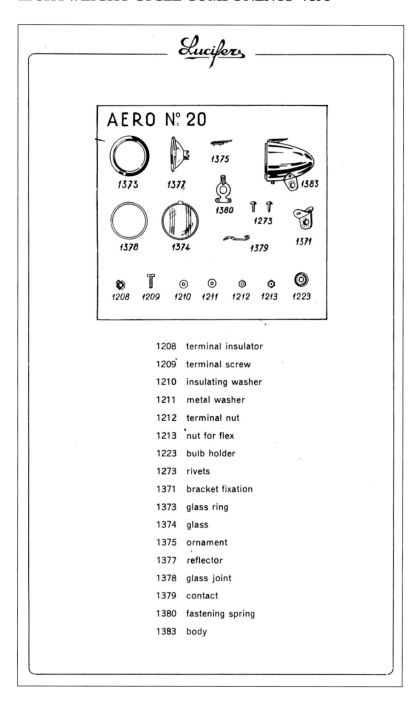

1208   terminal insulator
1209   terminal screw
1210   insulating washer
1211   metal washer
1212   terminal nut
1213   nut for flex
1223   bulb holder
1273   rivets
1371   bracket fixation
1373   glass ring
1374   glass
1375   ornament
1377   reflector
1378   glass joint
1379   contact
1380   fastening spring
1383   body

REARLIGHTS

Securita

For fitting to the rearstay. The glass rim is fastened to the body by means of a bayonet device; the bulb can therefore easily be removed and replaced. The Lucifer rearlight "Securita" is an ornament for any cycle and differs from the usual rearlamps by its smartness and its careful execution which is the hall-mark of all Lucifer products. The rearlamp "Securita" is always supplied in black enamel with a chromium plated rim.

Weight complete with flex
and flex fasteners : 3³⁄₅ ozs.
100 grammes.

Reflecta

This rearlight is intended to be fitted on to the rearmudguard in place of a ferrylight-reflector. The fitting of this rearlight is very strong and practical.

This rearlight which is, like the "Securita", fed by the generator, is also provided with a reflecting lens, which gives the cyclist double safety and renders him independent of the light produced by the dynamo. The whole lamp is well protected against dust and dirt.

The rearlight "Reflecta" is supplied in aluminium finish. Unless special instructions are given, our rearlights are always supplied complete with flex.

Weight complete with flex
and flex fasteners : 2 ozs.
60 grammes.

Securita had
been withdrawn
by the late 40s

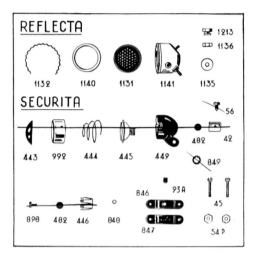

42	terminal	847	bracket
45	screw	848	insulating tube
54 P	nut	849	washer
56	flex tightening screw	898	terminal screw
93 A	contact screw	992	glass rim
443	red glass	1131	red glass
444	glass spring	1132	glass spring
445	reflector	1135	washer
446	bulb holder	1136	nut
449	body	1140	glass joint
482	insulating washer	1141	body
846	bracket	1213	flex tightening nut

BRACKETS

All Lucifer brackets are extremely strong, smart and yet light. They are supplied in black enamel, white cadmium plate or at a slightly increased price in chromium plate. — Please specify what is desired.

Dynamo brackets

The same type of bracket can be used with all Lucifer dynamos. All generators are supplied with brackets. To fit dynamo brackets to narrow section stays special liners are available. See also our special bracket to be soldered on to the fork.

Standard bracket for fork or seat stay

		ozs.	g
Ordinary dynamo bracket		3¹⁄₂	90
Liners for narrow section stays, pair		³⁄₅	15
Brackets for soldering on fork		2	60

Fitting instructions at disposal

Headlamp brackets

There are 11 models. We would ask our customers kindly to state in their orders which type of bracket they wish to receive. — The mostly used brackets are: A for lamp holder; U, "universal" can be fitted on to all bicycles.

		Steel		Aluminium	
		ozs.	g	ozs.	g
Bracket A		1³⁄₄	50		
Bracket B		4	110		
Bracket C		2²⁄₅	70		

1.57 ins. 40 mm.

4.13 ins. 105 mm.

3.15 ins. 80 mm.

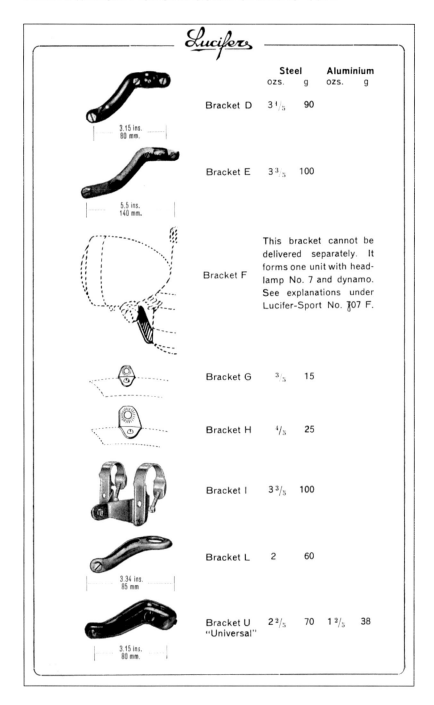

		Steel		Aluminium	
		ozs.	g	ozs.	g
Bracket D		3 1/5	90		
Bracket E		3 3/5	100		
Bracket F		This bracket cannot be delivered separately. It forms one unit with headlamp No. 7 and dynamo. See explanations under Lucifer-Sport No. 707 F.			
Bracket G		3/5	15		
Bracket H		4/5	25		
Bracket I		3 3/5	100		
Bracket L		2	60		
Bracket U "Universal"		2 2/5	70	1 2/5	38

3.15 ins. / 80 mm.

5.5 ins. / 140 mm.

3.34 ins. / 85 mm.

3.15 ins. / 80 mm.

BULBS

Weight : 2 grammes
31 grains

Unless special instructions are given, our headlamps and rearlights are supplied with our "Lucifer" bulbs which are included in the price. These bulbs are silk frosted and ensure a good and even diffusion of the light.

For the "Lucifer" lighting sets we particularly recommend the use of our "Lucifer" bulbs wich are especially manufactured for our sets. The lighting effect obtained with these bulbs is more satisfactory and they last considerably longer.

The "Lucifer" bulbs recommended are the following :

3 1/2 Volts — 0.2 Amp. for pilot light in Battery headlamp No. 9
4 1/2   »   — 0.35   »   » old Lucifer dynamos
6   »   — 0.35   »   » Lucifer-Baby dynamos
10   »   — 0.45   »   » Lucifer-Super 12 dynamos
6   »   — 0.04   »   » all Lucifer rearlamps.

CABLES

Cables of sufficient mechanical resistance and of the required electrical section should be used. We supply first class cables, either separately or in bundles of approximately 110 yds. Except by special agreement, our sets are supplied with cables. Dynamos alone are supplied **without** cables, headlamps and rearlights alone **with** cables. Unless otherwise specified, we supply cables for fixing to frontwheel.

SPARE PARTS FOR DYNAMOS AND HEADLAMPS

We supply all spare parts for our generators and headlamps. They are illustrated and numbered in our special price lists for spare parts.

Box containing the most usual spare parts and tools

Ask for quotation

Weight complete : 5 ¹/₂ lbs.
2480 grammes

Artistic Window Display

Particulars at your disposal.

Weight complete, with sets : 6 ⁵/₈ lbs.
2980 grammes
without sets : 3 ¹/₈ lbs.
1410 grammes

TERMS

Prices

Our prices are, without engagement, valid for orders of at least 100 complete sets, or 200 generators or 200 headlamps alone, packed in standard cases suitable for oversea transport. For exceptional consignments by parcel post, prices are proportionately increased.

Delivery of orders

As a rule we are able to supply any quantity of sets from our stock.

Payment

Our goods are normally forwarded against documentary sight draft, payable through a bank on receipt of goods.

Insurance

We insure all shipments against damage and ordinary loss with a highly reputed Swiss insurance company, unless a special arrangement has been made with the consignee. In case any damage or shortage were to happen, an official statement, duly signed, is to be made out immediately on receipt of goods. Claims in respect of parcel-post should be addressed to the Post-Master who will make out a detailed statement. These documents should be sent to us immediately for lodging the claim with the insurance company.

Packing

Always free of charge.

Alterations of models

We reserve the right to alter and improve our models at any time.

Guarantee

We guarantee all our products for two years from the date of delivery against faulty construction or material. This guarantee is limited to free replacement of any defective parts. Expenses incurred in connection with the return of defective sets to our works are at the buyer's charge.

INSTRUCTION FOR ORDERING

For complete sets and headlamps put the letter corresponding to the bracket wanted at the end of the Order No. or the Cable Code (example : 720 D, or BAAED).

In order to get the weight

add the weight of sets or the headlamp and the headlamp bracket you want.

Bulbs

are included in price and weight. If sets or headlamps have to be sent without bulbs please specify it.

Flexes

are always joined to the headlamps and not to the dynamos. Unless otherwise specified, we supply cables for fixing to frontwheel.

Prices for Spare Bulbs

without extra charge for freight if delivered together with sets.

Prices for Spare Parts

for goods delivered FOR Geneva unless delivered together with sets.

Order No.	Cable code	Specification	Bulbs	Finish	Glass diam. inches	Flex length inches	Weights with dynamo bracket but without headlamp brackets net-net Gr.	net Gr.	rough
		Complete sets with Dynamo Baby No. 900, 6 V. - 0.45 Amp. and :							
807	BASP-	headlamp SPORT No. 7	1	chrom.	1 5/8	F 3	480	540 G	
809	BABA-	» BATTERY No. 9 resistance built in	2	»	3 5/16	G 8	705	620 F	
811	BATO-	» TORPEDO No. 11	2	»	3 5/16	24	590	700	
814	BAOB-	» AERO-Bi No. 14 with switch on the body	1	»	2 1/4	24	580	690	
815	BABI-	» BILUM No. 15	1	»	3 5/16	24	660	770	
820	BAAE-	» AERO No. 20	2	»	2 1/4	24	540	650	
900		**Dynamo Lucifer-Baby No. 900 alone, 6 V., 0.45 Amp. with bracket :**					410	460	
700	canut.	CINBA	headlamp with rubber driving pulley for " sprints "				410	460	
		Headlamps alone :							
7	F	headlamp SPORT No. 7 mudguard fixing only by means of bracket G cannot be delivered separately	1	chrom.	3	3	60		
7	SPORG-	» SPORT No. 7	1	chrom.	1 5/8		60		
9	TERI-	» BATTERY No. 9 built in resistance	2	»	3 5/16	24	295		
11	TORP-	» TORPEDO No. 11	2	»	3 5/16	24	180		
14	ARBI-	» AERO-Bi No. 14 with switch on the body	1	»	2 1/4	24	170		
15	BILU-	» BILUM No. 15	1	»	3 5/16	24	250		
20	AERO-	» AERO No. 20	2	»	2 1/4	24	130		
		Lamp brackets : for bicycles with lamp holders (for all headlamps but not No. 7)				H 8			Weights of brackets
A		» handle bar stem fixing					50		
B		» handle bar stem fixing					110		
C		»		ebony or chrom.			70		
D		»					70		
F		»					90		
G		» for mudguard fixing (only for Sport headlamp No. 7) cannot be delivered separately, forms one unit with Baby dynamo headlamp No. 7					10		
H		» handle bar fixing (American) for all head lamps but not No. 7					15		
I		» handle bar fixing (only for Sport headlamp No. 7)					25		
J		» handle bar stem fixing					20		
L		»					130		
U		»					60 alum.		
		Rearlamps : (delivered with flex fasteners) reflexible, mudguard fixing (with bulbs 6 V. — 0.04 A.)	1	alum. ebony	1 5/8		50		
		polished glass, rear stay fixing	1	ebony	1 5/16		35		
Reflecta Securita	REFLE SECUR	reflexible, mudguard fixing				75	60		
						75	60		

Packed in standard cases of 100 sets. In order to obtain the rough weight add 19 Kg. for the case to the **net** weight of every 100 sets.
Example for 100 sets 720 D :
71.5 + 9.0 + 19.0 = 99.5 kg. rough weight.

L U C I F E R

No. 800 — LUCIFER-BABY

(Weight 12 OZS)

This 6 volt. 0,5 amp. (3 watt) capacity dynamo, finished in chromium-plate is the result of many years scientific research and practical experience. A good beam of light is obtained at 3 miles per hour with a normal output at 7 miles per hour.

No 800 F for dynamo with attached bracket for No. 7 F lamp.

Price : for No. 800 or 800-F   32/6

No. 807 F — COMBI

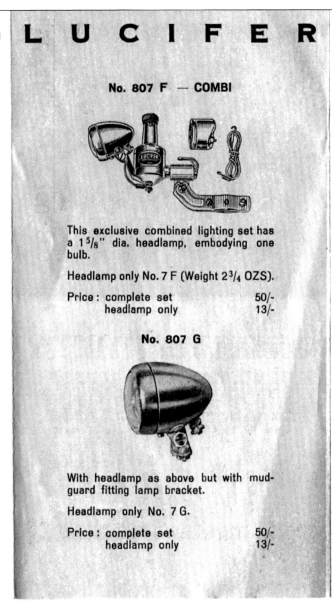

This exclusive combined lighting set has a $1^5/_8$" dia. headlamp, embodying one bulb.

Headlamp only No. 7 F (Weight $2^3/_4$ OZS).

| Price : complete set | 50/- |
| headlamp only | 13/- |

No. 807 G

With headlamp as above but with mud-guard fitting lamp bracket.

Headlamp only No. 7 G.

| Price : complete set | 50/- |
| headlamp only | 13/- |

No. 820 A — AERO

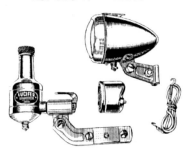

With streamlined $2^1/_8$" dia. headlamp, embodying one bulb.

Headlamp only No. 20 A (Weight $4^1/_2$ OZS).

| Price : complete set | 55/- |
| headlamp only | 17/3 |

No. 814 A — AERO-BI

With headlamp similar to the above but embodying 2 bulbs and two-way switch.

Headlamp only No. 14 A (Weight $5^2/_3$ OZS).

| Price : complete set | 59/6 |
| headlamp only | 21/6 |

Lucifer Catalogue c 1954 produced by Walter Flory, importers to the UK

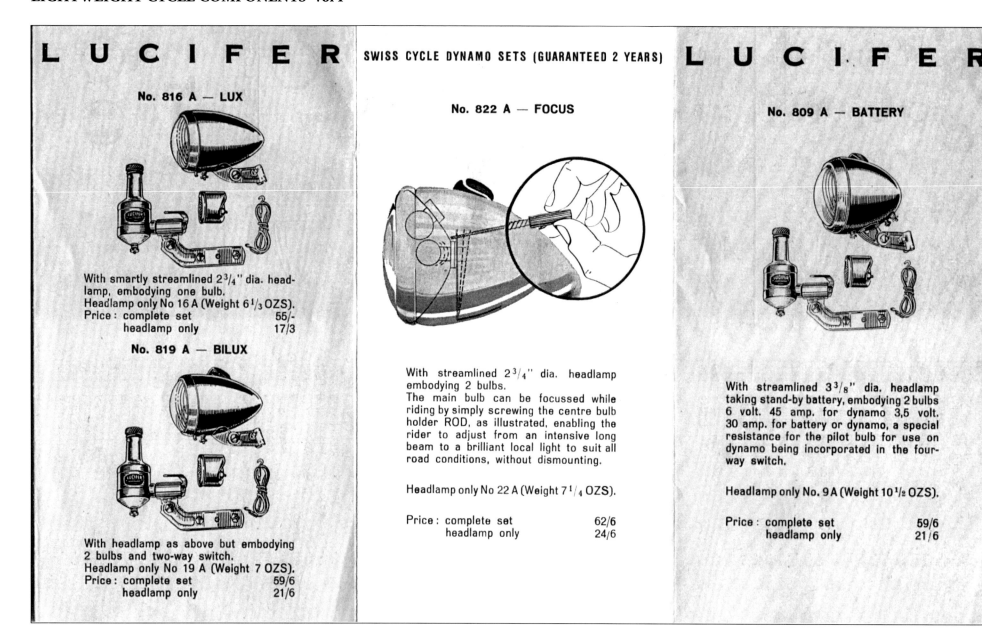

LUCIFER

No. 816 A — LUX

With smartly streamlined 2³/₄" dia. headlamp, embodying one bulb.
Headlamp only No 16 A (Weight 6¹/₃ OZS).
Price : complete set   55/-
      headlamp only   17/3

No. 819 A — BILUX

With headlamp as above but embodying 2 bulbs and two-way switch.
Headlamp only No 19 A (Weight 7 OZS).
Price : complete set   59/6
      headlamp only   21/6

SWISS CYCLE DYNAMO SETS (GUARANTEED 2 YEARS)

No. 822 A — FOCUS

With streamlined 2³/₄" dia. headlamp embodying 2 bulbs.
The main bulb can be focussed while riding by simply screwing the centre bulb holder ROD, as illustrated, enabling the rider to adjust from an intensive long beam to a brilliant local light to suit all road conditions, without dismounting.

Headlamp only No 22 A (Weight 7¹/₄ OZS).

Price : complete set   62/6
      headlamp only   24/6

LUCIFER

No. 809 A — BATTERY

With streamlined 3³/₈" dia. headlamp taking stand-by battery, embodying 2 bulbs 6 volt. 45 amp. for dynamo 3,5 volt. 30 amp. for battery or dynamo, a special resistance for the pilot bulb for use on dynamo being incorporated in the four-way switch.

Headlamp only No. 9 A (Weight 10¹/₂ OZS).

Price : complete set   59/6
      headlamp only   21/6

Late 1950s catalogue issued by Walter Flory

LUCIFER

First in 1910

Foremost today

will

give you YEARS

of good service

and make night

riding a pleasure

Stockist :

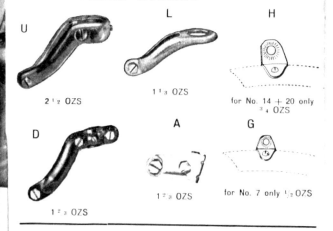

SWISS CYCLE DYNAMO SETS (GUARANTEED 2 YEARS)

DYNAMO BRACKETS

Y   Z   LV

2 ¹⁄₂ OZS   1 ³⁄₄ OZS   ³⁄₄ OZS

Showing standard dynamo bracket « Y » supplied with all dynamos.

Z, LV adjustable dynamo bracket for braze-on front stay.

HEADLAMP BRACKETS

U   L   H

2 ¹⁄₂ OZS   1 ¹⁄₃ OZS   for No. 14 + 20 only ³⁄₄ OZS

D   A   G

1 ²⁄₃ OZS   1 ²⁄₃ OZS   for No. 7 only ¹⁄₂ OZS

LUCI-Grip No. 1892 assures smooth and easy running in all weather conditions.

LUCIFER

All LUCIFER Dynamo sets are supplied with LUCI Dynamo Pulley Grip No. 1892.

All LUCIFER Headlamps are made of brass highly chromium plated.

All LUCIFER Bulbholders are specially ridged enabling the bulb to be focussed.

All LUCIFER Lamp Switches are constructed so as to give an un-interrupted light whilst switching from one bulb to another.

All Headlamps are supplied with Standard « A »-Bracket.

REARLAMPS are with 1¹⁄₂'' Reflectors for mudguard fitting as illustrated, but a stay fitting bracket is supplied with each set, which will shortly be replaced with one with adjustable stay fitting bracket only, torpedo shaped, highly chromed, with 4' cable.

Price : complete with cable & bulb 5/-

BULBS for No. 800 dynamo
     Headlamp 6 volt. .45 amp.
     (2.7 W).   Price :   -/10
     Rearlamp 6 volt. .05 amp.
              or .10 amp.
          Price :   -/10

BESIDES BROOKS

Other British Leather Saddle Makers for Lightweights

"The great advantage of a stretch leather saddle is, once broken in, saddle comfort is a given." (Quote from a letter in the *CTC Gazette*)

Other British saddle makers have been somewhat neglected. Like Brooks these companies were based in Birmingham (with the exception of Middlemores of Coventry). Clearly, Birmingham was an established centre of leather working. The companies covered in this article are Wrights, Mansfield, Wilby, Lycett, Middlemores and Leatheries. I am solely concentrating on their lightweight models, although they all made a range of sprung saddles. Many of their products were copies of Brooks and especially the B17, but there was also an element of innovation; for example, as early as the late 1920s Mansfield offered saddles with alloy frames.

Leather is, of course, one of the less durable materials used on cycles, and not surprisingly the cheaper models have an even shorter life. Lower quality saddles can often be identified by the use of a support layer on the underside made from plastic, card, or even felt. Another indication of a poorer quality saddle is the use of textured leather on the top. Brooks used this technique on a later version of the B5.

It is an indication of Brooks' dominance and influence in this market that they took over three of their competitors, some of whom had already adopted the Brooks system of a letter prefix for their models,

Fig. 1 Leatheries badge from an L99 saddle (their version of the B17). The saddle was made from the late 1930s but this is the badge used post war after they made been taken over by Brooks. (Stephen Tremaine)

based on the first letter of the company name. Thus Wrights W3 and Leatheries L99 (Fig. 1). Confusingly, Middlemores used a B prefix and their B89 was similar to the B17. Although Brooks took over Lycett in the 1920s they continued to offer saddles badged as Lycett well into the 1960s, so the consumer would still think they were a separate company. Unlike other saddle makers, Lycett chose more exotic names for their saddles, for example 'L'Avenir'. Figs. 2 and 3 show a couple of pre-war Lycett saddles.

" LYCETT " AEROBUTT
Leather Top with Flat Girder Base Frame and Elastic Cord Springing (as fitted to Spring Seat Saddles).
Race Model. Size 11″ × 5½″.
No. 25/S204b/*804*   ..   each **11/9**

Fig. 2 & 3 Two Lycett saddles from the 1939 Brown Brothers catalogue. Note the description of the Aerobutt as having elastic cord springing

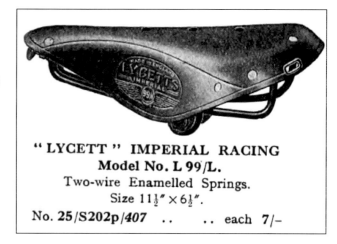

" LYCETT " IMPERIAL RACING
Model No. L 99/L.
Two-wire Enamelled Springs.
Size 11½″ × 6½″.
No. 25/S202p/*407*   ..   ..   each **7/-**

Like Lycett, Leatheries were taken over by Brooks, but in the late 1930s. For a short period Brooks used this trade mark but I do not think its use continued for long after the Second World War. Lycett also used the La Grande trade mark in the 1920s and 1930s for their cheaper models. One very unusual design in the mid 1930s was the model LB1 with a swinging cantle plate.

Bicycle makers at the lower end of the market, such as CWS, often fitted Leatheries saddles. Wrights had probably the highest volume of all these saddle makers and were taken over by Tube Investments (TI) in 1958 (according to Grace's Guide). TI's British Cycle Corporation merged with Raleigh Industries in 1960, so when Brooks was acquired by BCC in 1962 it was inevitable that Wrights and Brooks would be amalgamated. The Wrights trade name continued to be used and many Raleigh and Carlton sports bikes in the 1960s and 70s were fitted with the Wrights W3, similar in shape to the B17 Narrow, but of far inferior leather (with a grained top). These, and similar saddles, were not very durable. Wrights and Lycett offered a Swallow copy, the CL3 and L15, respectively, the latter being similar to the Brooks B15. In the 1940s to 60s Wrights made badged saddles for Dawes, often for lightweights as a copy of the B15 with perforated edges.

In many ways Wilby has a typical history. It was a Victorian rivet manufacturer, founded by Arthur Ernest Wilby, which took advantage of the cycle boom in the 1890s to manufacture saddles. Products were in the main at the lower priced end of the market and the range and production gradually declined until production ceased in the late 1950s.

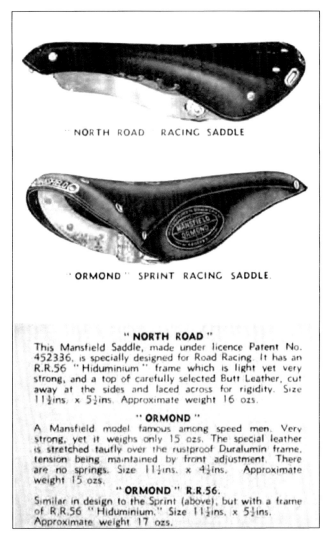

" NORTH ROAD "
This Mansfield Saddle, made under licence Patent No. 452336, is specially designed for Road Racing. It has an R.R.56 " Hiduminium " frame which is light yet very strong, and a top of carefully selected Butt Leather, cut away at the sides and laced across for rigidity. Size 11½ins. x 5¼ins. Approximate weight 16 ozs.

" ORMOND "
A Mansfield model famous among speed men. Very strong, yet it weighs only 15 ozs. The special leather is stretched tautly over the rustproof Duralumin frame, tension being maintained by front adjustment. There are no springs. Size 11½ins. x 4½ins. Approximate weight 15 ozs.

" ORMOND " R.R.56.
Similar in design to the Sprint (above), but with a frame of R.R.56 " Hiduminium." Size 11½ins. x 5¼ins. Approximate weight 17 ozs.

Fig. 4 Two classic Mansfield alloy framed saddles. Of leather of any saddle, although it still had saddlebag loops. National Cycle Library

Mansfield offered, I think, the most interesting range of all these makers. As early as the late 1920s they offered alloy-framed models (Fig. 4), and these and the steel framed Bath Road (Fig. 5) were

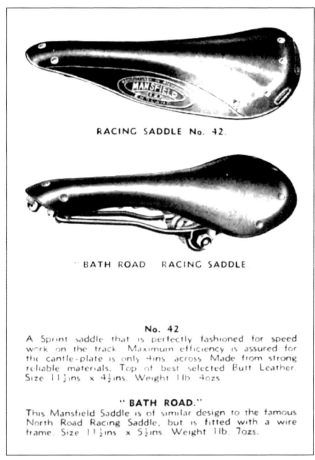

No. 42
A Sprint saddle that is perfectly fashioned for speed work on the track. Maximum efficiency is assured for the cantle-plate is only 4ins. across. Made from strong reliable materials. Top of best selected Butt Leather. Size 11½ins. x 4½ins. Weight 1lb. 4ozs.

" BATH ROAD."
This Mansfield Saddle is of similar design to the famous North Road Racing Saddle, but is fitted with a wire frame. Size 11½ins. x 5½ins. Weight 1lb. 7ozs.

Fig. 5 Mansfield's other 'famous road' saddle and a sprint saddle both with conventional wire frames. National Cycle Library

high quality products. These saddles clearly had an appeal as they were offered as alternatives by many of the small builders in the 1930s and 40s, for example, Macleans, Bates and Hetchins. The alloy frames had a reputation for cracking (Brooks had a similar problem with their alloy cantle range B27, 37 and 57) so careful treatment is essential. Post-war Mansfield used Evelyn Hamilton extensively in

Fig. 6 Evelyn Hamilton must have found sufficient comfort from her Mansfield 38N. National Cycle Library.

their advertising (Fig. 6). According to their 1952 catalogue she had recently cycled 12,000 miles in 100 days using a Mansfield model 38N saddle. They survived until around 1968, their output and range gradually dimishing.

During the 1930s Mansfield and Lycett offered what the 1937 J A Grose catalogue called 'spring top Aero-Race saddles' (Fig. 7). This was a stretched leather saddle in either B17 or Swallow shape but with mattress springs underneath for increased comfort. Lycett even had a model with a duralumin chassis, so there was a degree of innovation, as this was not a design offered by Brooks.

One disadvantage of these saddles was that there was no means of tensioning the leather, so they tended to sag (and they were heavy). Mansfield and Leatheries, like Brooks, made touring bags, Mansfield offering the novelty of dyed leather.

Middlemores, an old established maker of horse saddles (known until c1920 as Middlemore and Lamplugh), continued to make a limited range of saddles after the 1960s, gradually reducing the range at the end of the 70s. About this time cheap plastic saddles from the Far East began to dominate the market, driving out any demand for more affordable leather saddles. It is interesting to

note that at the end of the 1980s, the best known French company, Ideale, also disappeared. As an aside, are French cows different from British? I have always found Ideale leather completely different from British, being very difficult to break in.

Although Brooks tried to break into the ATB market with the sprung Conquest, leather saddles became a declining market in the 1990s. In the twenty first century they now have retro fashion appeal. It strikes me that Brooks have very successfully tapped into this market and are fast becoming the Burberry of the cycling world, able to massively increase the price of their saddles by creating an image of solid British provenance, sustainability and quality.

References

Catalogues for Wrights, Brooks and Mansfield in the National Cycle Museum/V-CC Collection. 1937 J A Grose catalogue. 1937 and 1952 Brown Brothers catalogues. 1930s CTC Gazettes, specifically the Show review number (usually November or December). The reviews always included saddles, often with illustrations. Various Flickr saddle groups (I even found an image of the last Mansfield factory). A Google search reveals a number of Birmingham local history forums which have details on addresses and some recollections by ex-staff.

Location of Birmingham Based Saddle Makers

Leatheries: Sampson Road North. Lycett: Arthur Street. Mansfield: three addresses, but latterly Heathfield Road, Handsworth. Wilby: Holloway Head. Wrights: Dale Road (1950s/60s)

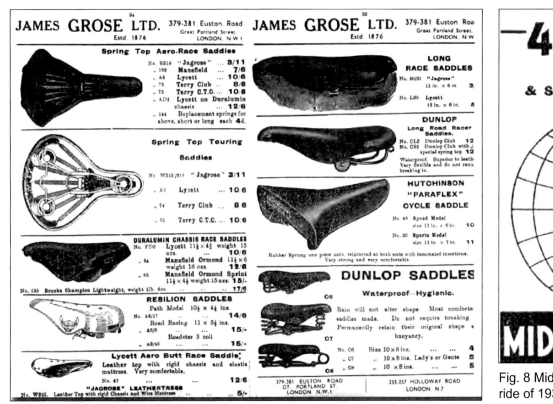

Fig. 7 Pages 94 and 95 of James Grose 1937 catalogue

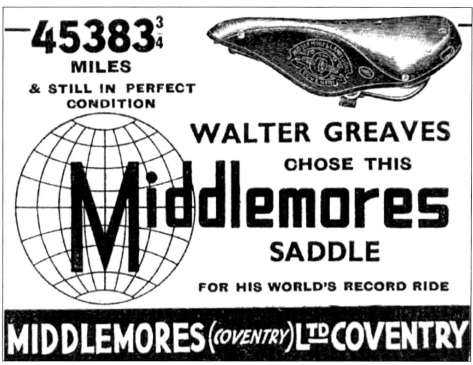

Fig. 8 Middlemores' advertisement celebrating Walter Greaves' record breaking ride of 1936

Acknowledgments

Thanks to Alvin Smith, Stephen Tremaine and Nick Hando for additional information.

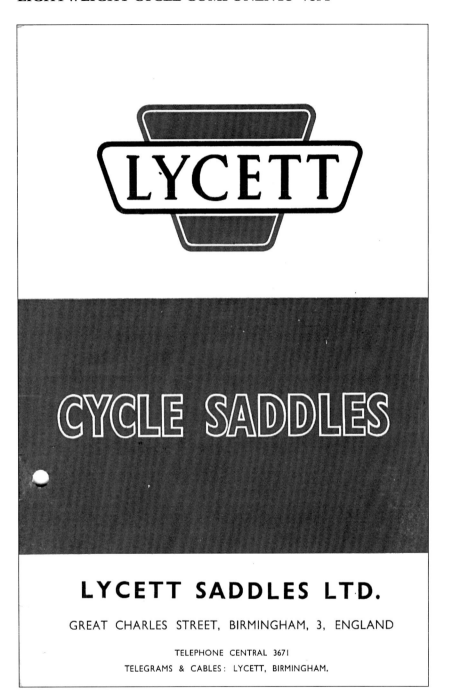

LYCETT

CYCLE SADDLES

LYCETT SADDLES LTD.

GREAT CHARLES STREET, BIRMINGHAM, 3, ENGLAND

TELEPHONE CENTRAL 3671
TELEGRAMS & CABLES: LYCETT, BIRMINGHAM.

Here is a full new range of Cycle Saddles bearing the well-known LYCETT name—a name which has been a guarantee of satisfaction for many years.

Our aim is to produce saddles of outstanding comfort, strength and reliability, and, whatever your choice, you will find a LYCETT saddle to suit your particular need.

We are always freely available to advise on all saddle problems.

TWO WIRE

L.15 NARROW

Sports model, with solid leather top. Mounted on light, sturdy two-wire frame.

Finish: Black Enamel. Size: 11 × 6 × 2⅞ in.
Weight: 1-lb. 7-ozs. Price 23/9.

L.15 STANDARD

Similar in design to the L.15 Narrow.

Finish: Black Enamel. Size: 11 × 6¾ × 3⅛ in.
Weight: 1-lb. 11-ozs. Price: 23/9

Where **COMFORT** *counts choose a*

FOUR WIRE

L.72

A tourist model fitted with a single loop four-wire frame. Solid leather top.

Finish: Black Enamel. Size: 10½ × 8¼ × 2¼ in.
Weight: 1-lb. 11-ozs. Price: 23/9.

L.72.L (Ladies' Model)
Finish: Black Enamel. Size: 9½ × 8¼ × 2¼ in.
Weight: 1-lb. 9-ozs. Price: 23/9.

L.70

Lighter than the L.72, having a solid leather top, mounted on single-loop four-wire frame.

Finish: Black Enamel. Size: 10 × 8¼ × 2¼ in.
Weight: 1-lb. 7-ozs. Price: 20/6.

L.70.L (Ladies' Model)
Finish: Black Enamel. Size: 9¾ × 8¼ × 2¼ in.
Weight: 1-lb. 6-ozs. Price: 20/6.

LYCETT

THREE COIL

L.73

A tourist model with solid leather top. Three coil springs bolted to a four-wire bracket.
Finish: Black Enamel. Size: $10\frac{1}{2} \times 8\frac{1}{4} \times 3\frac{7}{8}$ in.
Weight 2-lbs. 4-ozs. Price: **23/9**

L.73.L (Ladies' Model)
Finish: Black Enamel. Size: $9\frac{3}{4} \times 8\frac{1}{4} \times 3\frac{7}{8}$ in.
Weight: 2-lbs. 3-ozs. Price: **23/9.**

L.71

Lighter and smaller than the L.73. Solid leather top mounted on three coil springs with four-wire bracket.
Finish: Black Enamel. Size: $10 \times 8\frac{1}{4} \times 3\frac{7}{8}$ in.
Weight: 2-lbs. 2-ozs. Price: **20/6.**

L.71.L (Ladies' Model)
Finish: Black Enamel. Size: $9\frac{3}{4} \times 8\frac{1}{4} \times 3\frac{7}{8}$ in.
Weight: 2-lbs. 1-oz. Price: **20/6.**

Where **COMFORT** *counts choose a*

TWO COIL

L.66

Tourist model with solid leather top. Four-wire upswept bracket with two coils at rear.
Finish: Black Enamel. Size: $10\frac{1}{2} \times 8\frac{1}{2} \times 2\frac{7}{8}$ in.
Weight: 2-lbs. 5-ozs. Price: **23/9.**

L.66.L (Ladies' Model)
Finish: Black Enamel. Size: $10 \times 8\frac{1}{2} \times 2\frac{7}{8}$ in.
Weight: 2-lbs. 4-ozs. Price: **23/9.**

JUNIOR LEATHER

L.3

Carefully proportioned solid leather top. Improved single-wire frame, with eye bolt fitting. ($\frac{5}{8}''$ or $\frac{9}{16}''$)
Finish: Black Enamel. Size: $8\frac{1}{4} \times 6\frac{1}{2} \times 2\frac{1}{2}$ in.
Weight: 11-ozs. Price: **8/6.**

LYCETT

LOOP FRONT

L.90/3

Designed for rough going. Solid leather top, six-wire bracket, double loop front and stranded wire rear coil springs.

Finish: Black Enamel. Size: $11\frac{1}{2} \times 9\frac{1}{4} \times 4\frac{1}{8}$ in.
Weight: 3-lbs. 7-ozs. Price: **37/6.**

L.33/1

Smaller than the **L90/3**, with single loop front and plain rear coils on six-wire bracket.

Finish: Black Enamel. Size: $9\frac{3}{4} \times 8 \times 3\frac{5}{8}$ in.
Weight: 2 lbs. 6 ozs. Price: **21/-.**

Where **COMFORT** *counts choose a*

MATTRESS

S.21

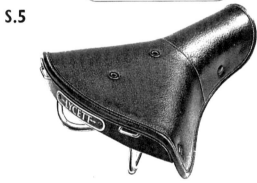

Very comfortable saddle, suitable for Ladies or Gents. Multi-spring mattress, girder frame. Four-wire bracket with two rear coils. Patent nose-piece adds to comfort and appearance. Finest quality black leathercloth covering tailored felt.

Finish: Black Enamel or Chromium Plated. Size: $9\frac{3}{4} \times 8\frac{1}{2} \times 2\frac{3}{4}$ in.
Weight: 2 lbs. 8 ozs. Price: Black Enamel **16/-**: Chromium Plated **19/-.**

JUVENILE MATTRESS

S.5

Mattress spring construction on two-wire frame. Tailored felt and the top covered with finest quality leathercloth. Finish: Black Enamel.
Size: $8\frac{3}{4} \times 6\frac{1}{2} \times 3$ in. Weight: 1-lb. 8-ozs. Price: **13/9.**

LYCETT

The CARRADICE STORY

"AS BRITISH AS THE UNION JACK"

A former editor of the CTC magazine, Tim Hughes observed that the presence of a cotton duck saddlebag on a cycle seen abroad proclaims the riders nationality as clearly as a GB sticker or Union Jack.

Carradice have been making cycle bags since 1929 and have achieved pre-eminence in this field seeing the disappearance of all their British rivals. This article attempts to trace not just the history of the firm but also their role in cycling over the last 80 years.

Since the early days of cycling much thought has been given to the best way to carry a load. It has long been axiomatic that it is better to let the bike carry the load, this being safer and far more comfortable (although many mountain bike riders don't seem to understand this) (1). A variety of materials have been trialled .Up to WW1 leather was predominant; however it is expensive, heavy and not good in the wet. In the 1930's leather cloth with a fibre insert for stiffness was used by a number of manufacturers for example Brooks, as was canvass. Chossy used printers felt for their bags (2) and Dunlop who was a major manufacturer of bags used a rubber based material. In the early 1930's Wilf Carradice would seem to have been the first to use treated cotton duck (original colour used dark tan).It seems likely that Wilf worked in a weaving mill, at the time Lancashire being the cotton mill centre of Britain.

Cotton duck is extremely hard wearing being able to put up with abrasion caused by leaning cycles against walls. It is specially treated to be rot protected and waterproof. Wilf began by making saddlebags for himself and his club mates in Nelson. Early on he hit upon the classic design of the large (18-24 litre) saddlebag with two side pockets, a rounded wooden dowel running the length of the main compartment for stiffness, an option of a 10 cm extension to the flap and an attachment on top to hold a cape. Other features included chrome leather straps and side pockets that could be opened when riding. Their largest bag, the Camper has remained in the catalogue (known first as the Camper's) with only cosmetic change, eg new logo, a reflective strip and even today a bracket for an LED rear light. It is large enough for a hostelling/ bed and breakfast tour. The saddlebag's position is ideal having very little effect on the handling of the bike. It can be fitted to most machines providing there are bag loops on the saddle and in the case of heavy loads a bag support/carrier is necessary.

Carradice had a number of rivals in the cycle bag market these included Baycliff, Brooks, Hutchinson, Midland, Dunlop, Chossy and after WW2 Karrimor who originally were in nearby Rawtenstall. Karrimor branched out into walking and climbing equipment and were in the mid 1970s, the first to market a nylon saddlebag (3). In

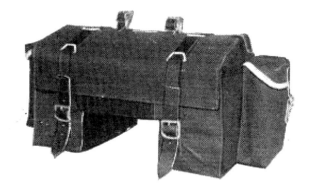

Fig. 1 From the 1951 Catalogue - a solution to the problem of lack of saddle height

the 1980's they converted their entire range over to nylon. Carradice responded with the Overlander range in blue and red nylon.

The relative merits of cotton duck verses nylon have been debated many times amongst cycletourists. The main drawback of cotton duck is its weight (the Camper weighs 1150g compared to 550g for a comparable nylon based bag). For me the drawbacks of nylon is the gradual lose of waterproofing over time and the poor resistance to the inevitable wear caused by leaning the bike against walls. Also nylon tends to sag when empty which is not the case with the stiffer cotton duck.

The Carradice Range

Carradice have focused on making their core products essentially saddlebags & panniers.

Pre- war they marketed equally to walkers as cyclists making tents, rucksacks and sleeping bags. In the 1940's to 1960's they made gauntlet gloves, moped and motorcycle panniers. They have added handlebar bags as these have increased in popularity being originally a French innovation. Carradice continue to make bag supports, saddlebag attachments and rainwear made from waxed cotton. They have made bags specific to certain cycles for example to fit on a Moulton and more recently for a Brompton (a rack top cuboid shape bag). The Super C range was introduced in the early 1980's , essentially this was cotton duck brought up to date with the use of nylon inserts, zips, drawstrings, quick release buckles and red trim to give more modern appearance.

Until the early 1970's they made bags in two grades:

Made of thicker cotton duck, with aluminium cape strap loops and large leather patch underneath to prevent wear to the carrier/mudguard. With leather trimming and the option of white stitching.

Standard material, slotted leather cape strap pieces and double material to prevent wear underneath.

The latter were about 20% cheaper but still had the same good design principles.

Sometimes there is confusion between what is a Camper or Nelson as the latter is only slightly smaller. The main distinguishing feature is that the former has aluminium cape strap loops whilst the latter has the slotted leather strap pieces. Also the

Camper is deeper although the width of the bags is the same.

Some of the model names are based on local places: Nelson, Kendal and Pendle. A solution to the problem of having little space between saddle and carrier was provided by the Low Saddle, the side pockets being deeper than the main portion of the bag. The earlier version of this was the Low Down (*see Fig. 1)* half saddlebag, half pannier. In some clubs this was known as the Marble Arch . Carradice has always produced a range of small day saddlebags, including the Junior without any side pockets. Other models include the Cadet and the smallest bag, another local name Barley (the village about 5 miles from Nelson with the last remaining Clarion Club House nearby).

The Appeal of Cotton Duck.

There is something peculiarly British about the use of a saddlebag and even more so about using proofed cotton duck. Amongst many CTC and RSF (Rough Stuff Fellowship) members of an older generation they would not consider using anything else.

The benefits include:
- Waterproof
- Long lasting (I have got 10 years out of a Nelson in almost daily use).
- Does not affect the handling of the bike unlike panniers.
- The long flap means capacity of even a full bag can be expanded.
- Side pocket right size to take a tool kit so no need to root about in the bag for tools the other

pocket can be used to carry a stove or now maybe a flask.
- Cape/waterproof can be carried outside avoiding the need to open the bag when it's raining.
- Don't show the dirt and need no real looking after.

I have always felt Carradice bags were designed by cyclists, for example they were the first British manufacturer to introduce a handlebar bag support that took the bag away from the bars enabling full use of all hand positions.

Apart from all the practical advantages there is for me an aesthetic appeal. Somehow the bags look just right on many of the understated British clubman's bikes which themselves were often black.

Dating

Many bags have remained in production with only cosmetic changes this is particularly true of the Camper and the Nelson. The best way to date older bags is by the address on the oblong label (3cm x 1cm). This was always in Nelson, Lancs.

- Pre World War II   16 Bedford Street
- From mid 40's to 1960   Leeds Road
- 1961 to 1979   North Street
- 1980 to 1983   Brook Street
- 1984 to present day: St Mary's Works Westmoreland Street. (A former weaving mill)

Carradice Today

When Wilf retired the company was bought in 1974 by Neville Chadwick a keen cyclist who has maintained the quality and core products. It is currently owned by his son David. Carradice still produce a full range of cotton duck bags (more recently with the option of green cotton duck) plus the Super C range which is aimed at cycle campers and expedition cyclists and the cheaper nylon based Cordura range. Many of their products are exported to Japan and the USA where they have acquired a retro cult status. (a market that Brooks since their takeover by Selle have sought to tap into by re-introducing bags). Nearer home they had the contract for producing panniers for Royal Mail cycles (these are appropriately red) which ceased in 2009. Currently their best selling bag is their smallest, the green cotton duck Barley (7 litres) with honey coloured leather straps.

References

1. *Cycle* (magazine of the CTC) December 2008 advocates using rucksacks for off road trips on the grounds it makes the bike easier to manoeuvre! This claim met with howls of protest from more experienced CTC members.
2. Chossy was the trade name of C.T. Osborne. Based first in London and latterly Epson, Surrey they continued in business until the 1990's. Pre war they seem to have wanted to keep their material a secret as in the 1935 Lightweight Cycling Exhibition Catalogue they refer to it as "an exclusive material" p 34.
3. *Cycletouring* CTC Magazine   April 1972 pp 90/91.

Other sources:

1951 *Carradice catalogue* in the Veteran Cycle Club library reproduced on the following pages.
1964 & 1967 *Carradice catalogue*.

Selection of *Carradice catalogues* including 1936 provided by Carradice themselves plus their own website www.carradice.co.uk which has useful data eg weights and dimensions.
Adverts in the *CTC Gazette* (1958 to 1963), *Cycletouring & Rough Stuff Journal.*
1982 *Richmond Cycles Catalogue*
1983 *Freewheel Catalogue* pp 68/69 (leading mail order firm of the late 70's to 90's).

Finally my thanks go to Margaret at Carradice for dealing with my long list of questions.

Cycle Saddle Bags

IN STRONG PROOFED DUCK

Made in sizes to suit every purpose and shaped to fit the cycle. Correct suspension is assured by the design and construction ; the bags hang easily and do not swing awkwardly under the saddle. *See back of List for details of construction.*

"CLUB"

The bag for Club Cycling and to carry average equipment. Size 12in. long ; 7½in. deep ; 6⅝in. wide. Two pockets, 7×4½× 1½in. Weight 24oz.

Capacity 596 cubic inches.

"LONG-RUN"

A fine bag for touring and long runs when extra kit is carried. Size 13in. long, 8¼in. deep, 7in. wide. Two pockets 7½ × 4½ × 1½in. Weight 26oz. Capacity 775 cubic inches

"CAMPERS"

The bag for camping, youth hostelling, and tandem work when height of rear saddle allows (say 1½in. or more out of frame). Size 14in. long ; 9in. deep ; 7½in. wide. Two large pockets 8½×5× 2½in. Will hold half-pint stove Outfit, etc. Pocket tops are eyeletted and can be drawn up when pockets are only partly filled, so that contents are secure. Weight 30oz. Capacity 950 cubic inches.

LONG-FLAP "CAMPERS"

Also available with 4in. longer top flap, with two sets of straps. Makes capacity 950/1,120 cubic inches. Useful when bag is almost always over-filled. Not essential for average use.

Straps

SADDLEBAG STRAPS, Chrome Leather, as fitted to our bags, 8in. long, ⅝in. wide.
CAPE STRAPS for Cycle Bags. Chrome Leather, Roller Buckles, ⅝in. wide.
　　　To take One set of Oilskins .. 　.. Length 17in.
　　　To take Two Sets of Oilskins .. 　.. Length 23in.

"LOW-SADDLE"

A bag of less depth than preceding bags, but of good length to give capacity. Size 14in. long ; 6½in. deep ; 7in. wide. Two pockets 6 × 4 × 2in. Weight 27oz. Capacity 660 cubic inches.

"LOWDOWN"

A large capacity bag, designed for use on cycles with very low saddle position. The centre gap will fit on any Carrier or Support up to 6in. in width. Size 14in. long, 9¾in. deep, 9in. wide. Centre depth 6in Two pockets 8 × 4¼ × 2¼in. Weight 32oz Capacity 880 cubic inches.

"BIG BAG"

Large pocket inside one end for tools, etc. Leather Cape-strap slots on top. Size 14in. long ; 9in. deep; 7½in. wide. Weight 28oz. Capacity 950 cubic inches.

"CLUB MINOR"

Pocket inside one end for tools. Leather Cape-strap slots on top. Size 12in. long ; 7½in. deep ; 6⅝in. wide. Weight 20 oz. Capacity 596 cubic inches.

"DAY" BAG

Size 10½in. long ; 6½in. deep ; 6in. wide. Pocket inside one end for tools. Cape-strap rings on saddle straps. Weight 16oz. Capacity 410 cubic inches.

CAPE CARRIER

Designed to carry oilskins and tools. Can be fitted direct to saddle or to cape loops of bags. Tool pocket inside roll. Stays in position when undone.
Solo size 15in. × 9½in. wide. Weight 8oz.
Large size (holds two capes). 18in. × 9½in. Weight 10oz.

Front Panniers

Lined top flaps with long straps. Side flaps with tie tapes. Straps round head and between bags.

Made in depths to fit 19, 20, 21, 22 and 23in. frames. Other sizes to order. (21in. size is 9½in. deep ; 6in. long ; 4½in. wide. Weight 14oz. Capacity 452 cubic inches.)

STANDARD PATTERN

Standard panniers occupy 4½ inches of top tube. (*For cycles with three-speed controls which cannot be set back to leave 4½ inches clear, see below.*)

THREE-SPEED PATTERN

For Sturmey-Archer type top tube controls set less than 4½ inches back. The bridge of this pattern is of leather, open 1⅛in. to admit the control, and may be further cut away if necessary. Stiffeners in backs prevent sagging where cut away.

DERAILLEUR PATTERN

For top tube controls having large levers which fall well forward. State this when ordering and a size less in panniers will be supplied, with longer leather bridge to allow pannier tops to be below lever when in forward position.

TANDEM REAR TUBE

Made with tapered foot to clear the heels of front rider. Can be used over cable-covered gear wires. In usual rear frame sizes. (Also in DIVIDED PATTERN for use with uncovered gear wires, as Sturmey-Archer. These panniers being joined together by straps which pass beneath the gear wire.)

Carrier Panniers

Suspended from the carrier by three stout leather bars, sewn and rivetted. Backs reinforced against wear. Lined flaps. Long fastening straps. Side flaps with tapes. Two anti-sway straps. Carrier top straps hold bags in position.

"SOLO" SIZE. 11in. long, 8in. deep, 5½in. wide. Two pockets 7¼ × 4 × 2in. on rear ends. Weight 36oz. Capacity 968 cubic inches. Fit carriers up to 5¾in. wide.

"TANDEM" SIZE. 12in. long, 9in. deep, 6in. wide. Two pockets 8 × 4½ × 1½in. on rear ends. Weight 47 oz. Capacity 1,296 cubic inches. Fit carriers up to 7in. wide.

All "Tandem" *size panniers are separable, being joined by strap and buckle carrier bars. Useful for hostelling.*

"Limit" Carrier Panniers

Will carry the outsize outfits. Aluminium loops on top of each bag allow of tent poles, capes, etc. being carried outside. Separate bags make for easier handling of bulky packs.

Plywood inside back of each bag. Leather covered bars outside to space bags out from frame. Saddle-bag fitting by strong straps to carrier. Two anti-sway straps. Long top flaps, lined. Side flaps with tie tapes.
SIZE—12½in. long, 11in. deep, 7in. wide. Two large pockets, 8in. × 5in. × 2½in. on rear ends. Weight 3½lbs. Capacity 1,925 cubic inches.

"Triplet" Carrier Panniers

Maximum carrying capacity for low-seat machines.

The side bags are raised 4in. above carrier, with a centre case to utilise space on carrier top. Constructed as a unit, and easily slipped on or off machine. Hold steady by two anti-sway straps. To fit carriers 5in. to 6in. wide.

Plywood stiffener in back of each bag. Leather covered bars to space bags out from frame. Underside of centre case leather covered to protect against chafing. Lined flaps. Side flaps with tie tapes. Size 12½in. long, 13½in. deep, 5½in. wide. Centre case 12½in. long, 6in. wide, 4in. deep. Two Pockets, 8 × 4½ × 1½in. on rear ends. Weight 3½lbs. Total capacity 2,156 cubic inches.

Saddle-Spring Guard

A square of leather for protecting bags from wear by coil springs. Size 6in. × 6in. Punched to slip on saddle straps of any bag.

Gauntlet Gloves

THUMB AND FOREFINGER PATTERN

Genuine Chromed Horsehide hands. (Horsehide all round, not palms only.) Leather Cuffs. Thick, long-wearing, Yorkshire woollen lining all through hand and gauntlet. Sewn by nine-cord thread.

THUMB ONLY PATTERN

Made to take all fingers together ; thumb only being separate. Quality, size and make-up otherwise exactly as Standard pattern described above.
Each type made in—LADIES' SIZE, MEN'S MEDIUM SIZE, MEN'S LARGE SIZE, MEN'S LARGE BROADHAND SIZE.

Rucksacks

IN SUPERIOR QUALITY PROOFED DUCK

Leather bindings round sack and pocket flaps, gusseted pockets. Best leather straps, brass buckles and adjustable slings are features of these Rucksacks.

HANDY RUCKSACK

Size 16in. × 16in. Base 2½in. wide. One pocket 7½ × 5 × 1½in. Weight 18oz.

TWO-POCKET PATTERN

Measures 17in. × 17in. Base 2½in. wide. Two pockets 8 × 5 × 1½in. Weight 22 oz.

SHAPED BASE RUCKSACK

The D-shaped base of this Rucksack gives greater carrying capacity, with a flat surface to rest against the back. Measures 16in. wide at base ; 16in. high, base 7in. wide. Three Pockets, 8 × 5 × 1½in. Weight 27oz.

Cycle Pannier Carrier

A sturdy and rigid lightweight carrier of tubular construction. Brazed up joints. Side Frames clear all brakes. Adjustable seat-stay clips. Size 16in. × 5in. Weight 26oz. Enamelled Black

Motor Cycle Panniers

MADE FROM HEAVY PROOFED DUCK.

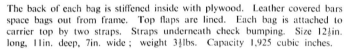

The straps attaching bags to machine can be adapted to most makes of motor cycles.

The back of each bag is stiffened inside with plywood. Leather covered bars space bags out from frame. Top flaps are lined. Each bag is attached to carrier top by two straps. Straps underneath check bumping. Size 12½in. long, 11in. deep, 7in. wide ; weight 3½lbs. Capacity 1,925 cubic inches.

Also available with Two Rear End Pockets, 8in. × 5in. × 2½in.

For machines without carriers, joining straps can be supplied which join the bags together, when they are simply slung over the mudguard. Straps round front of pillion prevent bags slipping down mudguard. These sets of straps are supplied as extras.

Haversacks

FOR WALKING OR MOTOR CYCLING.

Made from strong Duck. Sling has leather strap adjustment. Solid brass buckles. Top flap lined. Size : 14in. long, 9½in. deep, 5½in. wide ; tapering to 3in. at top. Front pocket, 8×5×1½in., with leather-bound flap. Weight 18oz.

PAGE 7

CYCLE BAGS AND PANNIERS

The Cycle Bags, Panniers, etc. in this list are made from Best Quality Proofed Cotton Duck. This material stands up to the hardest wear, giving years of unfailing service.

STRAPS are cut from Chromed leathers and are of ample length and width to permit easy fastening and overloading when necessary. Roller buckles are fitted.

BAG CORNERS are bound with webbing, sewn and rivetted, preventing bursting of seams when forcing bulky articles into the bags.

TOP FLAPS are lined, and gussets extend to form flaps which tie across with strong tapes.

ALUMINIUM CAPE STRAP LOOPS, inserted under chromed leather bands, and large leather patches to take mudguard or carrier wear, are fitted to most bags.

POCKETS have leather-bound hooded flaps.

THONGS for buckles and saddle-pin straps are securely rivetted.

THREAD is Nine-Cord shoe thread throughout.

The capacities of all Bags and Panniers (exclusive of pockets) are given in cubic inches. These figures are a useful guide in comparing the different types of bags and panniers for any particular purpose.

Prices of bags are *less* cape straps. *These are listed on page 2.*

————o————

GENERAL INFORMATION

Carradice Equipment is obtainable from Lightweight Cycle Dealers, etc. There is no reason why you should accept substitutes : a list of stockists in your area will be sent on request. In case of any difficulty, write direct to the works ; we pay carriage in these special circumstances.

GUARANTEE. Every article made by us is guaranteed sound and serviceable ; any defective part will be replaced free of charge if the defect is proved to be due to faulty material or workmanship.

Accidentally damaged equipment, of our manufacture only, can be put into serviceable condition. Quotation free on receipt of damaged article.

Correspondence, etc. should be addressed—
H. W. CARRADICE, *Leeds Road Works,* **NELSON,** *Lancashire.*
Telephone : Nelson 1286. *Works close* 5.30 p.m. ; *Closed Saturday.*

Veevers & Hensman Limited, Burnley

BAYLISS WILEY
The Bicycle Bearing Specialists
"line from a January 1937 advertisement in the *CTC Gazette*

I have always felt Bayliss Wiley was an under-rated company. Their products were consistently excellent yet they were never that highly rated. Their hubs were seen as second best to British Hub Co and their bracket fittings inferior to Chater-Lea. They produced at least two highly innovative components in the 30s the freehub and the oil bath bottom bracket.

Their products can be classified into:
* hubs and related fittings eg hub brakes, wing nuts, track nuts, freewheels
* bottom bracket fittings
* headset fittings

Founded in 1919 by Cecil Bayliss and Arthur Wiley, throughout the 20s and 30s they produced a wide range of bracket and hub fittings for all types of bike from carrier to lightweight, always of high quality and durability. Pre-war they only made small flange hubs including an alloy flanged model design to compete with BHC's Airlite. The pre-war version can be identified by the screw in dust cup covers.

Their most interesting development was the freewheel hub (fig.1) ie a combined hub and freewheel body which of course thanks to Shimano has become the standard fitting for all except the cheapest bikes over the last 20 years. Launched in 1937 and featuring four sets of bearings (including

Fig. 1: Freewheel Hub – 1937 to mid 1950s

a double sided cone) it was all steel which added to the weight. The length of unsupported axle on the gear side contributed to a number of axle breakages which may explain why it was not a commercial success. Certainly this is one of the most common components that turn up at cycle jumbles in new old stock condition. One advantage of using the freehub on a rebuild is that you can use fixed wheel sprockets and you should be able to use four 3/32" or three 1/8". The only difficulty is finding a sprocket larger than 20t. Pre-war freehubs can be identified by the stamping *patent applied for* on the barrel.

In the Newcombe Circulating Notebooks [1], a corresponding circle of CTCites started in 1950

there are a number of references to the freewheel hub. The general consensus seems to be that the idea is an excellent one. Freewheels of the time were a source of problem (for example weak pawl springs). However in practice the hub is just not robust enough to cope with loaded touring often on rough stuff. There are a number of reports of axle breakages on the long unsupported gear side. Speaking to other V-CC members who have experience of using it they all complain about the chain jamming and hitting the chainstay when you free-wheel or try and pedal backwards. As one person pointed out it on the workshop its perfect but on the road with the weight of the rider the best thing to do is just keep pedalling all the time!

The modern freehub was first developed by Suntour in the late 1960s. It was not a commercial success because they made the mistake of launching it as a bottom of the market product. It took Shimano marketing skills in the late 1980's to make it the standard fitting. Campagnolo were initially slow to respond, being limited by the terms of the Shimano patent. Their first version is visually very similar to the Bayliss Wiley, if not a copy certainly inspired by...

Post- war large flange hubs or as they were known 'continental' became popular. BW produced two versions. First in 1946 with only five cuts outs in the rear alloy flanges and four in the front (fig 2) and later in the early 50's a version

Fig 2: First version of the large flange hub with the smaller number of holes in the flanges (five in the rear and 4 in the front)

with the more conventional nine cut outs (fig 3). The former are I think a very distinctive and an attractive design. With the move towards using derailleurs BW introduced a longer cone (about 2cm long) which meant that adjustment could be made to the cone without having to take the freewheel off, a real innovation.

BW bottom brackets were produced first in nickel and black and then chromed plated. In the early 50's they introduced a featherweight bracket set comprising a hollow axle and lightened cups including a hexagonal adjusting cup. The locknut was of special design with 8 slots. These are of first rate quality, look superb and right on any 50s lightweight. Although I would be the first to admit the weight saving of 50g is of dubious benefit.

In the early 30s they introduced an oil bath bottom bracket which was used on frames including Paris and RO Harrison which were not threaded, a very useful item in rescuing a frame where the bracket threads had stripped. (fig 4). It came with a special lockring with a flanged inner side which was used to hold it firm in the frame.

Bracket numbering for lightweights with 68mm bottom bracket shell (all cottered) NB the featherweight hollow axles kept the same numbering:

Number	Use	Overall Length
15	For non gear case clearance (ngcc) ie for single speed or Sturmey	120mm
23	Slightly wider for some narrow doubles eg Chater or four/five speeds	124mm
14	For wider doubles eg Williams C1200	127mm
8	Even wider for BSA pattern 5 pin cranks eg Stronglight Competition where a greater clearance is required on the chain side Described by BW as for balloon tyre machines.	134mm

Fig 3 .Continental large flange hub 1950 until 1960

Fig. 4: Oil bath bottom bracket - early 1930s onwards

For a 73mm bracket shell there is the number 22 the same width as a number 8

Bayliss Wiley were taken over by Renold Chains in 1959; this was effectively the end of the line for them .This was a consequence of the massive decline in the cycle market and the increasing preference for European products by the lightweight market. BW had not kept up with the market, for example they did not make any cotterless axles or quick release hubs. The bracket and head fitting market was taken over by TDC whose quality was nowhere near that of BW.

Illustrations

All thanks to Peter Underwood of:
www.classiclightweights.co.uk

References

[1] The Newcombe Circulating Notebook is in the V-CC online library. For a summary of its contents see my article in *The Boneshaker* no. 174 summer 2007 p20

Bayliss Wiley components feature in *Brown Brothers* and *Holdsworth Aids*. After their demise in 1960 they continue to feature in the latter with a warning note about stock diminishing.

BW advertised extensively in the *CTC Gazette*, the following are useful as the illustrate the item and indicate date of introduction:

No 23 wider axle for 5 speeds, March 1953

Featherweight bottom bracket set, July 1953

Lightweight racing hubs small flange January 1957 (the last new product)

BAYLISS WILEY - PERRY BROCHURE FROM 1953

What must surely be the most attractive bottom bracket set, although the weight saving was tiny

In the early 50s Bayliss Wiley linked up with Perry, by the end of the decade they were both owned by Renolds Chains

LARGE FLANGE HUBS

HOLLOW RACING BOTTOM BRACKET AXLE

No. 19
FRONT HUB

PRICE
26/1

This large tapering flange racing hub has a centre machined from the solid for maximum strength, $\frac{1}{4}''$ ball bearings to give maximum smoothness in running, and spoke flanges machined from hiduminium—an aluminium alloy of very high tensile strength. The spindle is hollowed for lightness and is fitted with chrome finish washers and lock-nuts.

No. 23R
" The Featherweight "

PRICE
5/3

No. 21
REAR HUB

PRICE
30/5

Specification as No. 19 Front Hub but with larger tapering flanges which provide for a common spoke length for the pair. Made specially for use with Derailleur Gears. Fixed gear model No. 20 available at same price.

The cycling enthusiast wants lightness *without sacrificing strength*. This special " Featherweight " racing axle is precision-made from a high tensile steel forging, drilled and counter bored. Guaranteed for strength, *it is $2\frac{1}{2}$ ozs. lighter in weight than the solid axle.*

B. W. BEARINGS MAKE THE BICYCLE !

WILLIAMS
A Guide to Crank and Chainring Identification

This guide has been produced because:

1. Williams are wrongly in my view judged by their base model the C34. Would we judge Brooks by the B5 or Campagnolo by the Valentino gear?
2. It can be difficult to identify different models. Their advertisements before 1955 are often Professor Eddywilly cartoons, which although are amusing are not helpful to identification.
3. Williams were an important manufacturer whose cranks were fitted to virtually every type of bike by a wide range of manufacturers as original equipment. They can be found on a Hetchins and on a Carrier bicycle.

Other products

Adaptor to fit 5 pin TA /AB77 cranks and take 151mm PCD chainrings (Campagnolo's original design until 1967 when they changed to 144mm PCD). Williams also made a version to fit 144mm rings

Alloy 151mm PCD chainrings 44 to 56.

Williams accepted special orders, this included rings up to 64t, special chainring design and bevelled edge cranks.

Pre-war made special flush fitting cotterpins and dureel fixed sprockets. For an 18t this saved 37g over a steel sprocket. These had a special bottom bracket made by BW.

> **STOP PRESS !!** Williams Latest Patent Cottering. The invisible Cotter ! ! Extremely neat appearance. Weight saved. No further fitting. Complete sets, with correctly fitting bracket axle and extraction tool.
> Extra on Williams C34 and C1000 Sets 4/-

From 1936 *Holdsworthy Aids*

Chainring fittings

Until 1954 all Williams cranks used the small screw square bolt method of attachment (also used by BSA). With the introduction of the C45 a larger splined hexagonal sleeve fitting was introduced . The main reason for this switch was the latter was far easier to accommodate double chainrings, which were becoming more widespread. Well into the 60's Williams continued to offered cranks with the original square bolt fitting. With the LC1232 the outer ring to crank was splined but the 6 point inner to outer ring was square bolt

The square bolt is very easy to round and damage if you don't use a special tool. The BSA multi purpose spanner is the best one to use.

"Williams the conquerors of transmission troubles" (long running strap line to advertisements, a pun on William the Conqueror)

Their telegraphic address: 'Sprockets, Birmingham'

Abbreviations used by Williams in their literature

- B 5 pin BSA Made from 1913
- D for tandem as prefix or double chainring as suffix e.g. C45D
- F fixed ring
- LC fluted and sleeved fitting for doubles 3/32
- SD semi detachable eg for tandem one ring fixed
- NGCC & GCC none and gear case clearance, C34 offered in both versions
- J joggled fixed ring made by stamping no flange- cheapest and often poor quality as the metal can distort

Dating/Marking:

All products are either marked E.B.W. with the sword trademark in the middle and/ or stamped Williams (on cranks). The latter is etched very lightly into the chrome surface only and often is lost in rechroming.

C1232 outer ring marked: RD 874905
C45 rings marked: REGDAPPDFOR
C28 rings marked 410207
Alloy adaptor is marked: regd 909182 (the patent number).
Alloy 151 PCD rings: regd 908786 for the original pre 1967 Campagnolo cranks

1912/3 A I	1936 Y	1958 AY
1914 B J	1937 Z	1959 AZ
1915 C	1938 AA	1960 ZA
1916 D	1939 AB	1961 ZB
1917 E	1940 AC	1962 ZC
1918/19 E	1941 AD	1963 ZD
1920 F	1942 AE	1964 ZE
1921 G	1943 AF	1965 ZF
1922 H	1944 AG	1966 ZG
1923 I	1945 AH	1967 ZH
1924 J	1946 AI	1968 ZI
1925 K	1947 AJ	1969 ZJ
1926 L	1948 AK	1970 ZK
1927 M	1949 AL	1972 ZM
1928 N	1950 AM	1973 ZN
1929 0	1951 AN	1974 ZP
1930 P	1952 AP	1975 ZS
1931 S	1953 AS	1976 ZT
1932 T	1954 AT	1977 ZU
1933 U	1955 AU	1978 ZW
1934 W	1956 AW	
1935 X	1957 AX	

Year of manufacture codes

Size

The majority of Williams cranks were available in 6½" and the C34 in 7" The exceptions were the LC1200 and C1200 only in 6 ¾"

Demise

In the June 1968 CTC Gazette there is a note to the effect that the Williams advert in the Feb 1968 issue would be their last. They were ceasing production of steel cranks and rings and only making the AB77 alloy set. This may have been linked to the balance of payments and credit squeeze crisis which it is noted affected a number of regular advertisers to the CTC magazine

In the late 70's production was taken over by Nicklin who made a greatly reduced range based

around the C34. Nicklin (of Wildenhall, Staffordshire) were a trade competitor established in 1894; their products were copies of the C45/C34/B100 range made in oval and square cranks. One innovation was that in the early 1960s they marketed a triple crank based upon the C45 design (1). Options offered were 52, 44, 36 and 48, 46, 42. Their products can be identified by the indented 'N' on the crank inside. Nicklin were a major supplier for large British manufacturers e.g. Raleigh, Dawes, Falcon etc They had made a fluted version of the C34, the N34 since 1963 when Williams ceased production of this model.

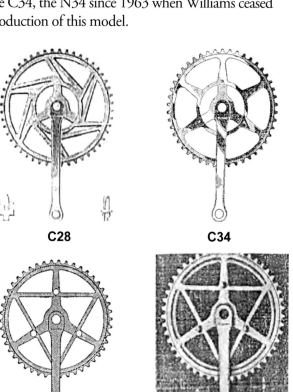

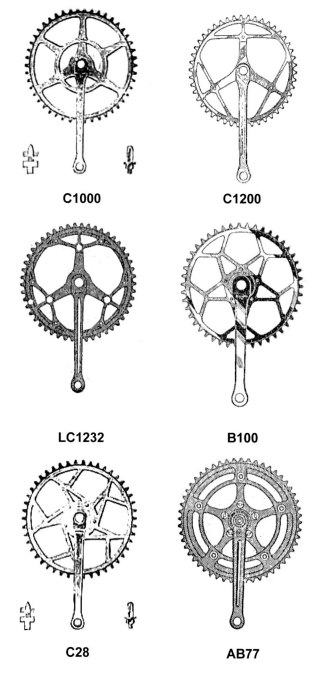

C1000

C1200

C28

C34

LC1232

B100

C45

C45 Double

C28

AB77

A GUIDE TO WILLIAMS CRANK AND CHAINRING IDENTIFICATION.

MODEL	DATE	RING SIZE	PCD*	DETAILS
C28	Mid 20's/30's	44,46,48	C34	Pre-war only same cranks as C34 but different chaining design. Marked 410207
C34	Late 20's to 62	32 –60 even. One inch pitch 16 -30	88mm 3 arm	Most common model plain cranks normally. Usually 6 ½. Swaged on ring arms. Chainrings flanged on outside only. Production stopped in 1962 but chainrings continued to be made until the end of the 60's. Fluted version 1s 4d extra in 1962 . Single and double fluted made. Sleeved fitting 1s 8d more expensive in 1962. Cranks in 3 options: -square -half round -fluted
D34	30's to mid 60's	Front 42 & 44 Rear 42, 44 46 ,48 ,52	Outer C34	Tandem version detachable rings inner fixed to outer 160 PCD, 5 arms. Cranks are strengthen at bottom bracket fitting and have slightly wider Q
No number Direct Drive for tandem	30's to 50's	Front 32 Rear 32 & 48	C34 large bolt .Inner bolted to outer at same pitch	Described in 1939 Brown Bros as for Sun or Brampton tandem fitting
SC31	31 to early 50's	44,46,48, 52	160 6 arm	Tandem inner ring fixed ,outer 6 arm detachable
C45 & C45D double	54 to early 60s	44 46 47 48 49 50 3/32 & 1/8	C34	Triangular ring pattern designed to allowed easy chainring removal i.e. without taking off pedal (gives 100mm bore). Same cranks as C34, sleeved only.
C1000	36 to mid 60's	As C34	C34	Described as club racer set, lighter cranks than C34, weight with 46t, 756g. Cranks are thinner and l/h is cutaway back of cotter end. Both cranks at pedal end raised on the inside
C1032	Early 50's to 61	44 – 52 even	C34	Double: square screw fixing of both rings (version of C1000).The 32 stands for 3/32 chain
C1200	39 to 67	44 - 54 including odds 47 & 49 no's	116mm continental size. Open claw design	THE TOP MODEL. 6 ¾ only. Fluted only top quality forged right crank one piece. Rings driven by bosses on ring not chainring bolts, better design than Chater-Lea. Both sleeve and screw ring fitting .Weight with 46t, 700g

MODEL	DATE	RING SIZE	PCD*	DETAILS
C1232	54 to mid 60's	As above 3/32 only	As C1200	Double version of C1200 same quality
LC1232	54 – mid 60's	46 – 54 including odds 47 & 49 3/32 only	As C1200 but inner ring 160mm PCD fixed to outer.	Double sleeve fitting to crank. Inner ring six screw bolt fitting to outer marked Pat 874905. Different ring design and wider crank arms (like C34) than C1200. The 32 stands for 3/32 chain.
LC 1200	61 to late 60's	44-50	As C1200	Single. Replaced the C34. Fluted 6 ¾ only. Wider chainrings arms than C1200 ,swaged on .Sleeve fitting only
B100	1913 to early 70's	26 to 56 also one inch pitch	BSA 5 pin	Plain cranks . Number of options eg double flanged, toughed cranks for carrier cycles ,gcc and ngcc. Chrome and nickel plated (1939). With fettling interchangeable with TA rings
B1100	Mid 30's to late 40's	44,46,48	As B100	Club racer set cranks without inside flange to suit narrow built lightweight frames. Weight with 46t same as C1000 756g
B109	Pre-war	44,46,48	As B100	Dureel ring, weight with 46t 560g.. Same cranks as B100
F100 F45 F27	30's to 60's 54 to late 60's	44.46 48	n/a	Fixed ring version chainring design as per model letter eg F45 as C45 except F27 =C34
AB77 Cotterless	62 to mid 70's	Minimum 42 made by Williams but interchange-able with TA minimum 26. also adaptor see below	5 pin as TA	Splined b.b & cups made by TDC (poor quality). High quality cranks, all alloys. Benefit over Gnutti splined is that no need for special tool to remove cranks. 6 ¾ only. Only British made cotterless crank made in any quantity.

*PCD : pitch circle diameter.
Diameter of circle joining the centre
of the crank bolt holes also known
as BCD, bolt circle diameter.

References

(1) 1963 Nicklin catalogue

Other references:

Holdsworth Aids, 1952 to 1969

Williams Catalogues

Brown Brothers Catalogues

Adverts in *CTC Gazette* 1958 to 1963 & Sporting
Cyclist 1959 to 1965

Show Reports in the *CTC Gazette* and *Cycling* from
1923 onwards

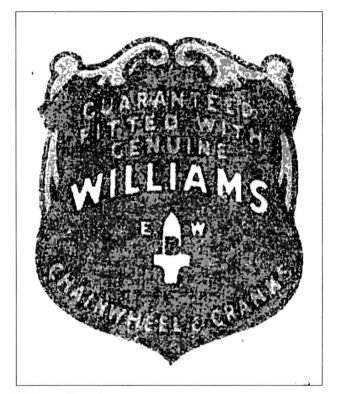

Williams Decal

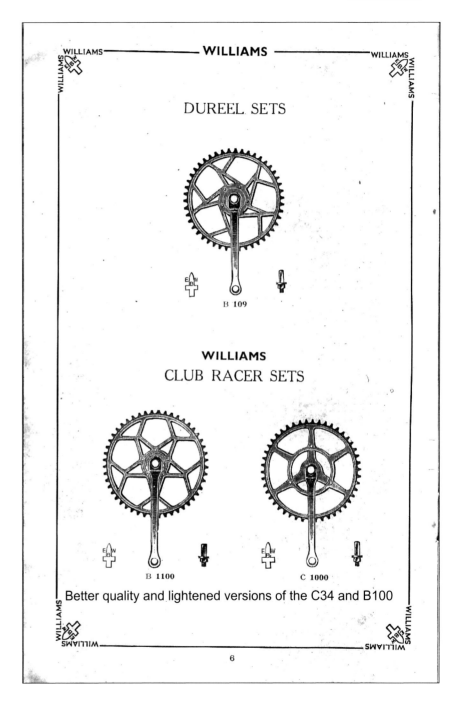

WILLIAMS

DUREEL SETS

SUPER LIGHT RACER SET

A Standard WILLIAMS Dureel Set consists of a specially treated Duralumin 5 pin detachable chain wheel of suitable design.

A pair of extra light high tensile steel cranks 6½in. long, with cotters. Chromium plated.

Standard wheel sizes : 44, 46, 48т. ½in. pitch × ⅛in. width of tooth.

Weight of 46т ½in. × ⅛in. wheel with 6½in. cranks = 1 lb. 4 oz.

Extra Léger "Dureel" Serie de Cours.	Extra Leichte "Dureel" Garnitur fuer Renner.	Super Light Dureel Race Stel.
Une Serie Courante **WILLIAMS** Dureel comprend : Une roue dentée en Duralumin traité par procédé spécial ; du type avec 5 vis et dessin choisi. Une paire manivelles d'acier de grande tension très légère chromé, 6½ de longeur, avec calles. **Dimensions de Roues** 44 46 et 48 dents ½ × ⅛". **Poids** de 46т ½ × ⅛ roue avec 6½ manivelles 567 gram.	Eine normale **WILLIAMS** Dureel Garnitur besteht aus : Einem besonders bearbeitetem Duralumin Kettenrad geeignetes Dessins von 5 Shraubenbefestigung t y p e ; Einem Paar extra leichte hochwertige verchromte Stahlkurbeln, mit Keilen. **Kettenradgroesse** sind 44, 46 & 48 Zähne ½" Teilung ⅛" Zahndicke. **Kurbelgroesse** 6½" ohne Kettenkastenraum. **Gewicht** einer 46т ½ × ⅛" Dureelrad mit 6½ Kurbeln 567 gram.	Een standaard **WILLIAMS** Dureel stel bestaat uit een speciaal behandeld afneembaar profiel, en bevestidg met vijf boutjes. Een paar bizonder lichte cranks 6½ van groote trekvastheid met crankspieën—chroom vernikkeld. **Standaard wielmaten :** 44, 46 & 48 T. ½" steek × ⅛" tandbreedte. Gewicht van een wiel 46 T. ½ × ⅛ met 6½ cranks 567 gram.

Complete Set	..	..	..	
Chain Wheel only	..	..	..	
Right Hand Crank only	..	..		
Left Hand Crank only	..	..		
Cotters, per pair	..	..		
Screws	..	..	..	per set.

WILLIAMS

CLUB RACER SETS

A Standard WILLIAMS Club Racer Set consists of a Cold Forged Steel Chain Wheel of special light design, and without inside flange to suit narrow built machines.

A pair of specially treated light weight Cranks with Cotters.

Standard Wheel Sizes : 44, 46, or 48 teeth, ½in. pitch, ⅛in. wide.

Non-Standard Wheel Sizes : 40 or 42 T.

Cranks : 6½in. or 7in. long, without Gear case Clearance.

Weight of 46т ½in. × ⅛in. 6½in. B1100 or C.1000, 1 lb. 11 oz.

Series de Cours Club WILLIAMS.	WILLIAMS Klub Renn Garnitur	WILLIAMS Club Race-Stellen.
Une Serie courante de Cours Club comprend une roue dentée en acier à rebord de chaine, forgé à froid, de dessin léger et sans rébord a la cote gauche. Une paire de manivelles légère trempée avec calles. **Les Dimensions des Roues Courantes** 44 46 et 48 Dents, ½" écartement, ⅛" épaisseur. **Les Dimensions des Manivelles** 6½" ou 7" de long sans écartement pour carter. **Poids** de 46 ½ × ⅛ 6½" B 1100 or C 1000 765 gram.	Eine Standard **WILLIAMS** Klub Renn Garnitur besteht aus : Einem patentierten Stahlkettenrad in eigenartiger leichter Ausfuhrung ohne Innenrand ; Einem Pear spezialbearbeiteten leichten Kurbeln mit Keilen. **Normale Groessen** sind 44, 46, od 48 Z ½" Teilung ⅛" Zahndicke. **Normale Kurbelgroessen** sind 6½" und 7" ohne Kettenkastenraum. **Gewicht** fuer 46 Z ½ × ⅛" 6½" B 1100 or C 1000 765 gram.	Een standaard **WILLIAMS** Club Race Stel bestaat uit een koud gesmeed stalen tandwiel van bizonder licht profiel en zonder binnenrand, passend voor nauw gebouwde machines. Een paar speciaal behandelde cranks met crankspieen van licht gewicht. **Standaard wielmaten :** 44, 46 of 48 T., ½" steek ⅛" tandwijdte. **Cranks** 6½" of 7" lang, zonder ruimte voor kettingkast. **Gewicht** van stel 46 T ½" × ⅛" 6½ B 1100 or C 1000 765 gram.

	Nickel Plated		Chromium Plated	
	B1100	C1000	B1100	C1000
		Per Set		Per Set
Complete Set	..	..		
Chain Wheel only	..	..		
Right Hand Crank only	..			
Left Hand Crank only	..			
Cotters, per pair	..			
Screws, per set				

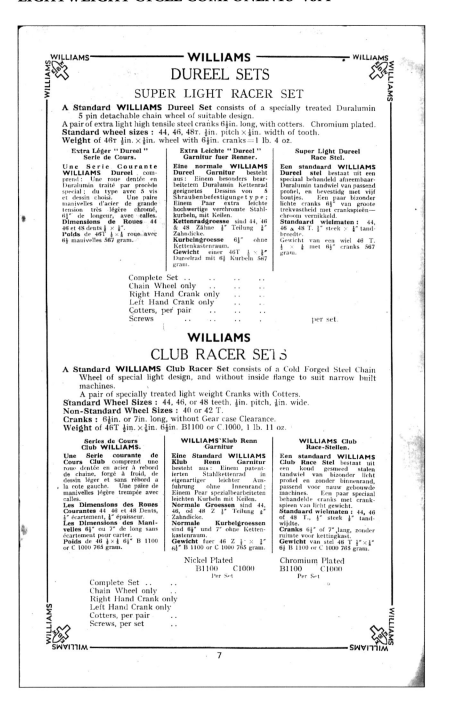

WILLIAMS

CARRIER SETS

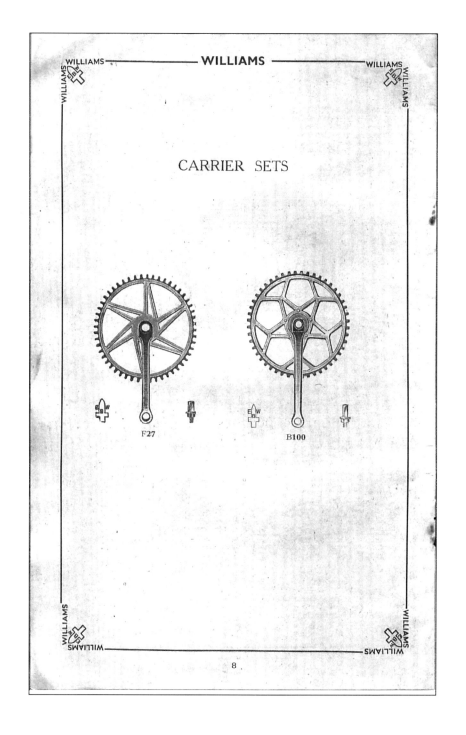

F27   B100

Left page (14)

DIRECT DRIVE TANDEM SETS

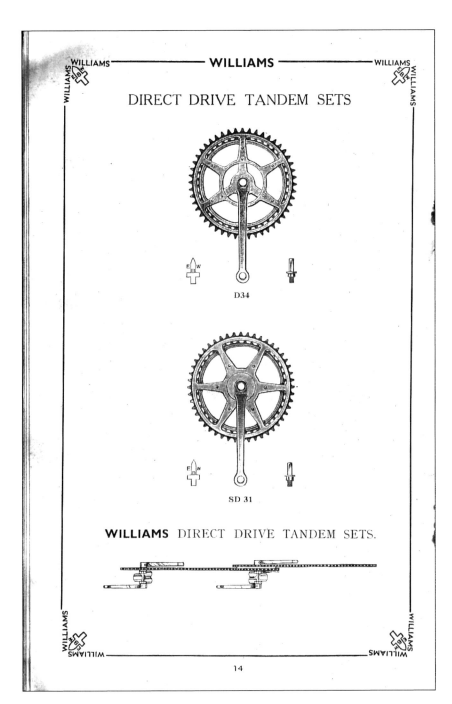

D34

SD 31

WILLIAMS DIRECT DRIVE TANDEM SETS.

Right page (15)

DIRECT DRIVE TANDEM SETS

Consist of The Front Drive and Combination Gear Sets.

The former is a 3-pin detachable Cold Forged Flanged Chain Wheel with improved Bevelled Edge Cranks, and the latter comprises a 6-pin detachable Cold Forged Steel (inside and outside) Combination gear, together with a pair of specially treated, Bevelled Edge Cranks complete with Cotters. All Chain Wheels are specially cut to ensure both pairs of Cranks being parallel or in line.

Standard Combinations : 42 :: 44, 46, 48, or 52 × ¼in. × ⅛in. with 6½in. or 7in. cranks
44 :: 46, 48, or 52 × ¼in. × ⅛in. with 6½in. or 7in. cranks.

	Nickel Plated.	Chromium Plated. Black Enamelled
Complete Tandem Set	..	.. ..
Front Drive Set	..	..
Combination Set	..	.. ..
Front Chain Wheel	..	.. ..
Outside Combination Gear	..	..
Inside Combination Gear	..	..
Right Hand Crank	..	..
Left Hand Crank	..	..

WILLIAMS
Semi Detachable TANDEM SETS

Comprise a Front Drive and Combination Rear Set.

The former is a fixed type Cold Forged Flanged Chain Wheel with improved bevel edged cranks ; the latter consists of a fixed type Cold Forged Flanged Inside Gear with Cranks and a 6 pin detachable Cold Forged Outside Gear which registers on the central boss of the inside gear to maintain true running.

The Chain Wheels are specially cut to ensure both pairs of Cranks being parallel or in line.

Cotters are included with complete sets.

Standard Combinations : 42 :: 44, 46, 48 or 52T × ¼in. × ⅛in. with 6½in. or 7in. Cranks.

	Nickel Plated	Chromium Plated Black Enamelled
Complete Tandem Set	..	
Front Drive Set	..	
Combination Set	..	
Front Chain Wheel and R. H. Crank	..	..
Rear Inside Wheel and R. H. Crank	..	
Rear Outside Wheel	..	
Left Hand Crank	..	
Cotters per pair	..	

WILLIAMS Cross Over Drive Tandem Sets can also be supplied if desired.

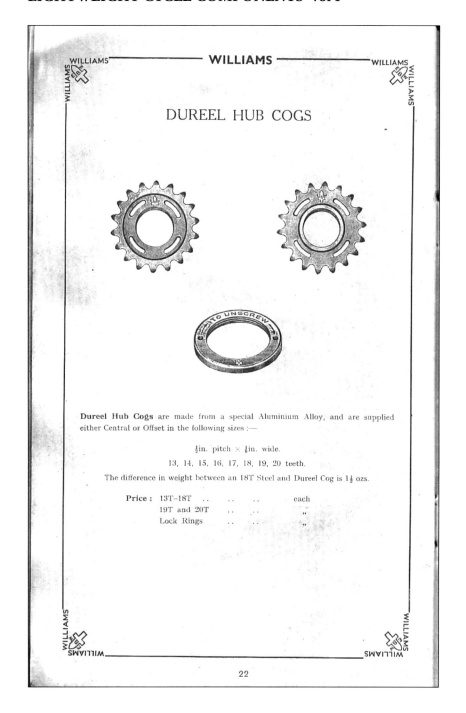

WILLIAMS · WILLIAMS · WILLIAMS · WILLIAMS

DUREEL HUB COGS

Dureel Hub Cogs are made from a special Aluminium Alloy, and are supplied either Central or Offset in the following sizes :—

½in. pitch × ⅛in. wide.

13, 14, 15, 16, 17, 18, 19, 20 teeth.

The difference in weight between an 18T Steel and Dureel Cog is 1½ ozs.

Price : 13T–18T .. .. .. each
19T and 20T .. .. ,,
Lock Rings .. .. ,,

22

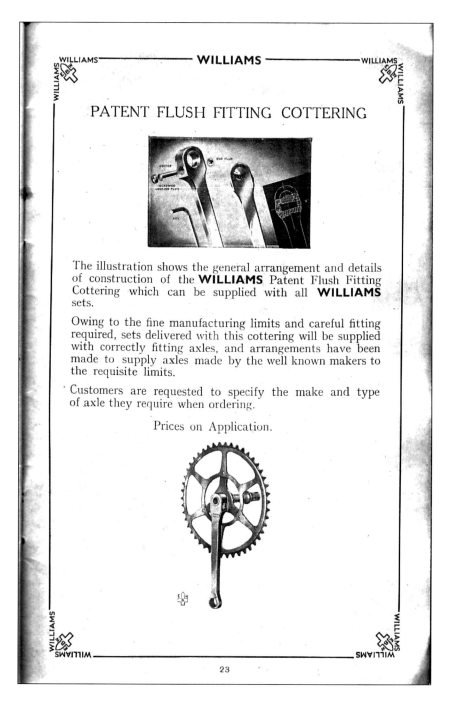

WILLIAMS · WILLIAMS · WILLIAMS · WILLIAMS

PATENT FLUSH FITTING COTTERING

The illustration shows the general arrangement and details of construction of the **WILLIAMS** Patent Flush Fitting Cottering which can be supplied with all **WILLIAMS** sets.

Owing to the fine manufacturing limits and careful fitting required, sets delivered with this cottering will be supplied with correctly fitting axles, and arrangements have been made to supply axles made by the well known makers to the requisite limits.

Customers are requested to specify the make and type of axle they require when ordering.

Prices on Application.

23

The BLUEMEL'S STORY
As Light as a Feather

"Mudguards are one area where a British company, Bluemel's has achieved pre-eminence, no doubt due to our weather" Tim Hughes, *Adventure Cycling* 1978.

"When price is not the only consideration": a long running line used in advertisements.

The first quotation demonstrates just how dominant and highly regarded Bluemel's became.

I doubt if there are many V-CC members who do not have a bike equipped with Bluemel's mudguards and a Bluemel's pump. The second quote shows that Bluemel's sought to sell on quality rather than price.

Bluemel's was founded by three brothers of the same name at the end of the nineteenth century. It was originally based in Stepney, East London. In 1902 they purchased the old artificial silk works at Wolston. The location was chosen deliberately to cater for nearby Coventry's fast developing cycle and motor industries. At the time of the last remaining brother's death in 1938 a local newspaper described the growth. From a small start the workforce had grown to over 600 at the time of Mr Bluemel's death. Described as a modern factory, its chief products were plastic mouldings in bakelite, steering wheels, and pumps, and to a lesser degree, bicycle mudguards and gear cases.

Bluemel's essentially focused on producing items for both the cycle and motor trade manufactured from plastics. In the early days this was bakelite and celluloid. The trademark of the feather within the letter *B* has it origins in the fact that Bluemel's products were replacing those made from far heavier material, i.e. metals. Featherweight, No-weight and Lightweight products are names that are continually used by Bluemel's. Their advertising focuses on just how light Bluemel's accessories are and with regard to mudguards the fact that they can be detachable

I am struck by how much innovation there was in the first decade of the twentieth century. I have for example a Bluemel's Directon, a direct connection pump, an innovation I assumed belonged to the 1960s.

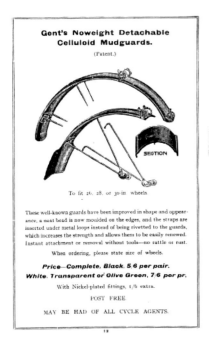
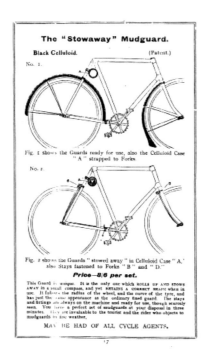
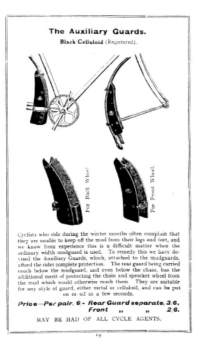

Fig. 1 From 1904 catalogue: page 12 Peerless mudguards, page 17 Stowaway guards, and page 19 auxiliary guards

Core Products

These can be classified as :

- mudguards
- pumps
- handle bar grips
- reflectors

For mudguards and pumps for many years the top range was the Noweight followed by the Lightweight and then the Featherweight. The Noweight featured alloy rivets and the open end of the stays were threaded, which provided the adjustment rather than the conventional bolt. Before 1914 there was also another top model, the Peerless. One product that disappeared in the 1920's was collapsible mudguards, Bluemel's versions was called the Stowaway. The idea was that it could be rolled away and stored behind the fork crown and seat stays. I have never seen a surviving example which is perhaps evidence they were not a success or at least not durable. Another innovation was telescopic mudguard stays which had about 2cm of adjustment. They were stainless steel, with brass adjusters, which added quite a bit of weight. I was left wondering the purpose. How often after setting up mudguards would you want to adjust them? I suppose maybe if you were fitting different tyre width. Bluemel's also made a range of mudguard accessories e.g. rear and side extensions plus front spearpoint.

Bluemel's positioned themselves as suppliers of quality products, a 1937 advertisement suggest if you bicycle cost less than five pounds it would not be reasonable to insist on Bluemel's. If it was around five or six pounds it should have Featherweight accessories and if more than that Noweight! (Fig. 5)

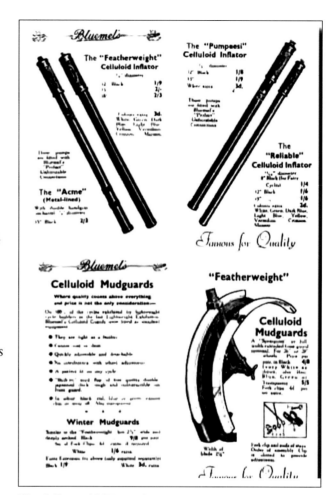

Fig. 2 From 1937 catalogue page 4-5 pumps, page 10 -11 mudguard extensions

Bluemels also made a range of alloy guards from the ultra narrow Continental to the much wider Airweight and Tour de France. The stays and fitting were the same as their plastic guards a marked difference to French guards. I have always found these rattle or transmit road vibrations one cure is to paint the insides with primer.

Fig. 3 Early 1920s advertisement on a *Cycling* cover

Other products

Bluemel's also marketed dynamos and lights. They seem to have been badge engineered in the 30s made by Miller and in the 70s the Bluemel's Featherweight Dynamo set was in fact the French Soubitez model. Up to World War One they made saddles, chain cases, bags, brakes and levers. There was also in the 1930s a celluloid horn. By the 1930s the vast majority of their output was for motor vehicles, products including number plates, steering wheels etc.

Fig. 4 1923 Trade advertisement in both French and English

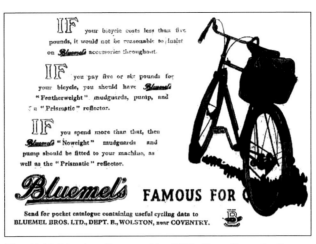

Fig. 5 1937 advertisement in CTC Gazette note the relating of price of cycles to their products.

Fig . 6 Range of mudguards in the 1970's from CTC Cycletouring June 1975

Dating

Up to the 1930s products are marked Bluemel's Bros and feature the feather logo, For the next twenty years the Bros was dropped, a reflection of the change in ownership. The spearpoint front mudguard was made until the late 1950s. From this time onwards products are just marked Bluemel's made in England in plain block letters. The last products made late 80s early 90s are marked 'Bluemel's SKS Made in Germany'.

Decline

By the end of the 1950's Bluemel's were the major British maker of mudguards and pumps. There were new model introduced in the early 1960's e.g. the Classique guards with a chrome effect strip down the middle. Their product range was centred on mudguards and pumps plus handlebar tape, grips and end plugs or as a 1974 advertisement put it:

Presenting Bluemel's bolt-on, clip-on, snap-on, screw-on, press-on, wind-on goodies. CTC *Cycletouring* February/March 1974 p38

Even in the 1970s they still made a wide range of mudguards (fig 6). The major new product was the Sovereign range made from direct connection pumps. Of the lightweight guards the narrow, central ribbed, Club Special has become the sought after model (fig 7). With a width of 1⅝″ it was introduced in 1955, it was second narrowest guard, the Continental (alloy) being ⅛″ narrower.

At 16/6 in 1955 it was the most expensive of Bluemel's guards being 3/- more expensive than the Noweight.

Not surprisingly the most common model you see is the cheaper plain Popular. Much of the range e.g. the Lightweight and Popular had been made unchanged for years. In the 1970s a sign of the times was the short so called 'racing guards' which were alloy and fitted to quite a few sports bikes of the 70s, but needless to say, offered no protection and were never used in races!

The first serous competition to the Bluemel's core product came in the 1970's from the German company Esge and their chromoplastic mudguards. These were pretty much unbreakable and quickly became popular for this very feature. Ironically it was SKS, another German company, who bought out both Esge and finally Bluemel's in the early 1990s.

In the early 80s Bluemel's were bought by a firm

Fig. 7 Two of the top 1970s models from CTC *Cycletouring* June 1975

Fig 8 Bluemel's building 2009 now part of a housing development (acknowledgment to Alexander von Tutschek)

of venture capitalists who then bought up Saracen, a major maker of Mountain bikes, and also the Ron Kitching business upon his retirement in 1984. However things did not go well and soon the only part of the organisation making any money was Ron Kitching's. You can read a somewhat biased version of events in Ron Kitching's autobiography *A Wheel in Two Worlds.* Ron was of an age when he had to retire, but did not really want to hand the company over to anyone else. Demand for the core Bluemel's product, mudguards, declined quickly with the rise of the Mountain Bike. Bluemel's invested heavily in a special pump for Mountain Bikes but it was a failure (*failed to inflate their fortunes* as Ron Kitching put it) and fairly quickly the end was near.

Today all that is left is a housing development and road with the Bluemel's name. The listed part of the original building has the famous logo engraved above the door. (fig 8).

A sad end to a company whose products were once so common and helped to define a unique British style.

References

1904, 1937 and 1962 Bluemel's catalogues in the V-CC library.

Bluemel's advertised extensively in *Cycling* and the *CTC Gazette* often with a good description of their products.

Brown Brothers catalogues are a useful guide usually having several pages of mudguards, Bluemel's and their competitors.

Acknowledgements

Norman Cole for Brown Brothers reference.
V-CC on line library for the Bluemel's catalogues.

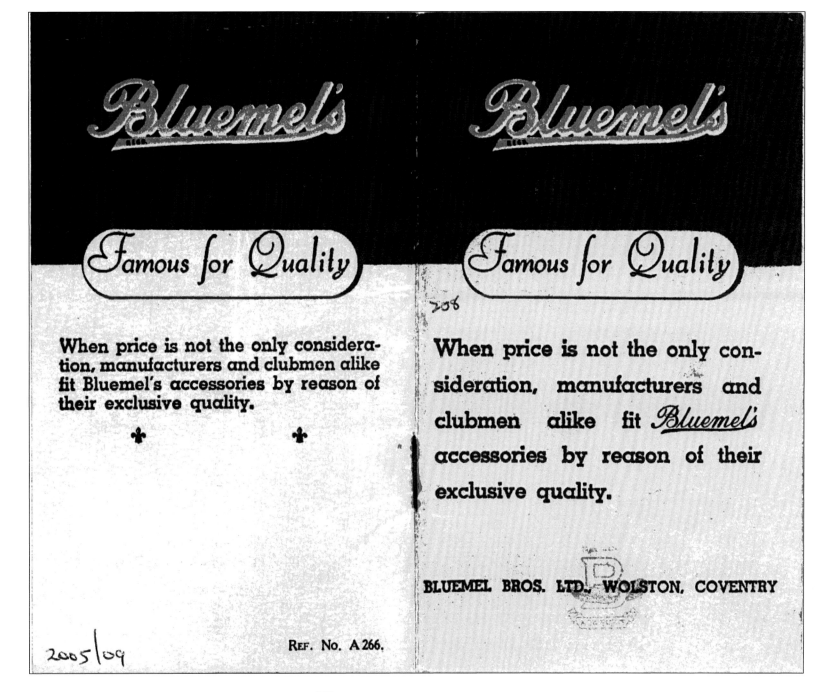

Bluemel's

Famous for Quality

When price is not the only consideration, manufacturers and clubmen alike fit Bluemel's accessories by reason of their exclusive quality.

REF. No. A 266.

2005/09

Bluemel's

Famous for Quality

208

When price is not the only consideration, manufacturers and clubmen alike fit *Bluemel's* accessories by reason of their exclusive quality.

BLUEMEL BROS. LTD. WOLSTON, COVENTRY

Because

 use only the finest materials irrespective of price :—First grade opaque celluloid of a rich jet black and a clean ivory white; translucent material of weak colour is less expensive.

Front mudguard flaps are of double extrastrong duck and cannot fray at the edges like American cloth and other cheap substitutes.

All stay wires are of high grade steel of our own specification specially treated in common with our other metal parts.

Accessories combine the best materials, faultless workmanship and fine finish.

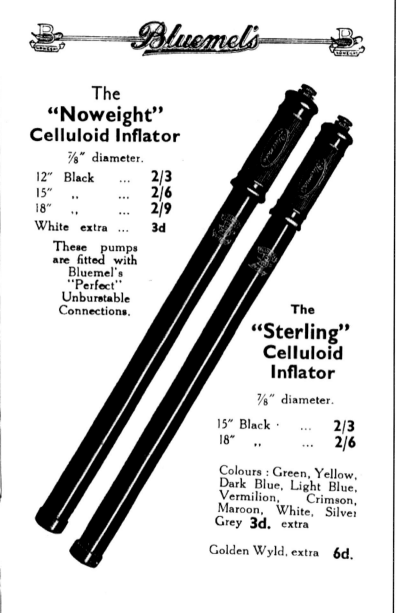

The "Noweight" Celluloid Inflator

$\frac{7}{8}$" diameter.

12" Black	...	**2/3**
15" ,,	...	**2/6**
18" ,,	...	**2/9**
White extra	...	**3d**

These pumps are fitted with Bluemel's "Perfect" Unburstable Connections.

The "Sterling" Celluloid Inflator

$\frac{7}{8}$" diameter.

15" Black ·	...	**2/3**
18" ,,	...	**2/6**

Colours : Green, Yellow, Dark Blue, Light Blue, Vermilion, Crimson, Maroon, White, Silver Grey **3d.** extra

Golden Wyld, extra **6d.**

2

3

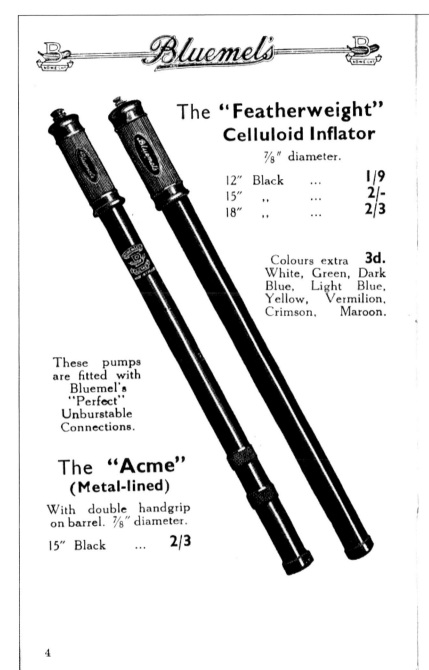

The "Featherweight" Celluloid Inflator

⅞" diameter.

12"	Black	...	1/9
15"	,,	...	2/-
18"	,,	...	2/3

Colours extra   **3d.**
White, Green, Dark Blue, Light Blue, Yellow, Vermilion, Crimson, Maroon.

These pumps are fitted with Bluemel's "Perfect" Unburstable Connections.

The "Acme" (Metal-lined)

With double handgrip on barrel. ⅞" diameter.

15" Black   ...   **2/3**

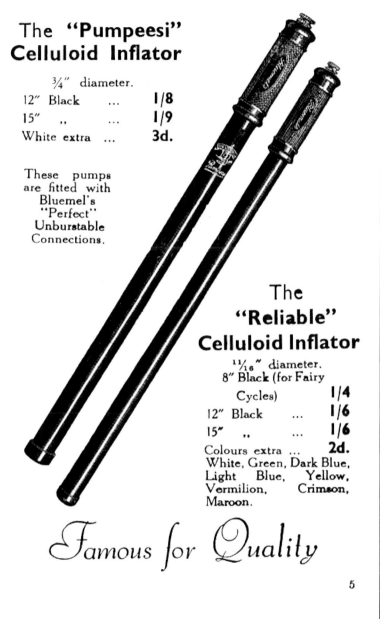

The "Pumpeesi" Celluloid Inflator

¾" diameter.

12"	Black	...	1/8
15"	,,	...	1/9
White extra		...	3d.

These pumps are fitted with Bluemel's "Perfect" Unburstable Connections.

The "Reliable" Celluloid Inflator

¹¹⁄₁₆" diameter.

8" Black (for Fairy Cycles)		1/4
12" Black	...	1/6
15" ,,	...	1/6
Colours extra	...	2d.

White, Green, Dark Blue, Light Blue, Yellow, Vermilion, Crimson, Maroon.

Famous for Quality

4

5

Bluemel's

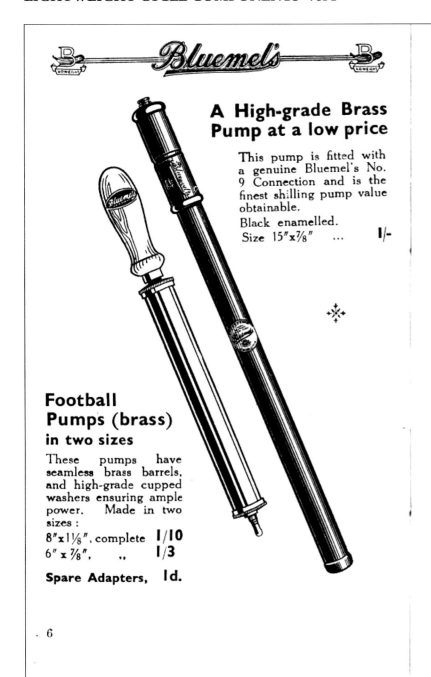

A High-grade Brass Pump at a low price

This pump is fitted with a genuine Bluemel's No. 9 Connection and is the finest shilling pump value obtainable.

Black enamelled.
Size 15"x⅞" ... **1/-**

Football Pumps (brass)

in two sizes

These pumps have seamless brass barrels, and high-grade cupped washers ensuring ample power. Made in two sizes :

8"x1⅛", complete **1/10**
6" x ⅞", ,, **1/3**

Spare Adapters, 1d.

. 6

Motor Cycle Inflators

FITTED AS STANDARD EQUIPMENT BY THE LEADING MOTOR CYCLE MANUFACTURERS.

The "MOTOBIKE"

	each
15" x ⅞" ...	**3/-**
18" x ⅞" ...	**3/3**

The "MOTOBIKE"

An extra strong inflator with seamless brass barrel, celluloid covered, and folding foot stirrup. Also a spring is fitted in the handle, and our best quality "Motobike" connection, 13" long.

The "POWERFUL"

A larger inflator similar to the "Motobike", with 15½" durable connection.

18"x1" price each **4/6**

Famous for Quality

7

Unburstable Inflator Connections

"COVENTRY", a low priced standard connection for cycles.

4d. each.

"PERFECT." For cycle inflators, 6 in. long. 6d. each, as below :—

NO. 9. Standard connection for Dunlop (Woods) Valves.

NO. 9a. For "Sclaverand" (French valve) also Dunlop High Pressure and Tabucci Tyres with "Presta" valves.

NO. 9b. For Schrader (American) to screw on outside of valve.

NO. 9c. With two male ends to screw *inside* "Schrader" valves, also for Constrictor Path Racing Valves.

NO. 10. As No. 9 but with large spring collar for metal pumps.

NO. 8. With two female ends for Dunlop (Woods) valve at both ends.

NO. 11. As No. 9 but 8" long, **7d.** each.

NO. 14. For "Motobike" pumps with "Schrader" swivel, also Dunlop Adaptor. 13" long, **9d.** each.

"Noweight" Inflator Clips

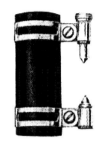

Well finished spring clips which can be instantly locked by tightening the milled nut at the top, thereby making the inflator quite secure.

Black enamelled or plated.

Per pair **9d.**

Inflator Washers

Oiled ready for use. 7/8", 3/4" and 11/16" diameter.
Price each ... **1d.**

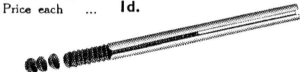

Trouser Bands

Celluloid covered in Black, Brown, White or Grey. Cannot rust, or damage the trousers. Per pair 6d.

Lacquered steel Per pair ... **3d.**

6d. per pair

Famous for Quality

8

9

Celluloid Mudguards

Where quality counts above everything and price is not the only consideration:—

On 100% of the cycles exhibited by lightweight cycle builders at the last Lightweight Exhibition. Bluemel's Celluloid Guards were fitted as standard equipment.

- They are light as a feather.
- Cannot rust or dent.
- Quickly adjustable and detachable.
- No interference with wheel adjustment.
- A perfect fit on any cycle.
- "Built-in" mud flap of first quality double-japanned duck, tough and indestructible—on front guard.
- In white, black, red, blue or green—cannot chip or wear off. Also transparent.

* * *

Winter Mudguards

Similar to the "Featherweight" but 2⅞". wide and deeply arched, Black ... **9/8** per pair.

Set of Fork Clips 4d. extra, if required.

White ... **1/6** extra.

Front Extension for above (only supplied separately)

Black **1/9**   White **3d.** extra.

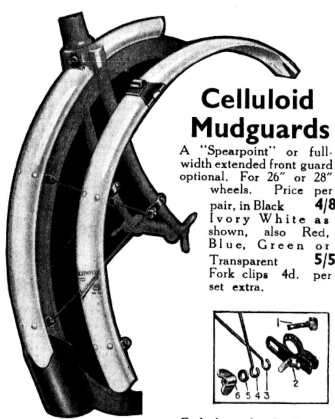

"Featherweight"

Celluloid Mudguards

A "Spearpoint" or full-width extended front guard optional. For 26" or 28" wheels. Price per pair, in Black **4/8** Ivory White as shown, also Red, Blue, Green or Transparent **5/5** Fork clips 4d. per set extra.

Width of blade 2¼".

Fork clip and ends of stays. Order of assembly. Clip is slotted to provide adjustment.

Famous for Quality

10

11

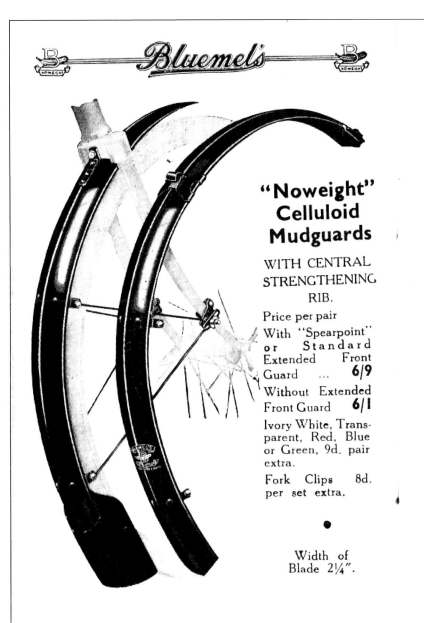

Bluemel's

"Noweight" Celluloid Mudguards

WITH CENTRAL STRENGTHENING RIB.

Price per pair

With "Spearpoint" or Standard Extended Front Guard ... **6/9**

Without Extended Front Guard **6/1**

Ivory White, Transparent, Red, Blue or Green, 9d. pair extra.

Fork Clips 8d. per set extra.

●

Width of Blade 2¼".

Celluloid Mudguards
Details of quickly adjustable Fittings ("Noweight" Pattern)

Fig. 1.

FIG. 1. The upper end of the stay screws into a swivelling nut on the mudguard bridge. This contributes towards a perfect fit.

Fig. 2.

FIG. 2. The flexible fork clip fits any size or shape of fork and need not be disturbed when the guards are removed. The long looped end of stay permits of adjustment.

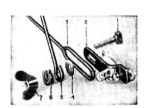

Fig. 3.

FIG. 3. Order of assembly. The securing T-bolt can be withdrawn through slot in fork clip without disturbing the latter.

Special fittings are available for tandems.

Famous for Quality

12

13

Another new feature :
"Duplex" Mudguards
with rear reflector moulded in!

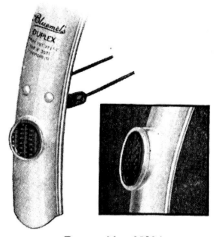

Patent No. 35284.
N.P.L. Certificate No. 151.

The neatest combined mudguard and reflector ever produced. Our Improved "Prismatic" lens is actually moulded into the guard.

Two patterns are supplied, "Duplex Featherweight" and "Duplex Noweight", at 1/- extra to the standard prices.

"Lightweight" Narrow-Section Celluloid Mudguards

WITH CENTRAL STRENGTHENING RIB.

"Spearpoint" Extended Front is standard.

For 26" wheels only.

Price per pair.
In Black ... **6/4**

Ivory White, Transparent, Red, Blue or Green, per pair extra **9d.**

Width of Blade 1¾"

Fork Clips per set extra. **8d.**

These guards are also supplied with our "Featherweight" pattern fittings at same prices as Featherweight Guards.

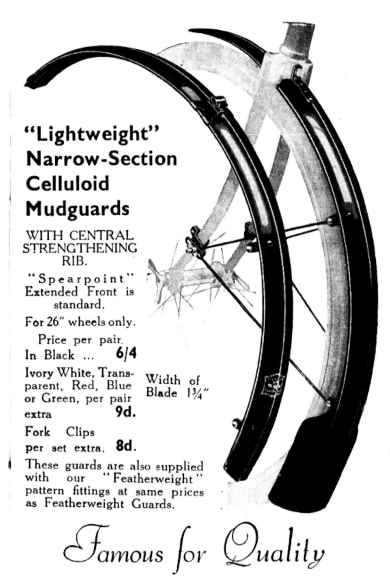

Famous for Quality

14

15

Celluloid Front Extensions

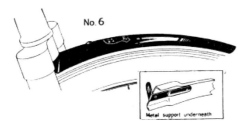

No. 6

Metal support underneath

A light, strong, V-section front extension moulded to follow the curve of the wheel.

No. 6. With bolt and spring washer for fork crown, Black **1/-**

No. 7. Standard fork clips, Black **1/2**

No. 6a. With a similar fitting to No. 6, but it does not taper towards the tip, which is square.

Black **1/-**

No. 2. Full width pattern as "Featherweight" Guard. Suitable for use with any other guards, Black **1/3**

Green, White or Transparent, extra   **3d.**

"Noweight" Celluloid Horn

Black or
White Body

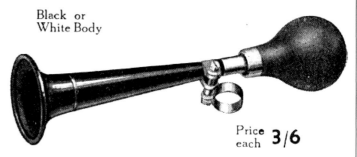

Price each **3/6**

This light celluloid horn has a clear, powerful and pleasing note. It is easily heard at dangerous cross roads and corners.
The polished celluloid body is rust-proof and cannot dent like metal.
With clip for ⅞" bar. The white celluloid model, in particular, looks most attractive.

Mud Flaps

Made of black double-japanned cloth. Very strong, durable material which will not crack. Secured by a flexible metal clip. Equally suitable for celluloid or metal guards. **6d.** each.

"PERFECTION"
Black Celluloid Flap.

10" x 6¾"   ...   ...   **11d.**
12" x 7⅜" **1/4**

Green, White or Transparent,
3d.   extra

Famous for Quality

18

19

Rear Extensions

Ideal for wet weather. Length 14½". Weighs only 5 ozs. complete with fittings. Width of blade 2¼". Bolts on to end of rear guard. Special stays fix on to existing fork clips.

Price complete :

In Black ... **2/–**
White ... **2/3**
Supplied without flap, **3d.** less.

Can be used as an extra long front extension.

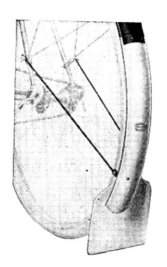

Celluloid Sideguards

Very light; quickly attached and detached; adjustable for width.

The front guard fits to within about 2½" of the ground. Swivel jointed adjustable metal clips fix on to the mudguard stays.

Price each
Front, Black ... **2/6**
Rear, Black ... **2/4**

To comply with "White Patch" Regulations

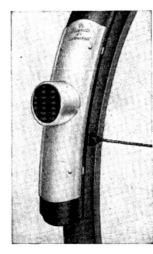

No. 1.

No. 3 "Safeguard"

A white patch primarily for road racing cycles without mudguards. For attachment with our No. 7, or similar stay-fitting reflector. Price **6d.**

Less Reflector.

No. 1 "Safeguard"

To meet the 1934 Lighting Regulations. No. 1 incorporates our Improved "Prismatic" Reflector (N.P.L. Certificate 151). Clips on guard. With or without rib down centre.

Price complete **1/6**

No. 2 without reflector **6d.**

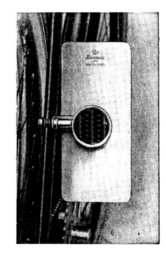

No. 3.

Famous for Quality

A white patch was a legal requirement in the 1930s and 1940s until legislation on compulsory rear lights was introduced in 1945

20

21

No. 24 "Prismatic" Reflector
in Rubber Case

(Pat. No. 425138. N.P.L. Certificate No. 151).

Here are a few of its advantages :—
New-type rubber body.
Cannot rust or chip.
Cannot dent.
Everlasting.
Fits any mudguard.
Concealed fitting.

Black or White   **9d.**

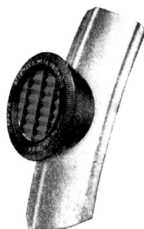

"Raylight" Reflectors
with double convex lenses

(N.P.L. Nos. 102 & 123).

The only reflector approved for use in the Channel Islands.

The celluloid case is strongly constructed and cannot dent or rust.

No. 8, stay fitting with clip ... **1/3**

No. 9 to screw on to centre of guard **1/-**

No. 14, to clip on to mudguard ... **1/-**

Improved "Prismatic" Rear Reflectors

(N.P.L. Certificate No. 151).

BE SEEN AND NOT HURT !

Why risk your life by failing to specify a dependable rear reflector? Modern traffic conditions demand a Bluemel "Prismatic" (or 'Raylight"). Every Bluemel reflector is of approved type, and its highly efficient lens reflects the poorest light with the steady glow of a lighted lamp. The polished celluloid case is rust-proof, dust and watertight. The models with white cases are particularly suitable for use with our white celluloid mudguards, and have a high degree of visibility at night.

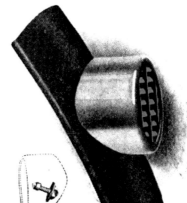

No. 10

(Pat. No. 316110. N.P.L. Cert. No. 151).

This model fits closely to the guard and is secured by a concealed nut and bolt. Used as a standard fitment by many leading cycle manufacturers.

each
Black celluloid case **1/3**
White celluloid case **1/4**

Famous for Quality

22

23

Improved "Prismatic" Reflectors

(N.P.L. Certificate No. 151).

No. 5, to screw on to the guard   **1/-**

No. 4
with mudguard clip
1/-

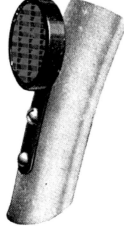

No. 5.

No. 7 stay fitting, with clip ...   **1/3**

*   *

White 1d. extra
on all models.

No. 7

Universal "Prismatic" Reflector

A very moderately-priced reflector combining our improved "Prismatic" glass with high-grade celluloid, rustless case. There are four types of interchangeable fittings as illustrated and the prices for any pattern complete are:

No. 27 - Mudguard Fitting

No. 28 - Stay Clip

Black Case

10d.

White Case

11d.

No. 29 - Stay Fitting

N.P.L. Cert. No. 151.
Prov. Pat. No 12455/35.

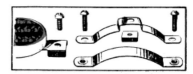

No. 30 - Mudguard Clip

Famous for Quality

24

Sixpenny "Prismatic" Reflectors
with metal cases

N.P.L. Cert. No. 151.

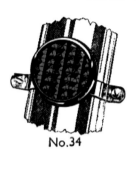

No. 34

No. 35

No. 26

No. 37

Our Improved "Prismatic" Reflector lens is used in conjunction with a metal case to make possible so efficient a reflector at the low price.

The popular fittings illustrated meet all requirements.

Price **6d.** each in all four fittings.

26

"DUALITE" Combined
Rear Lamps and Reflectors

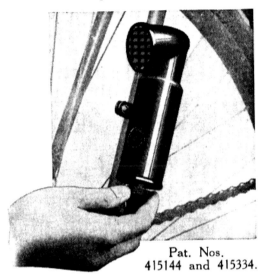

Pat. Nos.
415144 and 415334.

The red glass is a Bluemel Improved "Prismatic" reflector of officially approved type — a useful standby should the bulb or battery fail. The non-corrodible body is of stout celluloid which cannot chip, rust or dent.
No. 1 takes Ever-Ready battery No. 1839 and 2.5 v., .1 amp. bulb.
No. 2 takes Ever-Ready U.2 large capacity unit cell and 1.5 v., .1 amp. bulb, giving upwards of 35 hours light for 3½d.
Price each, with bulb and battery:
No. 1 **3/6** No. 2 **3/3½**
White body 3d. extra.
IMPORTANT. *Be sure to get correct replacement bulbs.*

Famous for Quality

27

"Lightweight" Dynamo Set for Cycles

(BRITISH MADE THROUGHOUT)

The following features of this highly efficient set will appeal to all experienced cyclists :—

- Dynamo 20% lighter than the average.
- Body of Dynamo is of a special shock-proof material which provides perfect insulation and is rust and corrosion proof.
- Smooth and easy running.
- Neat locating lever locks Dynamo securely in driving or off position.
- Headlamp with special glass and silver-plated reflector giving extra wide beam. No loose wires.
- Twin-bulb headlamp has latest type two-way switch giving light from self-contained 4.5 v. battery when Dynamo is not in use.
- Rear lamp incorporating Bluemel's Improved "Prismatic" reflector, officially approved. Can be used as either.

PRICES:

Complete set with necessary cable, British bulbs and Ever-Ready 1289 battery for head lamp	**23/5**
Set as above, but less rear lamp	**21/5**
Dynamo only, complete with cable ...	**14/-**
Headlamp only, with battery and British pilot bulb	**7/5**
Rear lamp, Black with cable (less bulb)	**2/-**
,, ,, White ,, ,, ,, ,,	**2/2**

28

"Lightweight" Dynamo Set for Cycles

HEAD LAMP

WEIGHT (less battery)	14 oz.
FINISH	Ebony with chromium parts
BULBS (all British)	Main bulb 6 v., 0.3 amp. gas filled
	Pilot bulb 4.5 v., .3 amp.
GLASS	3¼ in. diameter

DYNAMO

WEIGHT	23 oz.
BRACKET	Suitable for front or rear forks
CAPACITY	6 volts

REAR LAMP

BULB	6 v., .1 amp. vacuum
GLASS	Bluemel's Improved "Prismatic" red reflector
	(Approved Type), Patent No. 423,464
WEIGHT	1¾ oz.
BODY	Polished Black Celluloid
BRACKET	For seat stay

(It is important that the correct bulbs be specified for replacement purposes).

Famous for Quality

29

"Featherweight" Dynamo Set for Cycles

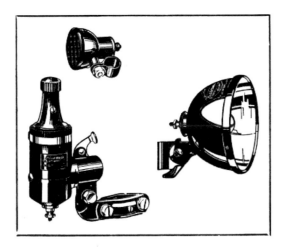

Full specification of the Dynamo and "Lightweight" Rear Lamp are given on page 29. "Featherweight" Head Lamp on page 31.

PRICES :

Complete Dynamo Set in Black with front and rear lamps, bulbs and cable **22/-**

Set as above less rear lamp **20/-**

Head lamp, white extra ... ... **3d.**

Rear lamp, white to match, extra ... ... **2d.**

30

"Featherweight" Head Lamp

Rustless, celluloid body of stout gauge. High-grade 3″ glass. Silver-plated reflector of exceptional brilliance. Patent clip which prevents theft of lamp or bulb. Radial bulb focussing. The prices below are with cable, but without bulb as this varies according to dynamo used. Weight, 5½ ozs.

Black ... **5/6**
White ... **5/9**

"Lightweight" Rear Lamp

This lamp can be used with any dynamo and as the glass is our improved "Prismatic" reflector it complies with the law even when the current is off. The prices shown include cable, but not bulb as this varies according to the dynamo used.

Black ... **2/-**
White ... **2/2**

Famous for Quality

31

Improved No. 3 Moulded "Litalite" Battery Lamp

The advantages of this handy dual-purpose lamp are :
- Neat folding handle enabling it to be used as a hand or cycle lamp.
- Improved quick-action clip-on back for battery or bulb renewals.
- Body of special material which cannot become sulphated or corroded from a spent battery, and provides perfect insulation.
- High grade silver-plated reflector.
- 2.5 v. bulb of first class quality (British made).
- Takes Ever-Ready battery No. 800 or similar.

RETAIL PRICES WITH THE STANDARD "800" BATTERY.

In Black, Green, Red or Walnut	...	**3/2**
In White	...	**3/8**

Green Transparent Eye Shade for Cyclists
(NON-INFLAMMABLE)

FOR LADIES OR GENTLEMEN.

They shield the eyes from dazzling head lights, from sun-glare and are useful for shading the eyes when reading or writing near bright lights. Nos. 3a and 4 can be carried flat in the pocket.

No. 2

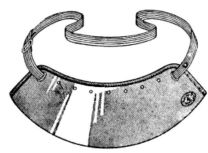

No. 2
With stiffening band at the top, neat binding at the edge and wide elastic.
Price ... **1/9**

No. 3
With wide elastic band and ventilation holes. Price **1/3**

No. 4
A slightly smaller model at a lower price ... **9d.**

No. 3a
Similar to No. 3 but with narrower elastic band ... **1/–**

Famous for Quality

32

33

Celluloid Handles

No. 142.
7½d. pair.

No. 264.
6d. pair.

No. 176.
7½d. pair.

The handle occupies the most exposed position on the cycle where it is subject to severe blows and, often, abuse. The Bluemel Handle is built to withstand rough use. Its tough foundation enables it to withstand severe treatment as will no other handle.

A range of neatly embossed designs, well-finished, coated on the inside with strong adhesive which only needs moistening before placing on the bar.

Celluloid-covered Handlebars

Handlebars can be covered in durable, thick celluloid, plain black or fine diamond check design, or the following colours:
Vermilion, Crimson, Maroon, Dark Blue, Green, Yellow.

Prices from your dealer.

34

Celluloid Chain Covers

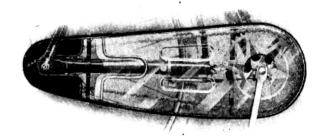

They are extremely light, quickly fitted or detached, and can be lengthened or shortened to suit cycles with centres varying from 18″ to 20½″. This adjustment ensures a perfectly fitting cover.

	Price each
Black	5/-
Transparent	5/6

Dress & Overcoat Shields

Strongly made, yet very light. Will fit any cycle.

	each
In Black Celluloid	4/4
Transparent	4/8

State whether for 26″ or 28″ wheels.

Famous for Quality

35

Head Offices and Works, Wolston

INDEX

Famous for Quality

36

GEAR TABLE
for 26in., 27in., and 28in. Wheels

No. of Teeth on small chainring	Number of Teeth on large chain wheel (⅛" pitch) and diameter (in inches) of road wheel.											
	40			42			44			46		
	26"	27"	28"	26"	27"	28"	26"	27"	28"	26"	27"	28"
12	86.6	90.0	93.3	91.0	94.1	98.0	95.3	99.0	102.2	99.6	103.5	107.3
13	80.0	83.1	86.1	84.0	87.4	90.5	88.0	91.3	94.8	92.0	95.3	99.0
14	74.2	77.1	80.0	78.0	81.0	84.0	81.7	84.8	88.0	85.4	88.7	92.0
15	69.3	72.0	74.6	72.8	75.7	78.4	76.2	79.2	82.1	79.7	82.1	85.8
16	65.0	67.5	70.0	68.2	70.8	73.5	71.5	74.2	77.0	74.7	77.6	80.5
17	61.1	63.5	65.8	64.3	66.7	69.2	67.2	69.8	72.4	70.3	73.0	75.7
18	57.8	60.0	62.2	60.6	63.0	65.3	63.5	66.0	68.4	66.4	69.0	71.5
19	54.7	56.7	58.9	57.5	59.6	61.9	60.2	62.5	64.8	63.0	65.4	67.8
20	52.0	54.0	56.0	54.6	56.7	58.8	57.2	59.4	61.6	59.8	62.0	64.4
22	47.2	49.0	50.9	49.6	51.5	53.4	52.0	54.0	56.0	54.3	56.4	58.5

	48			52			56			60		
	26"	27"	28"	26"	27"	28"	26"	27"	28"	26"	27"	28"
12	104.0	108.0	112.0	112.6	117.0	121.2	121.2	126.0	130.6	130.0	135.0	140.0
13	96.0	99.7	103.4	104.0	108.0	112.0	112.0	116.3	120.6	120.0	124.6	129.2
14	89.1	92.5	96.0	96.5	100.2	104.0	104.0	108.0	112.0	111.8	115.7	120.0
15	83.2	86.4	89.6	90.1	93.6	97.0	97.0	100.8	104.5	104.0	108.0	112.0
16	78.0	81.0	84.0	84.5	87.7	91.0	91.0	94.0	98.0	97.5	101.2	105.0
17	73.4	76.2	79.0	78.5	82.3	85.6	85.6	89.0	92.2	91.7	95.2	98.7
18	69.3	72.0	74.6	75.1	78.0	80.8	81.0	84.0	87.2	86.7	90.0	93.3
19	65.7	68.2	70.7	71.2	74.0	76.6	76.6	79.6	82.5	82.0	85.1	88.3
20	62.4	64.8	67.2	67.6	70.2	72.8	72.8	75.6	78.4	78.0	81.0	84.0
22	56.7	59.1	61.0	61.4	63.8	66.1	66.1	68.7	71.3	70.8	73.5	75.3

HARDEN HUBS AND OTHER CYCLE PRODUCTS PRODUCED BY THE HARDEN TOOL AND GAUGE COMPANY

Harden hubs: instantly recognisable and certainly the most distinctive and innovative British hub design. Harden's place in cycling history is assured by their use of cartridge bearings (caged non-adjustable ball bearings) not just for their hubs but also for the bottom bracket. If that wasn't enough in the late 1940s they produced a freehub 40 years ahead of Campagnolo and Shimano.

Mention of Harden hubs within the V-CC seems to produce two very different reactions. Firstly, they are regarded as one of the greatest hubs ever produced, light years ahead of their time. An engineering marvel combining free running with an appearance aesthetically pleasing to the eye. The contrary view is that they were expensive compared to quality cup and cone hubs of the period (e.g. Airlite and Bayliss Wiley) with bearings prone to failure and difficult to replace - simply not up to the job. Stories of axle breakage, especially in track racing are then quoted.

The purpose of this article is to outline Hardens history by reference to period sources, drawing on more recent research and recollections by a former employee, David Goss.[1]

The origins of Harden are to be found in the Jewellery Quarter in Birmingham in Vittoria Street. In the early 1930s one J. Kraut (a Swiss) was a maker of clock gears and parts. He also

1 Employed from 1936 for over 20 years at Hardens

Fig. 1 Harden's so-called Bacon Slicer hubs were the very first cycling product from the Harden Tool and Gauge Company

had the contract to wind and maintain the city's municipal clocks. J. Kraut died in 1935 and shortly afterwards the family sold up and returned to Switzerland. The purchasers were a J. Hart and a Miss Eden (the company secretary and principal investor). It was a combination of their names that gave rise to the company name Harden.

J. Hart sent his son Harold to the USA to be educated and become an engineer. When he returned the company expanded, starting to manufacture jigs and tools for the then rapidly expanding aircraft industry. In 1945 the Harts sold the company to Cecil Jordan who had been factory manager at Hobson carburettors in Coventry.

David Goss, upon whose recollections this article draws extensively, joined Harden in 1936.

Reprinted from
THE MOTOR CYCLE AND CYCLE TRADER
October 26th, 1945

A New Hub Set
Lightweight Pattern for the Enthusiast

The Harden Tool & Gauge Co., Ltd., of Regent Place, Birmingham, 1, have just marketed a set of hubs which should claim the interest of the discerning cyclist. They embody the principle of the annular bearing fixed in a standard shell of Duralumin with deep flanges, and the whole ensemble is exceedingly neat and light. The rear hub minus sprocket weighs 8¼ oz., and the front one an ounce less.

The point about these hubs, which are not a cheap job, is that they follow the best engineering practice in bearings, and are claimed to be trouble free, in addition to their obvious virtues of easy running and lightness.

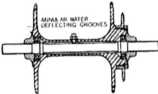

Sectional view of the new lightweight hub.

We have examined a hub that has been through some 2,000 miles of racing stress, and it certainly ran beautifully smoothly and looked the part of an aristocrat in fitments, simple in design and by that reason attractive to the eye.

Much has been written on the subject of annular bearings as applied to cycle engineering practice, but examples of this method of acquiring a greater perfection of trouble-free running have been few; hence the reason we think this new hub will be of general interest.

Our illustration shows the simple layout and details.

Fig. 2 The first announcement in the press of the Harden hubs from *The Motor Cycle and Cycle Trader* October 26th 1945

Initially this was as the family driver whose duties included taking Harold's children to school in a large American car. He then became an apprentice toolmaker and ended up as chargehand during the period of cycle component production. At the time of his marriage in 1940 his best man was Don Humpage, a well-known Midlands track cyclist who was then Harden foreman. That Harden ever made cycle components was very much down to Don's interest and motivation.

During WWII Harden made specialist alloy parts for the aircraft industry (in particular anti-icing devises for the Halifax bomber) and it was this expertise that Humpage applied to bicycle hubs. In the latter part of the war he had a number of prototypes made up including a front hub of magnesium alloy, which still survives to this day on his Joe Cooke cycle, which is owned by a V-CC member.

In 1945 Harden obtain a patent for the Humpage alloy hub design with cartridge bearings pressed on to the axle. Manufacture began at the end of that year. At the height of cycle component production they employed about 60 staff. Initially all hubs were large flange and undrilled, a style that became known in Britain as 'bacon slicers'. These were offered in versions typical for the time e.g. double or single fixed, gear/fixed and gear only. One problem with these hubs is that the spoke holes are drilled very close to the edge of the flange. This can result in the flanges cracking. This can be caused by a number of factors including spokes over-tightened, a chain coming off the rear usually fixed sprocket or now simply the age of the metal (around 60 years old).

Fig. 3 The drilled version of the large flange hub from the cover of the c1950 catalogue

With its elegant curve from flange to hub barrel and Tecalemit grease nipple they are some of the most attractive hubs ever produced. The front weighed 6oz and the rear 7½ oz. In 1947 a drilled version appeared described by Harden as 'with lightening holes'. Some of the drilled hubs clearly started off as bacon slicers as some lightening holes are drilled through the Harden logo. I take this as evidence that Harden supply was in excess of demand.

There were also small flange hubs although these are far rarer, by a ratio I estimate of 1 to 40. These were produced when the large flange sales tailed off in 1948, the idea being to compete with Bayliss-Wiley and Airlite. This plan failed, as Hardens were still significantly more expensive. They were produced by merely reducing the size of the flange and thus are identical in all other respects to the large flange hub. David Goss estimates Harden produced 100,000 large flange hubs and about half that number of the conventional cup and cone version (Flywate).

The only hubs exported were 500 cartridge large flange, in 1947 to Australia (to Bruce and Co). David records that they were extremely grateful for the food parcels received from the importer (remember this was the height of rationing, some items not rationed in the war were now rationed!).

Fig. 4 A small flange Harden rear hub seen in the single fixed version from the c1950 catalogue; it was available in double-fixed, gear/fixed and gear versions

Harden also produced track nuts (unmarked) and from 1947 marked wing nuts. These were designed by a relative of the Jordans. In 1948 they produced a cartridge unit bottom bracket designed to fit in an undrilled bracket shell. There was a serious design fault in that the axle tended to break where it was a drilled for a screw on the non-drive side for locking. The bearings by modern standards were somewhat undersized.

Fig. 5 Harden wingnuts and track nuts – these are really quite rare, one wonders just how many were made

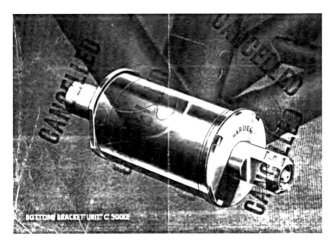

Fig. 6 The bottom bracket unit – seen from a c1948 catalogue which has had 'cancelled' stamped over it; presumably it had been withdrawn by the time this copy was sent out

In 1949 Harden marketed a cartridge bearing freehub, of a very innovative design. The weight of the unit minus sprockets was 14oz. It received a very positive test report in 'Cycling' being subject to the uses and abuses of a tandem tour in a mountainous region of France. Bearing in mind freehubs were not widely adopted until the late 1980s you quickly realise just how innovative this design was. Simplex and Bayliss-Wiley had both produced freehubs in the late 1930s, but these were based around conventional bearings. Both the freehub and the bottom bracket were produced in very small qualities, according to David Goss around 60 of each. .

Also in 1949 they advertised the Flywate, a conventional cup and cone large flange hub but there there was no small flange version. Some of these are not marked Harden but can be recognised by

Fig. 7: A sectioned rear freehub, maybe produced for show use

Fig. 8 The freehub from the catalogue

Fig. 9 The Harden Flywate plus first adverts for freewheel hub and tricycle axle from *The Bicycle* 25/10/49

the fact they used the Tecalemit nipple and the first version has the distinctive Harden profile. The later version has a curve similar to an alloy Campagnolo hub. Although these were cheaper than the cartridge bearing Hardens, they were still more expensive than their competitors and thus were not a commercial success. The switch to conventional

"CYCLING" TEST REPORT

NEW HARDEN FREEWHEEL HUB

Before Being Ridden on Continental Roads, this Hub "Covered" 26,000 Miles on Laboratory Tests. Its Condition is Still Perfect

SPLENDID results have been obtained from extensive tests recently carried out on a new freewheel unit hub produced by the Harden Tool and Gauge Co., Ltd. (51, Vittoria Street, Birmingham, 1). The hub, which has an alloy shell, has been fitted to a tandem with a three-speed derailleur gear and in a few, short weeks was taken over some of the worst pavé in France and was subjected to severe strains during high - speed descents of mountain passes.

The hub is primarily designed as a lightweight job for the racing and club man, but the standard of the test to which we have subjected it, by far exceeds the needs of these types of cyclists. The tandem on which it was ridden was a touring model and was fully loaded for a three weeks' tour. The highest speed stretch was a 1½-mile descent of a straight road with a 1-in-10 gradient; it was taken down this without any restriction by braking. On the other hand, there was considerable braking applied on the mountain descents, when on several occasions, from 6 to 10 down-hill miles were ridden at speeds constantly varying between 10 and 40 m.p.h.

It will be appreciated that under these conditions any flaw in the construction of a hub would quickly reveal itself, but the writer is happy (gloriously so) to relate that there was never a moment's anxiety. It was, therefore, with tremendous interest on the return to England, he dismantled the hub for a closer inspection.

It might well have been used for a 20-min. run up and down a flat road. The grease packings inside the hub remained undisturbed and no wear could be traced on any of the internals.

This is the first unit hub produced by the Harden company and it is constructed in the following manner:

The hub shell, which, in appearance, is similar to the familiar Harden hub with integral races, contains the free-wheel ratchet on an internal barrel within the shell on the driving side. The hub spindle passes through the hub centre and is supported by the fitting of two integral ball races which are retained in position by push-fit plates. A separate barrel carries the sprockets, this barrel having a cup on the reverse side containing the two free-wheel pawls. This barrel also carries two ball races. When the cup is inserted into the hub shell, the pawls engage with the free-wheel ratchet and the two ball races slip on to the hub spindle, the sprocket unit being held in place by a lock-nut screwed on to the spindle. Thus, when the unit is assembled, it runs on four integral ball races, two within the hub itself and two contained in the sprocket unit.

The hub unit will be retailed at 75s.

Showing how the sprocket unit, which runs on two integral ball races, is separated from the hub shell.

Again showing the driving side of the hub shell with the sprocket unit removed. The hub spindle, bearing one of its two integral ball races, is being inserted through the hub centre.

The ratchet can be seen in this picture within the hub shell. The sprocket unit has been removed and reversed to show the cup containing the free-wheel pawls. The hub spindle remains in position, supported by its two sets of ball bearings.

Fig. 9 The review from *Cycling*

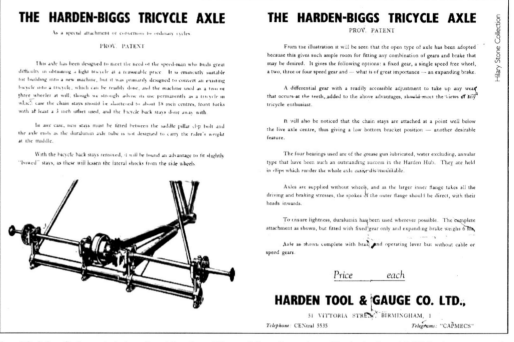

THE HARDEN-BIGGS TRICYCLE AXLE

As a special attachment or conversion to ordinary cycles.

PROV. PATENT

This axle has been designed to meet the need of the speedman who finds great difficulty in obtaining a light tricycle at a reasonable price. It is eminently suitable for building into a new machine, but it was primarily designed to convert an existing bicycle into a tricycle, which can be readily done, and the machine used as a two or three wheeler at will, though we strongly advise its use permanently as a tricycle in which case the chain stays should be shortened to about 18 inch centres, front forks with at least a 3 inch offset used, and the bicycle back stays done away with.

In any case, new stays must be fitted between the saddle pillar clip bolt and the axle ends as the duralumin axle tube is not designed to carry the rider's weight at the middle.

With the bicycle back stays removed, it will be found an advantage to fit slightly "bowed" stays, as these will lessen the lateral shocks from the side wheels.

THE HARDEN-BIGGS TRICYCLE AXLE

PROV. PATENT

From the illustration it will be seen that the open type of axle has been adopted because this gives such ample room for fitting any combination of gears and brake that may be desired. It gives the following options: a fixed gear, a single speed free wheel, a two, three or four speed gear and — what is of great importance — an expanding brake.

A differential gear with a readily accessible adjustment to take up any wear that occurs at the teeth, added to the above advantages, should meet the views of any tricycle enthusiast.

It will also be noticed that the chain stays are attached at a point well below the live axle centre, thus giving a low bottom bracket position — another desirable feature.

The four bearings used are of the grease gun lubricated, water excluding, annular type that have been such an outstanding success in the Harden Hub. They are held in clips which render the whole axle easy to dismountable.

Axles are supplied without wheels, and as the larger inner flange takes all the driving and braking stresses, the spokes of the outer flange should be direct, with their heads inwards.

To ensure lightness, duralumin has been used wherever possible. The complete attachment as shown, but fitted with fixed gear only and expanding brake weighs 6 lbs.

Axle as shown complete with brake and operating lever but without cable or speed gears.

Price _____ each

HARDEN TOOL & GAUGE CO. LTD.,

51 VITTORIA STREET, BIRMINGHAM, 1

Telephone: CENtral 5535   Telegrams: "CAPMECS"

Fig. 10 A leaflet explaining the Harden-Biggs tricycle axle – likely to be 1949 but never put into production

bearings was made all the easier as David Goss's sister-in-law was employed by a manufacturer of cup and cones.

In 1949 they advertised their final cycle product, a differential tricycle axle: the Harden-Biggs. During the course of my research I have been unable to either locate one or find any reference as to who Biggs was. It is possible it never progressed beyond the prototype stage, although it is referred to in an advertisement in 'The Bicycle' (26/10/49).

Harden continued in the cycle trade until 1953, but there was no further innovation after 1949. Indeed David Goss suggests that they did not produce any hubs after 1950 merely selling existing stock. Their departure from the cycle business seems to have coincided with Don Humpage leaving to form a sub-contracting company, Beacon Tool Company. Also at this time there was the general decline in the lightweight cycle trade with the start of the car boom.

Not long after their introduction cyclists began to experience technical problems with the hubs. Considerable numbers were returned usually with bearing problems, which cyclists and dealers believed to be irreparable. Harden advertised a special service for local cyclists: the opportunity to service your hubs by opening the factory on Saturday morning. For other cyclists they offered a 24-hour turnaround time. By 1951 this task had been given to outside contractors. By 1954 this service has ceased. Harden tried to fit stronger bearings, but to no avail.

Clearly there were problems but one wonders how much was caused by dealers and cyclists not understanding that it was possible to obtain replacement bearings and doing the job yourself. According to David Goss:

"We made more money [than selling hubs] setting up a repair service to replace the ball race bearings which had a very short life due to them being over-stressed for the job they were expected to fulfil"

Even *Cycling* magazine's technical expert, 'The Lightweight Man' writing 25th May 1960 stated that the bearings were not available. He was put right by a reader, R. E. Greenbury, a couple of weeks later who pointed out this was a fallacy and that they were easily available industrial bearings (he quotes Hoffman S3 and Fischer EE3). Greenbury advised new bearings could be fitted by removing the locknuts and dust caps, warming the bearing housing and taping the end of the spindle until the old bearings dropped out. Then fit new bearings while still warm and refit dust caps and locknuts.

I think there is a parallel with Cyclo and the uphill battle they had to introduce derailleur gears in Britain in the 30s. However unlike Harden, Cyclo issued very detailed instructions for fitting, servicing and repairing gears.   Perhaps because of the money to be made in servicing, Harden

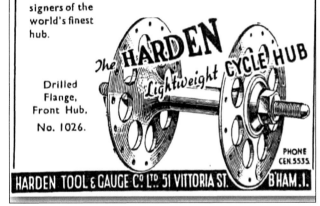

Fig. 11 An advert from *The Bicycle* 27/7/49 – in it Harden announces the Saturday morning service programme

deliberately refrained from issuing any maintenance instructions. Some of their adverts actually stated:

"never take your Harden hubs to pieces…simply lubricate occasionally with a grease gun".

During my research I came across a classic

example of cyclist ingenuity. A rider in Barrow in Furness who worked for the local bus company repairing ticket machines noticed that these used the same bearings as Harden hubs. He then had a very successful sideline in repairs with his club.

Hardens were far more expensive that other quality hubs. In a 1948 *'Cycling'*, Claud Butler offered a pair of Fiamme rims on Gnuttis for £4 12s 6d, the same rims on Hardens were £7 8s 6d. To many club cyclists this must have been far too much to pay. One reason for the high price was that the hub polishers belonged to a very powerful trade union and were able to demand high rates.

Harden advertised extensively in the cycling press in the late 1940s and employed one rider Wally Summers to use their hubs.

Hub Details

Early Hardens can be identified as they are stamped 'patent pending' later ones have the patent number 596137 stamped on the flange.

The centre section diameter varies, there seems to be two ranges:

14.3mm to 14.6mm

16mm to 16.6mm

This does not correspond to manufacturing dates, as hubs known to be sold as pairs have both diameters. This inconsistency extends to the Flywate range, furthermore it is not always the rear hub which is wider in diameter.

Some Flywates are not marked Harden. The first version of the Flywate uses smaller non-standard cones, the later ones use standard cones.

Cage bearing fit was 875" x 312" x 281"

The locknut was originally one piece, but with

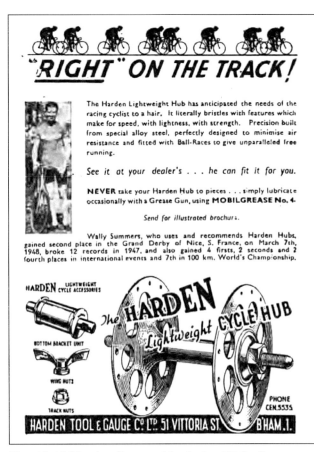

Fig. 12 1949 advertisement featuring Wally Summers the only rider to promote Harden. Note the rare sealed bottom bracket, the wing nuts and the track nuts that are stamped in tiny letters ' harden'

a change in supplier became two with a separate washer, this occurred around 1948.

Unique Hardens

A rear with lightening holes on one side only, this was a Holdsworth sales rep's sample designed to illustrate the two options in one hub. In November 2007 on eBay a Hi Lo Harden was

sold, that is a rear hub with one side large flange the other side small flange. Again this is thought to be a rep's sample designed to show both options in one hub. I have seen Hardens fitted with quick release axles, these are home made modifications. Similarly anodised Hardens, which turn up, were not done by the company.

Manufacture

According to David Goss the method of manufacture was as follows:

All Harden hubs were produced from 'hot drop stampings'. A hot billet of aluminium alloy was placed in situ on a steel mould (half the profile) and an identical steel mould was dropped from a height. This might happen a number of times, to force the plastic material into the final rough shape, ready for a clipping process to remove the resultant 'flash' surrounding the profile. This method of manufacture resulted in a much more homogenous structure and ensured that there was no danger of porosity to weaken the structure as could happen in castings

In 1953 the company moved to South Wales to take advantage of government grants to encourage relocation to assist in employment of disabled Welsh miners. They became known as Harden Valve Company based in Ammanford and continued in business until the 1990s but ceased to have any connection with the cycle trade.

Servicing

The following is a guide kindly provided by Peter Underwood:

- The original ball bearing races were Hoffman but if you go into a bearing stockist ask for bearing KLNJ 3/8 Y. High quality Swiss RHP bearings will cost just over £20 a pair. The British equivalent are about £12.
- The hub consists of the hub shell, the spindle made from high tensile (65 ton) special alloy steel, the two bearings, two alloy oil-seal discs and two alloy nuts which hold the whole assembly together.
- It is essential to remove the grease nipple first to avoid damage to the axle.
- The first job is to remove the outer nuts and it pays to remember that axle threads get slightly deformed where it sits in the fork ends. The Harden axle has flats so it is possible carefully to put the axle in a vice whilst getting these nuts off (best to hold in brass pads).
- Once they are off, take a fairly substantial polyurethane hammer and tap one end of the axle. After a few taps you will notice that the oil seal has come away so remove it from the axle and put to one side. Next to come away should be the caged bearing.
- Now it is possible to remove the axle from the hub and having done so support the inner edge of the attached ball race (say on a vice opened a fraction more than the axle diameter) and again tap with the hammer until the seal and bearing come off the axle. You should now have the shell and seven components including the axle.
- After carefully cleaning everything it is now time to

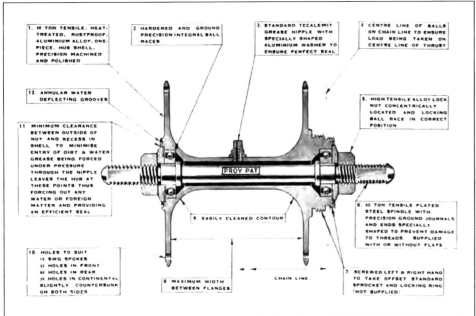

Fig. 13 Cut away view of a hub from the 1950 catalogue

Fig. 14 From *The Bicycle* 19/10/49

reassemble. Note that if you have a gear/fixed hub that the axle threads will be longer on the gear side.

- Take one of the cages (assuming that you have fingered grease into it from both sides) and slide it up the axle and then use the vice as before except this time to tap the axle in.
- Now feed the axle into the hub and slide on the other bearing – it is now possible to use the open vice again to support the bearing whilst it is tapped in by the opposite axle end.
- All that remains now is to slide on the seals and then the retaining bolts – you may have to hold the axle flats in the vice to stop them twisting.
- Hub assembly is made easier by heating to about 50 C.
- If there are no flats on the axle it is possible to

use two nuts locked together on a free part of the axle. These nuts can now be clamped in the vice to hold it whilst you work on it.

- Once assembled any looseness can be removed by tapping the axle and tightening the locknuts.
- These instructions work with hub only or with a built-up wheel. With the wheel you need the radius of the wheel clear on all sides.

Summary

Harden hubs clearly have a very special place in the history of lightweight parts. Thanks to the vision of one man, Don Humpage they produced some of the British cycle industries most technically innovative products. Throughout the last 50 years many high quality hubs have essentially refined

Hardens design, these include Maxicar, Mavic, Sachs and Phil Wood. Today all bottom brackets use sealed bearing, which are a direct descendant of the Harden design. Similarly the freebub and sealed bottom bracket are now pretty much ubitiquous, a classic example of British designs being taken and developed by a Japanese company (Shimano).

You may be asking at this stage is the author of this piece pro or anti Harden? To give a politicians answer I think there is something to be said for both views. Yes they were innovative, smooth running and aesthetically pleasing but there were certainly technical issues. According to David Goss the main problem was the bearings were insufficient for the task. Harden fitted 7/8" x 3/8"x 7/32" when he thinks they should have used 1

1/8" x ½ "x 9/32". This would have made them even more expensive and heavier!

Acknowledgements:
My thanks to the following people
Alexander von Tutschek who suggested the subject and supported the research
Peter Underwood for Harden servicing details
Hilary Stone for use of his *Cycling Plus* article: May 2004
Neville Bousfield for information on hub barrel diameters
Ray Miller for information from the V-CC library
Most of all David Goss for his recollections

Subsequent Info:
Don Humpage died 1954, his widow believed he was working on a pedal but design stolen

THE HARDEN LIGHTWEIGHT CYCLE HUB
Patent Applied For

DRILLED FLANGE FRONT HUB 1026

HARDEN A PILLAR OF INDUSTRY BIRMINGHAM

Talked into Fame By the Club & Racing Cyclist

The only Harden Catalogue

THE HARDEN CYCLE HUB

Since its introduction, the "Harden" Cycle hub has met with an enthusiastic response from the discriminating cyclist, who has been quick to appreciate the outstanding advantages offered by its unique design.

Exclusive features are :—

Lightweight—6 ozs. front, 7½ ozs. rear, combined with great strength by the use of heat-treated alloy forgings giving a tensile strength of 30 tons per square inch as against 6 tons for a cast alloy.

Polished rust-proof one-piece shell.

Easily cleaned contour.

Water deflecting grooves.

Large flanges for wide pitch spoke holes giving a higher crossing point to the spokes resulting in greater wheel strength.

Spoke holes *lightly* countersunk both sides to ensure good seating for spoke heads without reducing the effective thickness of the flanges—no broken or loose spokes.

Spindle made from high tensile (65 ton) special alloy steel, with precision ground journals and specially shaped ends to protect the end threads. Rear spindles are normally supplied to suit standard drop-out, but perfectly round rear spindles can be supplied if required.

Nuts concentrically machined from high tensile light alloy.

The greatest trouble with hubs has been to exclude water. This problem has been overcome by Harden engineers by the use of water-resisting grease (Mobilgrease No. 4), which is forced by pressure gun through the nipple and travels along the annular space between shell and spindle to reach the inside of the ball races. Passing through

STANDARD FRONT HUB 1000

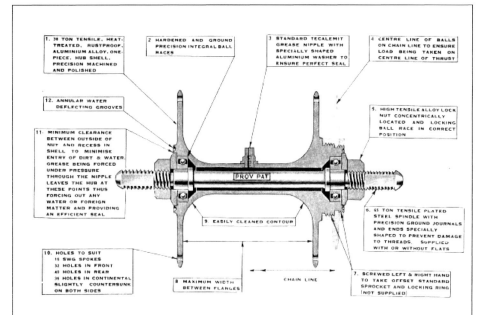

1. 30 TON TENSILE, HEAT-TREATED, RUSTPROOF, ALUMINIUM ALLOY, ONE-PIECE, HUB SHELL, PRECISION MACHINED AND POLISHED

2. HARDENED AND GROUND PRECISION INTEGRAL BALL RACES

3. STANDARD TECALEMIT GREASE NIPPLE WITH SPECIALLY SHAPED ALUMINIUM WASHER TO ENSURE PERFECT SEAL

4. CENTRE LINE OF BALLS ON CHAIN LINE TO ENSURE LOAD BEING TAKEN ON CENTRE LINE OF THRUST

12. ANNULAR WATER DEFLECTING GROOVES

5. HIGH TENSILE ALLOY LOCK NUT CONCENTRICALLY LOCATED AND LOCKING BALL RACE IN CORRECT POSITION

11. MINIMUM CLEARANCE BETWEEN OUTSIDE OF NUT AND RECESS IN SHELL TO MINIMISE ENTRY OF DIRT & WATER. GREASE BEING FORCED UNDER PRESSURE THROUGH THE NIPPLE LEAVES THE HUB AT THESE POINTS THUS FORCING OUT ANY WATER OR FOREIGN MATTER AND PROVIDING AN EFFICIENT SEAL

PROV PAT

6. 65 TON TENSILE PLATED STEEL SPINDLE WITH PRECISION GROUND JOURNALS AND ENDS SPECIALLY SHAPED TO PREVENT DAMAGE TO THREADS. SUPPLIED WITH OR WITHOUT FLATS

9. EASILY CLEANED CONTOUR

10. HOLES TO SUIT 15 SWG SPOKES 32 HOLES IN FRONT 40 HOLES IN REAR 36 HOLES IN CONTINENTAL SLIGHTLY COUNTERSUNK ON BOTH SIDES

8. MAXIMUM WIDTH BETWEEN FLANGES

CHAIN LINE

7. SCREWED LEFT & RIGHT HAND TO TAKE OFFSET STANDARD SPROCKET AND LOCKING RING (NOT SUPPLIED)

and filling the space between the balls, the grease finally leaves the hub by way of the small clearance between nut and shell. This tiny gap is the only clearance between fixed and moving parts, and this grease seal effectively prevents the entry of water or grit into the hub. All hubs are despatched from the works filled with this grease, and only this lubricant should be used in service, **it must be applied through the nipple by means of a grease gun.** If these instructions are ignored rusting may occur and our guarantee invalidated. Further protection is provided by the annular water-deflecting grooves in the hub shell which is recessed to take the bearing locknuts.

Bearings. The most exclusive feature of the Harden hub is the use of integral ball races in place of the usual cup and cone.

The 'line of thrust' of a ball bearing is across the points of contact, and in the cup and cone this line is at an angle from the vertical and results in a wedging action. Thus, although a cup and cone bearing feels

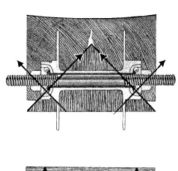

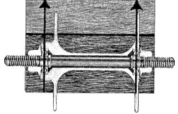

quite free when spun in the hand, the wedging action increases with the load, and the greater the load, the greater the wedging action, with consequent friction.

With the integral ball race, the load is taken vertically up and down through the centre line of the balls, and however great the load the free running qualities cannot be impaired.

To ensure this effect, it is essential that the ball races and housings should be correctly machined and positioned. The Harden hub section drawing shows that the centre line of the balls is on the chain line of the bicycle, the bearing thus both taking the weight of the rider and transmitting the thrust of the pedals.

The races are an "interference" fit in the hub shell which locks them securely in position. The inner portions of the races are an accurate fit on the ground spindles and are locked in position by the shouldered locknuts. No adjustment is provided as none is necessary; the locknuts should not be undone.

Service. Due to the extra efficiency obtained by the integral ball race the cost of these special races is approximately four times that of the cup and cone. Provided that the hubs are kept packed with grease, no replacements should be necessary for a considerable period. When service is required, no attempt should be made to take the hub apart. The complete wheel should be returned to the works where a fully equipped service department operates. It is important that advantage should be taken of these facilities as permanent damage can be done to the hub by incorrect service.

Models available. The original Harden hub range consisted of a plain flanged front hub, a single-sided fixed cog rear hub, and a derailleur hub.

SMALL FLANGE SINGLE SIDED REAR HUB 1038

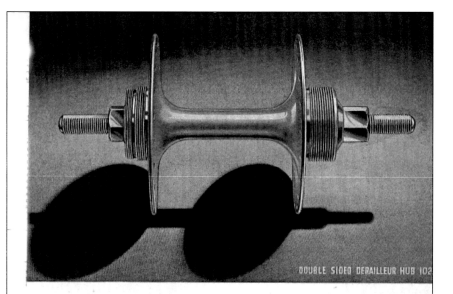

DOUBLE SIDED DERAILLEUR HUB 102

The single-sided rear hub was designed primarily for the racing man, who rarely required a double-cogged hub, and this enabled us to produce a hub with the maximum width between the flanges resulting in a very strong wheel. Similarly, the flanges were made plain for easy cleaning and "clean" appearance.

As a result of popular demand, we have now added two types of double-sided hubs to our range, giving five basic types and any of these types can be had with drilled holes if required. Similarly, limited quantities of small flanged hubs are available for those cyclists who prefer this type, although, owing to the exceptionally light weight of the shells, the saving in weight of either type is only $\frac{1}{2}$ oz. Full details and reference numbers of the complete range are shown on the back page.

Derailleur Hubs. The derailleur hubs are designed to take any of the usual types of 3- or 4-speed derailleur gears, and the fitting of a spacing collar of the correct thickness ensures that the chain line is always in the centre sprocket of a 3- speed or between the second and third sprockets of a 4-speed free wheel. Full details are supplied with each hub.

Packing. Each hub is packed in a specially designed box containing full fitting instructions. When ordering hubs to be built into wheels, the wheel builder should be asked for these instruction sheets.

Guarantee. See separate guarantee conditions on back page.

THE HARDEN CYCLE HUB

Reference Numbers. *For prices see separate list.*

		Plain Flange	Drilled Flange	Small Flange
Standard Front Hub	Ref.	1000	1026	1036
Single-sided Rear Hub	,,	1001	1028	1038
Single-sided Derailleur Hub	,,	1011	1030	1040
Double-sided Rear Hub (screwed for single sprocket at both ends)	,,	1020	1032	1042
Double-sided Derailleur Hub (screwed one side for single sprocket and locknut and opposite side for Derailleur)	,,	1023	1034	1044
Aluminium Spoke Guard	,,		1018	
Alloy Spacing Collars $\frac{1}{4}$" or $\frac{5}{16}$"	,,		1019	
Tecalemit Grease Gun (Type 7 M/c)	,,		1057	

Also made with spoke holes drilled 36/36—reference numbers similar to the above except that the first two figures are 36 instead of 10—thus 32-hole front hub reference number is 1000; 36-hole front hub reference 3600, etc.

TECHNICAL INFORMATION.

All hubs sent out are filled with Mobilgrease No. 4, and to ensure trouble-free running this brand of grease must be adhered to.

A grease gun should be applied to the nipple and sufficient lubricant inserted to force the old grease through the small clearance at the ends of the hub about every 200 miles. This operation prevents water and road grit from entering and gives the hub a smooth running and long life.

Mobilgrease No. 4 is marketed by the Vacuum Oil Company and can be obtained from dealers or from us.

DIMENSIONS.

Spoke Lacing. (Large Flanged Hubs.)

Leave six holes on the front hub and eight holes on the rear hub between every pair of parallel spokes, and alternate holes on the rim.

Length of Spokes as follows :—	26" Wheel	27" Wheel
Front, 32 spokes	$11\frac{3}{16}$"	$11\frac{13}{16}$"
Single-sided dished rear, 40 spokes	$11\frac{5}{16}$" and $11\frac{3}{8}$"	$11\frac{15}{16}$" and 12"
Single-sided dished derailleur, 40 spokes	$11\frac{1}{4}$" and $11\frac{1}{2}$"	$11\frac{7}{8}$" and 12"
Double-sided single cog rear, 40 spokes	$11\frac{1}{4}$"	$11\frac{7}{8}$"
Double-sided derailleur rear, 40 spokes (slightly dished) ...	$11\frac{1}{4}$"	$11\frac{7}{8}$"

	Sizes over nuts	Spindle lengths
Front hub	3·857"	5·482"
Single-sided and double-sided rear	4·138"	5·763"
Single-sided and double-sided derailleur	4·625"	6·250"

GUARANTEE.

1. The Harden Tool & Gauge Co. Ltd., will exchange or repair any Harden Hub which needs repair or replacement by reason of defective workmanship or defective material.

2. No claim can be considered unless the person claiming—(a) Returns the complete hub to the company's works, carriage paid. (b) Advises the Company that the hub has been so despatched and listing the complaint. (c) States date of purchase and dealer from whom purchased.

3. This guarantee shall not apply to any hub—(a) If the locknuts have been undone. (b) If lubrication instructions have not been carried out. (c) Which in the opinion of the Company has been damaged through wear and tear or unskilled handling. (d) Which has been used for any purpose other than that for which it is sold.

4. The liability of the Company is limited to exchange or repair under Clause 1 hereof. Every form of liability for every form of consequential loss or damage is hereby expressly excluded.

5. This Guarantee is given in lieu of and excludes every condition or warranty, whether statutory or otherwise, whatsoever not herein expressly set out.

HARDEN TOOL & GAUGE CO. LTD.

PRECISION ENGINEERS

Works: 6-8-10 REGENT PLACE, BIRMINGHAM 1

Offices: 51 VITTORIA STREET, ENGLAND

Telephone:
CEN. 5535 (2 lines)

Telegrams: CAPMECS, BIRMINGHAM 1
Code: BENTLEY'S

TOECLIPS - ALL CLIPPED IN

Cycling trivia pursuit question: *Which lightweight component never satisfactorily made the transfer from steel to alloy construction?* **Answer:** *Toeclips, although I would also accept saddle frames (as Brooks found out in the 1950s).*

Toeclips: one of the most effective aids to more efficient cycling, as well as a safety aid preventing the foot slipping. At the same time one of the least understood components by non- and occasional cyclists ("I wouldn't use those, be frightened of getting my feet stuck" is a commonly heard comment).

The sprung chrome plated steel clip (sometimes on copper), of which the Christophe (Fig. 1) was the most widely used, reigned supreme from the early 1930s until the 1990s with the introduction of clipless pedals. The Christophe clip was named after the French rider, Eugene Christophe, who is probably the most famous Tour de France rider never to have actually won the Tour, due his habit of breaking forks when in the lead. An oft repeated story of early Tours is that in 1919 he was given penalty points for having assistance from the black-smith's boy who operated the bellows during the repair. Christophe is also credited with inventing the wingnut.

Such was the popularity of these clips that sometimes they were the only French component on bikes manufactured elsewhere. The distinctive

Fig. 1 Classic Christophe toeclip

design included two rivets securing the toestrap slot (a good indication of whether clips of another make were actually made by Christophe) and the concave base shape. They were extremely durable and comfortable – an example of excellent design that stood the test of time.

With regard to markings , Christophe clips only changed in that latterly the C did not underline the entire word and the name was written in lower case. They were made by Afa (their name stamped on the underside with Brevette Made in France) and from early 1990s by Zefal (these do not have any markings on the underside). There were four sizes:

Size - Clip Extension	Marking	Extension from pedal (mm)
Small	D (Dames)	43
Medium	M	55
Long	L	65
Extra Long	X or XL	75

Christophe seems to be the only brand to offer extra long, advertised for shoe size 10½ (44) and over. Some of their clips are marked 'special' but there does not seem to be any difference to 'ordinary' ones.

One variant offered up to the late 60s was with the bends encased in leather. This was meant to prevent shoes being scuffed, but also had the benefit of preventing the clip from being scratched when wheeling the bike. In the 70s and 80s Christophe produced protector strips – black rubber sleeves edged in blue for fitting on the

Ref No.		Description	Price	
TOECLIPS				
T/100	BROOKS	No. 1. Chromed steel. Small, medium and large	5/9	Pair
T/105	CATOS	100. Adjustable, in polished alloy	4/6	,,
T/106	CATOS	101. Adjustable, in chromed spring steel	5/-	,,
T/107	CATOS	104. Fixed "Special" spring steel, plastic covered, in Red, Cream and Black	5/-	,,
T/108	CATOS	105. Fixed bright plated spring steel	3/6	,,
T/110	CHRISTOPHE	50 DAC. Short pattern, chrome on copper spring steel	6/6	,,
T/111	CHRISTOPHE	50 C. Medium pattern, as above	6/6	,,
T/112	CHRISTOPHE	50 SC. Long pattern, as above	6/6	,,
T/115	G.B.	"Professional" Stainless steel	6/6	,,
T/120	PATURAUD	9C. "Coureur" Cadmium plated piano wire	3/6	,,
T/121	PATURAUD	10B. "Super Champion" Ribbed chrome	5/9	,,
T/122	PATURAUD	16. "Grand Luxe." Chrome Medium and long patterns	6/6	,,
T/123	PATURAUD	22. "Grand Luxe." As above, but with leather covered front bars	11/6	,,
T/124	PATURAUD	18. "Femina." Grand Luxe, in short lady's design	6/6	,,
T/125	PATURAUD	18C. "Femina." As above, but with leather covered front bars	11/6	,,
T/126	PATURAUD	23. "Automatic." Chrome, adjustable, non-slip fixing	8/3	,,
T/127	PATURAUD	23C. "Automatic." As above, but with leather covered front bars	12/11	,,
T/128	PATURAUD	20. "Tourist." Chrome, with clamping plates and bolts to attach to rubber pedals	6/9	,,
T/129	PATURAUD	27. "Ville." Short chrome pattern for use without toestraps	5/3	,,
T/135	REG	207. Bright zinc plated spring steel	5/-	,,
T/136	REG	74. Chromium plated carbon steel, racing pattern	7/3	,,

TOECLIP COVERS

T/200	CHRISTOPHE	Leather Toeclip Shield, will fit easily to any type	4/-	Pair
T/210	PATURAUD	28. "Piescho." Solid leather, complete all round clip cover	25/-	,,

TOECLIP GUIDES

T/250	KAMZ	Pedal attachment designed to assist toeclip users to quickly guide the foot into the clip. Touch Kamz with your toe and VIOLA ! - your feet are in the clips	2/6	Each

TOESTRAPS

T/300	BINDA	The famous Italian quick-release strap, available in either Red or Natural	6/-	Pair
T/305	BROOKS	No. 1. De-Luxe non-stretch chrome leather, veined edges	4/6	,,
T/306	BROOKS	No. 1 Standard chrome natural leather, fitted quick-release buckle	3/9	,,
T/307	BROOKS	No. 2. Chrome natural leather, spring loaded buckle	2/6	,,
T/310	CONSTRICTOR	Strong natural strap with quick-release buckle	4/6	,,
T/315	CYCLO	"Oppy." Strong leather, cadmium buckle. Red. Blue or Natural	5/-	,,
T/320	LAPIZE	Quick-release chrome leather, cadmium buckle. Red, Blue or Natural	5/6	,,
T/325	LEDUCQ	Chrome leather, available in Red, Blue, Green or Natural, with cadmium quick-release buckle	6/-	,,
T/330	PATURAUD	15. "Eclair." Chrome leather quick-release cadmium buckle. Red, Blue, Green, Gold or Natural	6/3	,,
T/331	PATURAUD	30. "Super." Similar to above, with safety stop tie end	7/11	,,
T/332	PATURAUD	"Campionissimo." Highest quality chrome leather, with special buckle. Red, Blue, Green or Natural	7/11	,,
T/335	REG	23. Chrome leather, in Natural, Red, Blue or Green, with bright zinc plated special buckle	6/9	,,
T/336	REG	373. Chrome leather, racing pattern, with quick-release buckle, extra long strap with safety tie ends. Colours available as above	7/6	,,

TOECLIPS AND STRAPS

T/380	BARTHELEMY	Piano wire Toeclip, with quick-release toestraps	3/6	,,

81

Fig. 2 Ron Kitching range 1960

toeclip bends. If these were not securely glued on they tended to have very short life. A method used by some riders to protect the clips was to wrap the bends with handlebar or similar tape. One problem with any kind of covered clip is that moisture can get in and corrode the metal.

With the increasing popularity of Cyclo Cross in the late 60s a variant was designed to stand up to the rigors of this sport, that is repeated stamping on and hitting the ground. It was essentially two clips welded together.

The Christophe design was widely copied by Brooks, Cinelli, Campagnolo, ALE (main Italian makers based in Torino), Reg, Galli, Lambert, Lapize (also named after early Tour rider Octave Lapize who won in 1910), and Constrictor, amongst others. Whether Christophe actually originated this design is unclear. In the late 1930s Fonteyn imported a version, the Scherens, named after Jef Sherens, the Belgian rider who won the World Professional Track Championship from 1932 to 1937 inclusive. Does this make toeclips the most popular component to be named after a rider? Maybe, although handlebars give us numerous examples.

With regard to durability the Christophe is extremely tough. If the clip does fail it is usually at the bend above the pedal fixing after extensive use. The other cause of breakage is the toestrap slot becoming bent, usually by contact with the ground and snapping off.

Milremo had clips made in three sizes by Christophe. Ashby, the Birmingham based company, which also made saddlebag supports and racks, produced a version with a very un-English name – 'Monique' that was rivetless. The toestrap slot was just formed of bent metal. Another Birmingham

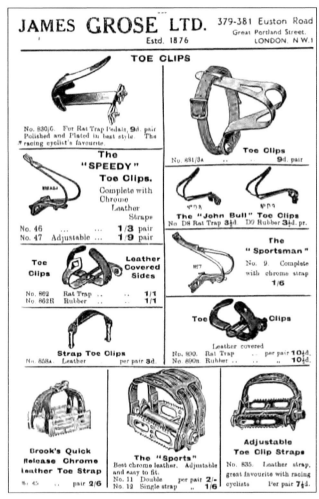

Fig. 3 James Grose 1937 catalogue selection

based company, Catos, made Christophe copies in both fixed and adjustable versions and some covered with coloured plastic.

Fig. 2 is from the 1960 Ron Kitching's 'Everything Cycling.' It shows the main marques and is a useful guide to relative prices. The toeclip covers listed were designed to offer bad weather protection, similar in concept to today's overshoes. Bernard Hinault, the mid 70s Tour winner, lent his name to a plastic pair.

Toeclips certainly go back to the nineteenth century as the earliest cyclists realised the benefits of some way of securing the foot to the pedal. The Data Book[1] has illustrations from 1911-12: the clip in its later forms is already evident. Fig. 3 from the 1937 J A Grose catalogue shows the range at this time. One type that did not survive post WWII was the wide strap without a clip. The rest of this article examines alternatives to the classic Christophe designs:

1. The Piano Wire

Good examples are the Oppy (named after Hubert Opperman, the Australian track and road champion who competed in the Tour de France, and took the End to End record in 1934) and Resto, both made by Cyclo from the late 30s until the end of 50s (Fig 4). Note the model for use with rubber pedals, which due to the flexible joint, has to be fitted to the rear of the front pedal block. Also in this style was the Python by Constrictor (Fig. 10).

Paturaud (a French company that only made toeclips and straps) offered a Coureur model available into the mid 60s and was in the Christophe shape (Fig. 5). Paturaud clips were not very durable, which explains why not many survived and the high prices they command on eBay. Catos made a range including an adjustable piano wire design, and their advertisements were a regular feature in the cycling press for over 40 years up to the 1980s (Fig. 6). Note the distinctive trade make of the extended 'C'.

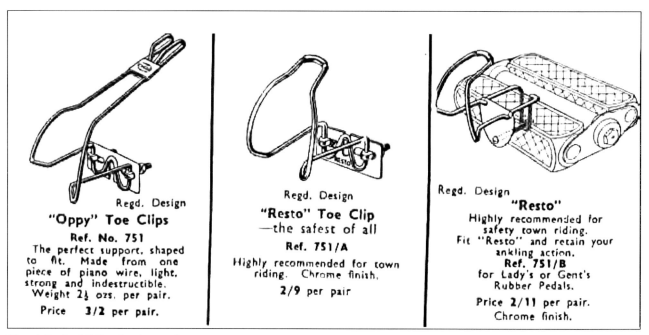

Fig. 4 Early 1950s *Cyclo catalogue*

2. The Adjustable

Fig. 7 shows an example from the 1931 Cycle Show produced by Ashby. With the aid of serrations the clip could be adjusted to fit the exact shoe size. The one illustrated has an amazing 16 different positions! Ashby continued to make an adjustable clip until the 1970s under the name 'Wanderlust' although this clip was of the Christophe pattern (Fig. 8). Paturaud also made a number of clips to this design (Fig 5, Nos. 20 and 23). The drawback to this design was that the toeclip could come loose or alternatively rust up solid. Also the elongated toestrap slot meant the toestrap was loose and could twist, making shoe entry difficult. Strata (a 1950's Lancashire based rival to GB) and Catos both made very attractive adjustable clips.

3. Other variants

GB produced a clip, the Professional, with a wider base (Fig. 9). Unlike Christophe the toestrap slot was not riveted, something they stressed in advertising as an advantage. British club cyclists regarded this as far more rust resistant than the Christophe. John Vaughan, a Director of Dawes Cycles, mentioned this in one of his highly regarded technical features in the CTC magazine *Cycletouring*:

"...among the few British components which are superior to imported ones are GB toeclips. The reason for this, of course, is that they are made from stainless steel. Apart from being virtually unbreakable they are non-rusting... GB for some reasons do not make any short ones so I fit

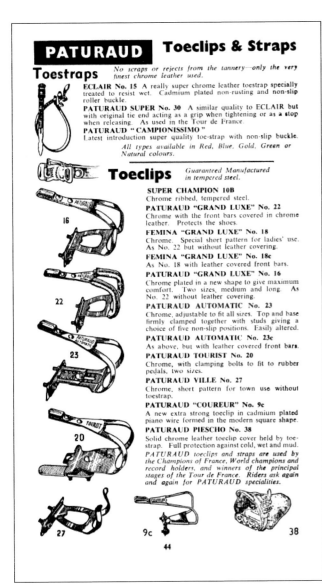

Fig. 5 Ron Kitching Paturaud range 1960.

Christophe to my wife's bike. *Within a few months the Christophe are red with rust while the GB are as bright as the day they were purchased.* The choice is

yours as long as you do not have small feet!"[2]

GB clips were made from 1954 for over 30 years, although latterly only in one size – long.

Surely the most fancy design was the Constrictor Boa (Fig. 10), which must be the leading contender for toe clip as art (clip art?). Unfortunately they were rather fragile. The last Constrictor clip, from the early 60s, had a gold finish, being made from bronze.

Christophe, Paturaud and others produced half or mini clips which did not need toestraps. They were marketed as either for the novice or for town riding. Clips were also produced in the 1980s and 90s by Christophe and ALE with widely spaced fixings to allow the fitting of pedal reflectors, which have became a legal requirement in many EU countries over the last 20 years.

4. Alloy Clips

Christophe, Cinelli and Milremo were amongst makers to offer an alloy toeclip in the 70s and 80s. The attraction was weight saving (about 35g a pair compared to steel.) Cinellis were made of Ergal and were available in silver, black, blue or gold. As I wrote at the start of this article these were simply not durable. Some of the more innovative French firms had tried this in the 40s and recognised the problem. Heavy forward pressure on the shoe could result in the clip shearing off, usually above the pedal fixing point.

5. The Last Generation

In the 1980s Shimano altered the fixing to a three-point triangular horizontal, designed to fit their aerodynamic shaped pedals. The clips were

Fig. 6 Catos advert from a December 1950 Cycling magazine.

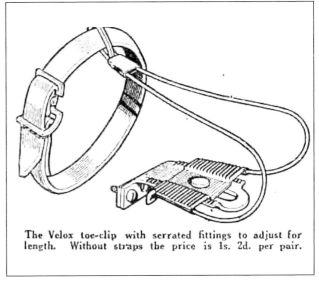

Fig. 7 The Velox toe clip from the Ashby report of the 1931 Show – Cycling 1931

offered in both chromed steel and plastic. The latter, of course, had the benefit of neither rusting nor breaking. However, plastic does has the disadvantage of permanently deforming under excess pressure, which could lead to overlap with the wheel or mudguard.

Campagnolo produced a similar design for their Victory and Triomphe pedals, which were of a horseshoe shape. Christophe produced a two point in line horizontal adjustable fitting for one variant of 1980s Campagnolo pedals and Maillard aero dynamic pedals of the same period. Earlier in the

Fig. 8 Ashby advert from an October 1950 Cycling magazine

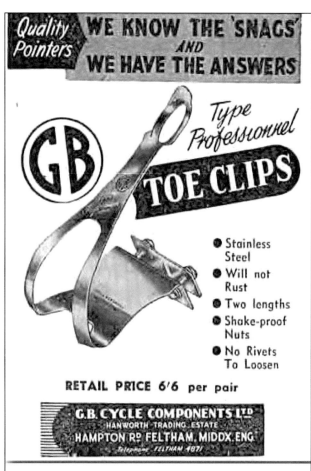

Fig. 9 GB Advert from a December 1960 Cycling magazine

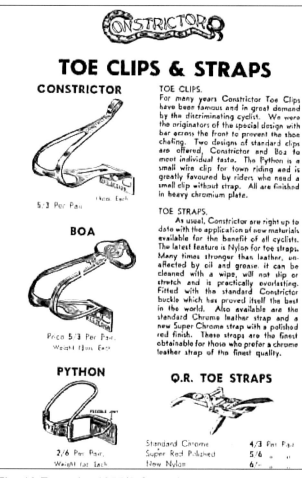

Fig. 10 From the 1955/6 Constrictor catalogue.

1980s they adopted the Christophe design to include a triangular pointed pedal pick up guide. The problem with both the above designs is actually finding the right toeclips; they are far rarer than the pedals and the standard toeclips do not fit.

The plastic toeclip was adapted for early mountain bikes, being stamp proof, and can still be found on lower priced machines. Some were shaped to allow the wearing of heavier shoes or boots. As the plastic is more flexible than metal, a variant was introduced with two upper slots for toestrap entry, so the clip is two pronged. Zefal still make a clip, the model 41, to this design. Since the clipless revolution of the 90s only MKS are producing a range of traditional pedals and metal toeclips, still based on the Christophe design.

Toeclips can be used with most shoes, although not with many modern 'trainer type' cycling shoes designed for clipless, because the front is too high to fit in the toeclip. The great disadvantage of the modern clipless designs (based originally on the system used for binding ski boots to skis) is that you have to use proprietary footwear. So if you just want to nip down to the shops you can't do it in any old footwear! The two main systems are SPD (Shimano Pedalling Dynamics) and Look (used by Campagnolo); they are not interchangeable.

Whilst researching this article I discovered the toeclip is not dead in the 21st century. Bruce Gordon, an American bespoke frame builder, has produced a half model made from titanium tubing priced at $74. Apart from weight saving they are very durable and when they get scratched they can be brushed with steel wool to look like new.[3]

REFERENCES

[1] *The Data Book 100 years of innovation in bicycle component and accessory design*, Van de Plas Publications p53. Note that p54 has a reprint from 1935 showing Christophe and Lapize clips.

[2] *Cycletouring*, June 1973, John Vaughan p128 (starting in August 1972 for nearly three year the CTC magazine featured an excellent series of technical articles only ended by John's untimely death.)

[3] *Vintage Bicycle Quarterly* Autumn 2005, Vol 4, No 1 p41 and www.bgcycles.com.

Other sources: *Holdsworthy Aids, Ron Kitchings' Everything Cycling*.

ATOM, MAILLARD, NORMANDY FAMILY

Resolving the confusion of interchangeable French Marques

ATOM, NORMANDY, PELISSER, EXCELTOO, MAILLARD, LE TOUR, AND SPIDEL

I have long been confused about the relationship between these names, never quite clear if they were in fact separate companies or just trade names for the one company. Regarding hubs I had thought it was quite simple: Atom were small flange, Normandy large and Maillard a name used in the 1980s. Imagine my confusion when I saw at a cycle jumble a freewheel box with all three trade names on it (Fig. 1). Also I have seen Atom hub boxes which also carry the Maillard trade name. Where do the other names, for example Le Tour and Pelisser fit in? I have also seen other similar French hubs but with different names, such as 'Sprinter' and 'Perrin'. This article is a bid to resolve the confusion regarding these trade names for pedals, hubs and freewheels.

Both Maillard and Exceltoo existed before the Second World War[1]. The curly M preceding the name stands for Maurice (Maillard), the founder. Their small flange one piece duralumin hubs were imported into the UK in the late 1930s. At this time hubs were usually all steel, or more expensive, a steel barrel with alloy flanges such as British Hub Company's top of the range Airlite. The one piece alloy hub was a significant advantage, being rustless, lighter and a stronger construction. Exceltoo, imported by Fonteyn and Co (who also handled

Fig. 1 Freewheel box with Atom, Normandy and Maillard names

Simplex), also made steel hubs, these being 50% cheaper than alloy ones. According to advertisements the Exceltoo hub featured ground cones and screw-in cone covers – post war every hub maker, including Campagnolo, adopted cheaper press-in cone covers.

Atom appeared soon after 1945 making hubs and freewheels and these were imported into Britain from the late 1940s. The core Atom product was their small flange one piece alloy hub, both with solid axle and later with quick release. The front hub was made with a distinctive step flange

at the ends of the barrel. Up to the late 1960s the hubs were marked 'Atom' in script; after this the name was stamped, together with a month and year. Small flange Atom hubs were for much of the 1960s and 70s the cheapest branded hubs you could buy. Nevertheless, they are quite serviceable and were widely used.

Atom also made pedals from the 1950s to the late 70s, offering a range of reasonable quality alloy pedals, the most common being a doubled sided rat trap, similar to the Lyotard 460D, and a higher quality series 600 quill pedal, fitted to Carlton and similar higher end sports bikes in the late 1970s. If not marked 'Atom' they can be identified by the name on the dust cap, or on earlier pedals by the slot across the diameter of the dust cap. Atom also made drum brakes for tandem use and in the 1940s a 'grande flasque' hub, incorporating two large riveted-on flanges lightened with two concentric sets of holes. Both pre and post war, in response to the demand for large flange hubs, a number of manufacturers, such as British Hub Co and Prior, another French company, used up their existing stocks of small flange hubs by riveting on a pair of large diameter flanges.

Atom's freewheels initially used the same two dog extractor as Regina, but then in the late 1960s moved to using a 2cm diameter splined extractor, which was a great improvement, though there was a drawback on some hubs, where it was necessary to remove the locknut to remove the freewheel. Atom freewheels were supplied in close ratio 3, 4 and 5 speed versions (Fig. 2).

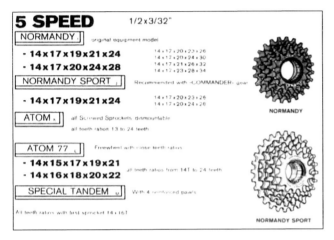

Fig. 2 1982 range of Atom and Normandy 5-speed freewheels, note the distinctive large diameter centres

Normandy hubs appeared a little after Atom and only seem to have been made with large flanges.[2] The 1950s versions with round cuts-outs are identical to the BH Company Racelite, which appeared in the mid 1950s. At the end of the 60s the design changed from round cut-outs to slotted ones. From the mid 1970s the barrels were stamped with the year of manufacture, providing a very useful dating guide. For quick release they used a separate black plastic wing nut similar to Simplex. In the 80s these hubs were initially marked Maillard and then Maillard-Sachs.

Normandy freewheels are distinctive in using a very large 3cm diameter 24 splined remover which was a very positive innovation, as there was no risk of the extractor shearing and damaging the

freewheel. This design also has the advantage of clearing the locknuts on all hubs, thus not requiring the axle to be removed. Some of these freewheels use a 3cm two dog extractor but these are the exception. They are credited with being the first company to make this innovation. I have found Normandy freewheels very durable and hard wearing. They are usually dated with the year stamped on the rear of the body, and have wide rations with the largest cog ≥24.

The Normandy large flange hub design also appears in the 1950s and 60s badged as Porthor and as Exceltoo. Both would appear to have been separate companies at this point. Exceltoo called their large flange all alloy hubs 'Super Competition'. They also made a small flange three piece hub. The latter brand reappeared in the 1970s with copies of the later slotted design, but oddly spelt Excelto.

At some point during the 1960s Atom and Normandy were taken over by Maillard. They were based at Incheville, France and effectively became the parent company.

Maillard became very successful in the 70s and early 80s, producing huge quantities of hubs and freewheels, which became standard original equipment used by many of the large manufacturers, such as Raleigh and Dawes, for their sports bikes. During this time large or high flange hubs became very fashionable hence the huge numbers of Normandy hubs you still come across. In the USA Schwinn had Maillard make them hubs which are marked 'Schwinn approved' some with an attractive three sided cut out. Ron Kitching had hubs made under his Milremo trade name that were direct copies of Atom and Normandy products. Le

Tour was a trade name used from the mid 60s to the late 70s, again for copy hubs. Maillard began to innovate in the late 1970s producing first the Normandy badged Luxe Competition and 600 series. Then the 700 Professional ranges (Figs. 3, 4 & 5), a top of the range series which included

Fig. 3 Maillard Professional 700 hubs

Fig. 4 Maillard 700 range – an advertisement from *Cycletouring*, June 1980

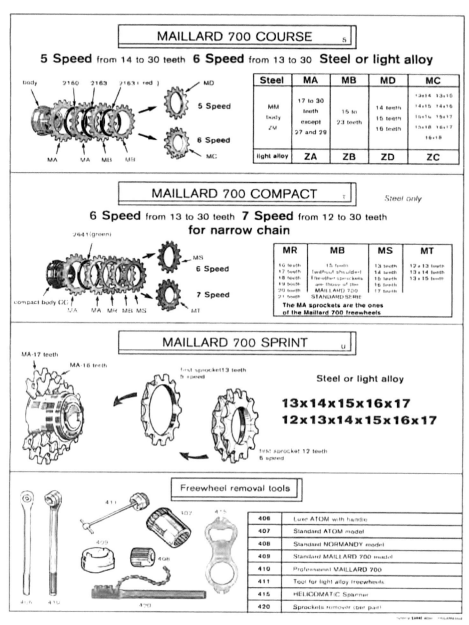

Fig. 5 Maillard 700 series freewheels plus range of remover tools, from their 1982 catalogue

sealed (annular) bearing hubs and alloy freewheels, the Course range. The alloy used in the latter was simply not durable enough and these have a very short life. There were also aerodynamic pedals, the CX series which required special toeclips. Other pedals included Campagnolo copies with both black and silver quill cages. Hubs were also produced in red, blue and gold and also under the name of Perrin-Maillard and Pelissier. I assume Perrin and Pelissier were both trade names Maillard had bought up.

In 1982 they introduced the Helicomatic hub (Fig. 6) which by use of a proprietary freewheel thread facilitated removal of the freewheel with only one light tool. The prime advantage was to enable gear-sided spokes to be easily replaced on the road without needing workshop tools. The remover is a very light flat tool that can also be used as a bottle opener (Fig. 5)! Although it gained some adherents – mainly cycletourists (it was fitted to the Dawes Galaxy for a short time) – it lost out to the freehub as developed by Shimano a few years later. The Helicomatic is, I think, a good example of a solution to a problem (that of broken spokes) which did not tackle the root cause of that problem, that is, badly built or overloaded wheels. During my research I found a website devoted to the Helicomatic hub, The Helicomatic Museum[3] and was surprised by the variety of different hubs made in this design (about eight) until it was phased out in 1988. This website advises against using the hubs on the grounds that you will not be able to get spare parts.

Spidel was not a manufacturer but simply a name adopted by a group of French manufacturers for high-end groupsets, in order to compete with those being marketed by the large manufacturers such as Shimano and Campagnolo. Maillard, Mafac, Simplex and Stronglight were the major companies initially involved in this venture.

DEMISE

In 1980 Maillard were taken over by the German company Sachs who had bought a number of other French companies, including Huret and CLB. The last all-Maillard product was the 'Diabolo' hub, incorporating a fatter barrel design for the emerging mountain bike market. After take-over products were initially marked Sachs-Maillard, but this ceased by the end of the decade and the trade name was lost. Essentially, screw-on hubs became a rapidly declining market with the rise to dominance of the Shimano Freehub (freewheel

Summary of Products

MAKE	HUBS	FREEWHEELS	PEDALS	COMMENTS
Atom	Small flange solid and q/r 1950s to 80s. Earlier ones have trade name in script. Range of threading gear only, geared and fixed and double fixed.	Up to 5 speed 40s to 60s, small splined remover.	Range of pedals both quill and double sided identified by the slot across diameter of dust cap. Atom 600 quill are a 70s product fitted to some Carltons.	Quick releases have both Atom and Maillard names on them.
Normandy	Large flange solid and q/r, 40s to early 80s. Earlier hubs have round cut-outs, later ones slotted. 70s hubs have date on barrel. In 70s made the Luxe Competition a higher quality model, q/r only identified by red or gold cone covers and decal in red/gold on barrel.	Identified by the very large (3cm) diameter splined freewheel remover. Popular in late 70s with tourists for their wide ratio blocks eg 14 to 32/34.	No	Some of the first Continental accessories to be imported after WWII. Quick releases are sometimes marked P1001, rather than Normandy. 50s/60s hubs identified by round cut-outs and by stamping of name: "Normandy".
Exceltoo	1950s large flange Super Competition model plus small flange all alloy and 3 piece hubs.	No	No	Also spelt Excelto, later hubs direct Normandy copies.
Pelissier	Both large and small flange, being copies of Atom and Normandy, plus some cheaper 3 piece steel hubs and tandem drum brakes. Used in the 80s for cup and cone copies of the 700 series.	No	No	Trade name disappeared in the late 70s. Pelissier made high quality products in the 30s and 40s, bought out in the 50s.
Le Tour	Both large and small flange mid 60s and 70s.	No	No	Large flange are Normandy copies, earlier ones slightly better quality. Originally imported by Holdsworth.
Maillard	Replaced both Atom and Normandy in the early 80s. Hubs are generally dated year and month. Hub barrels have gradual curve to the flanges unlike the stepped design for the Atom.	High quality freewheels. Series 700 and Course both steel and alloy.	1980s high quality pedals including a Campag copy and some with sealed bearings, series 700.	Hubs very widely used on sports bikes by big manufacturers. Q/Rs often marked P1001 or M. Maillard on one side and M.M Atom on the other.

integrated in the hub using cassette sprockets). Screw-on hubs were now the hallmark of a cheap machine and Sachs-Maillard couldn't compete in this market against Far Eastern competition.

Some comments on quality: the earlier hubs are greatly superior to the 70s product in terms of alloy used and quality of cones. For a quality 70s era bike it is worth seeking out the Competition Luxe range, as the cones and races are of a noticeably better standard. Standard Maillard cones can often be identified by the fact they are black and have a double concentric circle. The sealed bearing 600 and 700 series are of first rate quality.

So in conclusion there were a number of independent companies in the 1940s and 50s. Gradually they were taken over and Maillard became the dominant company. Until the end of the 1970s the main trade names were Atom and Normandy, but these were dropped in the 1980s, with Maillard becoming the sole trade name until the early 1990s when Sachs dropped the name.

Importers

There has been not only a number of different importers but also more than one at a time:
P Barwin: Normandy hubs, mid 1950s.
Walter Flory: Atom freewheels and Maillard products, 1950s to mid 1960s.
Ron Kitching: Exceltoo early 1960s and Maillard hubs 1960s/70s.
Cleminson: Maillard 1970s and 80s, all products.
RJ Chicken: Maillard, 1980s, all products.
Holdsworth: Le Tour hubs late 1960s.

References

1 In the Hicking of Hayes 1938 catalogue hubs are referred to as Hicking-Maillard. See also advertisements for Exceltoo hubs in *The Bicycle* 23 October and 17 November 1938.

2 *The Bicycle* 17 November 1954 Normandy hubs imported in the UK in the 50s by P Barwin.

3 See http://www.borgercompagnie. com/helico-matic/history.html

Fig. 6 Maillard Helicomatic hub, introduced in 1982 (from V-CC website)

PIERRE LYOTARD
A short history of one of the most widely used pedals in cycling

Given the long history of Lyotard (over 70 years) and their importance in the development of pedals it is surprising that virtually nothing has been written about them. The purpose of this article is to right this and provide information on a company who produced a solid range used by many racers and tourists. They may not have been top of the range but they were extremely widely used.

Throughout much of the post-war period, this French firm held a dominant position in the light-weight pedal market, being fitted both as original equipment by most of the major British manufacturers and sold as accessories via the two major importers Ron Kitching and Holdsworthy.

Pierre Lyotard founded the company in the early 1920s. During that decade Lyotard introduced the first version of the pedal, the Marcel Berthet platform pedal, which, I would argue, was their most innovative contribution to cycle development – see fig. 2.

Pre-war, Lyotard pedals were initially imported by Fonteyn and Co. Hicking of Hayes (importers of Caminargent) also imported pedals that bore a remarkable resemblance to Lyotard though they were not referred to as such in their catalogue, the models offered were different from those imported by Fonteyn. And Brown Bros must have also imported Lyotard as they are in their late 1930s catalogues with a slightly wider range than that offered by Fonteyn too. (Fig. 3)

In early post-war years, up to 1958 Fonteyn continued importing Lyotard pedals. Ron Kitching imported Lyotard from the middle 1950s.

A good example of Lyotard's range pre-war can be seen in fig. 4, taken from the 1939 Brown Bros catalogue. Post-war, Ron Kitching's *Everything Cycling* 1960 (fig. 5) shows that the range of Lyotard pedals available in Britain had increased markedly. And finally fig. 6 is taken from Holdsworthy's 1981 Aids and it is instructive to note how little change there was to the basic range of models over 21 years.

CLASSIFICATION OF THE LYOTARD RANGE
1 Platform Design

There was just one design, the Marcel Berthet platform pedal, which was given a few small modifications over the years. The foot rested on a wide platform, by its nature, it was extremely

comfortable especially for riders with broad feet. It needed to be used with toe clips as it was single sided.

It was named after Marcel Berthet, a French racing cyclist who held the hour record three times, twice in 1907 and once in 1913. He was the principal rival of Oscar Egg, the Swiss rider who later invented the Osgear.

The Marcel Berthet became known as the MB23 and remained in production until the mid 1980s.

Fig. 1 A letterhead for Pierre Lyotard from their early years

Fig. 2 The first version of the Marcel Berthet Lyotard platform pedal from the 1920s

Just before the war the shoe pickup plate ceased to be one piece, later examples are illustrated in figs 3, 4 and 5. The earliest reference I can find to this pedal in Britain is in an advert in the CTC Gazette in 1939, when it is referred to as the Continental. For a component with such a long history there were remarkably few variants, however, in common with other Lyotard pedals, there were later different thread lengths for steel or alloy cranks and the MB23 TF had threaded holes for toe clips. The pedal was very popular with cycle tourists due to the high degree of comfort. During the bike boom years of the 70s, Shimano, MKS and SR produced copies. One MKS copy, the 505, was counter-weighted so that the platform side always faced upward, making toe-clip entry easy. Pre and post-war, Constrictor copied the design with their Asp model. A very high quality copy was produced in the late 1970s by the British firm Barelli, based near Cambridge. This featured a range of detachable plates and is now extremely collectable.

2 Double-Sided

Of these, the most widely found is the 460. There were a number of versions of this design: a chromed steel range, a duralumin model and a wider version, the 240 – 4in as opposed to 3 1/2in. The 240 had P and L incorporated into the side plates, a style common to other pedal manufactures eg Chater Lea, BSA and Webb. Along with many other components of the period, the quality declined in later years. The main complaint from

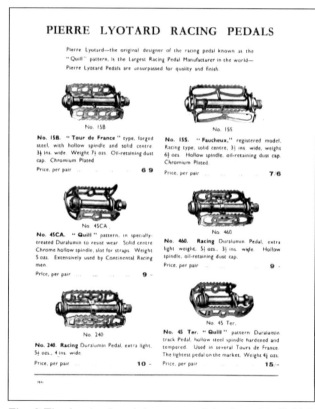

Fig. 3 The Lyotard pedal range as introduced to British cyclists in 1937 by Fonteyn & Co. From the 1938 Fonteyn Catalogue

users was that pedal frames creaked and needed to be removed from the crank and regularly hammered. However, there was one exception, the final 460 had reinforced axles at the crank end, a response no doubt, to complaints about breakages. In later years the steel version was the 460A – A for Acier (steel) and the aluminium version, the 460D – D for Duralumin (aluminium alloy).

The Tour de France no 15, which can be identified by having four cut-outs in the side plates, also had a very long history. This pedal was similar to some Victorian and Edwardian designs, a fact that did not escape Frank Whitt in his V-CC publication *The Restoration of Veteran Cycles* in which he recommends this model, stripped of its chrome and nickle-plated, as suitable for a much earlier machine.

An interesting variant of the 460 was the 46, which featured flat side plates on one side with concave on the other. This, it was claimed, allowed relaxation of the foot.

One of the great advantages of the double sided design is that the rider has choice whether or not to use toe clips.

Lyotard also produced a white split rubber pedal (ie with four pieces of rubber), a common fitting on women's bikes of the post-war period in France.

3 Quill

I do not agree with the statement in the 1960 Ron Kitching catalogue that Pierre Lyotard was the original designer of the quill pedal as I have seen turn of the century American Star pedals with this design. However he did develop the design and was the first to produce the modern quill pedal,

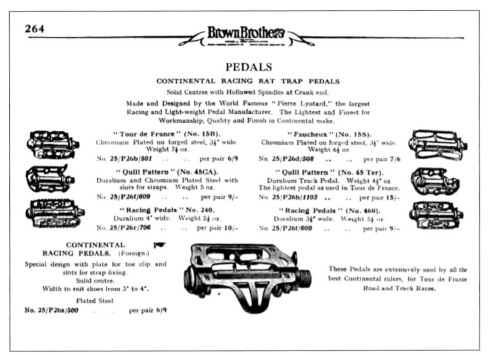

Fig. 4 Lyotard pedals from the 1939 Brown Bros wholesale catalogue

Pierre Lyotard, the original designer of the quill pedal produces an unrivalled range of light-weight pedals, each manufactured from the best of materials in either finest chrome steel or polished duralumin, every model designed for a particular purpose. Features of LYOTARD pedals include hollow spindles and solid centre barrels.

Duralumin Range

No. 460 COURSE
3¼" wide, extra light 12oz. pair

No. 240 COURSE
4" wide, 12½oz. pair

No. 45 CA. Piste
steel body, quill cage in duralumin. 3¼" wide, 12oz. pair.

Chrome Steel Range

No. 460 A. COURSE
popular double sided sports type 3¼" wide, 18oz. pair.

No. 15B Tour de France
solid centre barrel, double sided, 3¼" wide, 18oz. pair.

No. 15S Piste & Route
single sided, solid centre barrel, 3¼" wide, 16½oz. pair.

No. 23 Piste Marcel Berthet
platform type, solid centre barrel, 3¼" wide, 14oz. pair.

No. 45 PISTE
single sided quill, solid centre barrel, 3¼" wide, 16oz. pair.

No. 38 COURSE LUXE
double sided, solid centre barrel, 3¼" wide, 16½oz. pair.

FAUCHEAUX
new pattern single sided quill, solid centre 3¼" wide, 16oz. pair.

No. 46
Course and Cyclotouriste World patented design giving a choice of reach simply by reversing the pedal. The concave side gives a rational support for the foot and the reverse side being flat allows a relaxation of the leg. 3¼" wide, 15oz. pair.

Our LYOTARD pedals are made especially in British Standard threads and dimensions, and a full range of spare parts is always available.

Fig 5 Initially post-war the Lyotard pedal range offered by distributors was limited similarly to pre-war but by 1960 there was a much larger range imported by Ron Kitching. From the 1960 Ron Kitching catalogue

so widely copied in the 1960s and 70s by virtually every pedal maker.

The most common quill design was the no 45, which again was a very widely copied design. Like many of their pedals, Lyotard produced a number of different versions, which varied in the use of alloy and or steel.

One of their last pedals was of this design, the Mod 82, a robust one-piece cast model with a black plastic dustcap.

4 Single-Sided No Quill

Another model with a very long history, also named after a racing cyclist, was the Faucheaux, produced from the early 1930s for 40 years. This was a single-sided toothed model with the other side cut away (see the bottom of fig 3). It was named after another French cyclist Lucian Faucheaux who came second in the 200 meters sprint at the world track championships in Paris in 1922.

The earlier version of the Faucheaux had the side plates screwed on but this ceased about 1955, with cheaper riveting being substituted. They also produced the 462, a single-sided version of the 460. These pedals were slightly lighter than the quill version but they had the disadvantage of not having the protection of the quill for the pedal body.

PEDALS

LYOTARD

An excellent range of pedals from France. For the tourist or weight-conscious racer and at some of the best prices available.

65 A very high quality racing pedal with a one piece forged light alloy body and anodised alloy cage. Silk smooth bearings with hard nickel-chrome steel axle. Complete with toe-clip bolts. Weight 380g/13oz. £23.95

79 A light alloy quill pattern cage mounted on steel barrel. Weight 280g/9.8oz. £4.50

23 Unique platform pattern allows these pedals to fit any shoe width. Stainless steel plate on steel barrel with strap slots, shoe pickup and ridge for shoe plates. Weight 380g/13oz. £5.75

45ter Light pedal with one piece alloy body and alloy serrated quill frame. Weight 295g/10oz. £6.95

45CD Light alloy quill cage mounted on alloy barrel. Weight 310g/10.9oz. £7.00

45CDN As above with black cage. £7.75

45CA Same design as above but with steel quill cage. Weight 380g/13oz. £5.50

460D Full width all alloy double sided pedal with strong centre support. £3.65

460A Simple practical steel double sided pedal. £2.60

136R Double sided with reflectors. £2.65

36 A straightforward steel allround pedal ideal for everyday use. £2.20

Fig. 6 The range became more limited again in the 1980s though there were one or two new introductions. From the 1981 *Holdsworthy Aids* catalogue

PRICING AND THE LATER YEARS

Lyotard were, in terms of price, near the bottom of the market in later years. In 1962 they ranged from 9/- to 16/-, the latter being the MB23. Only Phillips was cheaper and to put these prices into context, Campagnolo pedals cost 72/-.

Lyotard's decline and the end of production in the late 1980s was caused by three factors. Firstly, the rise of the mountain bike, which used a wider, squarer type pedal. Secondly, the emergence of cheaper, Far Eastern manufacturers. Finally the move to clipless, which effectively ended the market for quality, traditional pedals. Since the early 1990s Campagnolo and Shimano have produced only clipless pedals. In common with other French component manufacturers, there was very little innovation. By 1980, their basic designs were at least 40 years old as a comparison of figs. 2 and 6 shows.

IDENTIFICATION AND DATING

Very few Lyotard pedals actually have the manufacturer's name on them, exceptions being the later Type 82 and the MB23 (which is anyway a unique design). The early models (pre- and early post-war) had either knurled dustcaps or caps with hexagonal clearly defined flats. With pedals from the 1960s onwards the easiest way to determine if a pedal is a Lyotard is by the dust cap. With the exception of a few later models this will be a screwed octagonal fitting with 'Lyotard Made in France' stamped on it. Later steel pedals, eg the 36, had a press-on dust cap, which the accountants presumably had worked out could save a few cents. It was a bad idea as they were often lost and various DIY tricks were needed to prevent this.

Pre-1960 versions of the Faucheaux, and other styles including the 460, featured oilers in the barrel. Another way of dating earlier versions is that the side plates were screwed on rather than riveted. This later practice ceased around 1956. Very late versions of most Lyotard pedals from the 1980s feature pedal spindles with four flats rather than two flats for pedal fitting and removal. Lyotard made pedals for Milremo, many of which are direct copies, particularly of the 460D and type 36.

Lyotard pedals tend to be available at cycle jumbles. Not commanding high prices, they remain probably the cheapest option for fitting to that period restoration. For me the MB23 and the 460 remain among the most comfortable pedals ever made, they won't cramp your feet or wear out cycling shoes.

REFERENCES

Fonteyn catalogues 1938–1958. Hicking of Hayes catalogues pre-WWII feature pedals which are almost certainly Lyotard. A wide range of Lyotard pedals are included in Brown Bros wholesale catalogues 1939 on. Holdsworthy included them in their 1939 Aids catalogues and from 1951. Both the Aids and Ron Kitching's Everything Cycling are a very useful source of information. For 80's models the Freewheel catalogues feature the final range. Adverts for Lyotard in the cycling press are extremely rare. F. R. Whitt *The Restoration of Veteran-Cycles* p27

The C.L.B. STORY: Braking French Style

CLB was second only to MAFAC as the leading post WWII French manufacturer of brakes. Like many French cycle component manufacturers the company was located in St Etienne, specifically the suburb of St Chamond. CLB history typifies the history of the French cycle component industry post-war – initially very innovative, then core products marketed for a long period of time. Decline in the 1970s was caused by a failure to understand, and respond to the changing market, and demise followed in the 1980s.

According to the National Cycle Library, CLB brakes first appeared in the mid 1930s, but were not widely distributed until after the war (Fig. 1). Brakes of the 1940s/50s are marked either just ALP or CLB ALP, the ALP name being dropped by the mid 1950s. The full business name was 'Angenieux CLB SA'. CLB are the initials of the founder, Charles Lozier Bourgoin. CLB also used the initials for advertising slogans, for example 'Ce Le Bre' and 'Cha Leger Bloque'.

CLB's Heyday – The 1940s and 1950s

A number of French companies had marketed alloy brakes pre-war and the most successful of these was LAM, who realised that it was necessary to use more metal when switching from steel to alloy to avoid brake flex and consequential poor braking. LAM is also credited with being the first company to offer a hooded lever (mid-1930s), which enabled the lever body to be used as a position for the hands.

Fig. 1 1930's advertisement from the NCL/V-CC website

CLB took on both these LAM innovations. Their top product in the 1940s/50s was an alloy side pull available in two depths: Standard (46-63mm), Competition, and short (35-54mm), which was oddly named 'Hi-Life'. Of all the alloy brakes of the period they are the most effective, a fact I attribute to the thickness of the arms and the quality of the alloy, which reduced flexing. The brakes soon became a favourite with top racing cyclists in France and BLRC riders in this country. CLB brakes were offered as an option by Paris and Stallard to name but two of the more progressive builders of the time. The Competition and Hi-Life models have a distinctive profile, a unique quick release with a cable adjuster, and brass bolts (Fig. 2). A variant of the Competition was the Professional, introduced in the mid 1950s. These are the classic CLB brakes and at the time the best stoppers available. The design originated in the late 1930s and the quick release enabled rapid wheel change, proving themselves in the early post-war Tour de France races, when many of the roads were still war damaged. Their only design weakness was that under repeated heavy braking the central bolt could bend.

CLB also made a range of basic side pull brakes, model 650, 700 and 800 – the higher the number the bigger the drop. They also made heavy duty brakes for cyclemotors. Products other than brakes that featured in the 1951 catalogue included crank shorteners, chainguards, wing nuts and handlebar stems with a recessed bolt for the handlebars.

With the introduction of MAFAC centre pulls in 1951/2 CLB popularity suffered a serious decline. As period photographs show, MAFAC rapidly became the brake to have. Tour riders very quickly took to them as did many riders in this country. The more conservative British rider stuck to GB, leaving a very small market share for CLB, so they were no longer in the forefront and played second fiddle to MAFAC.

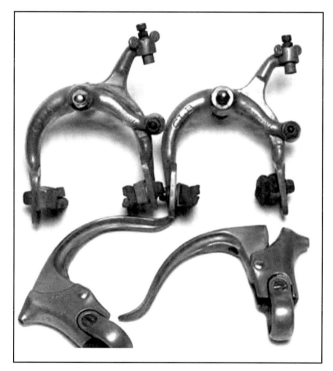

Fig. 2 Competition brakes and cast levers

Levers

Until the late 1950s CLB levers have the clip as part of the lever body. This was also a feature of LAM, Burlite, and early GB levers, an idea soon

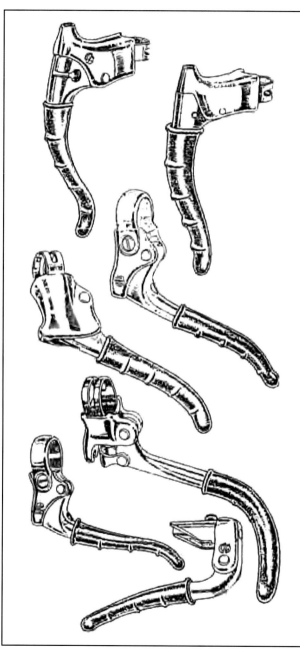

Fig. 3 1961 lever range

dropped by manufacturers due to the high incidence of fracture.

From the early days CLB made levers in different sizes, in contrast to MAFAC, which made at most two sizes. Tony Oliver, the highly regarded British frame builder of the 1980s and 1990s, praised this attention to detail, using it as an illustration of French attitudes where cycling is 'number one'.[1] This feature was particularly useful for riders with smaller than average hands, who might struggle with standard brake levers. They also experimented with the curvature of the lever and thus you will find a greater variety of CLB levers than any other company, however, this can make it difficult to match odd components. Their drop bar levers are designed to follow the curve of the handlebar, resulting in an extremely comfortable lever. The grip around the hood is far wider than, say, a Campagnolo hood, and thus gives a feel of greater security. The rubber hoods (usually with the CLB 'sun' logo often referred to as model Sulky) were made of softer rubber than MAFAC or Weinmann. They were not as durable but provided a high degree of comfort. Some of the later levers had nylon bodies, which made them even lighter. CLB were also keen on rubber and plastic sleeves for the lever blades, something that never found favour with British riders. Fig. 3 illustrates the range of levers available in 1961.

CLB also made other levers, including an inverted version (Fig. 4) that fitted in place of the bar end plugs, a short 'city' type lever for flat bars and, like MAFAC, a Guidonnet lever which fitted under the flat portion of drop bars and followed the curvature of the bar. The latter was aimed at tourists,

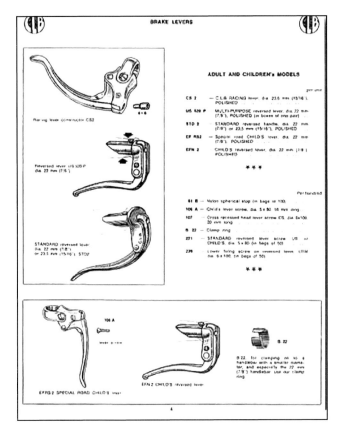

Fig. 4 Reversed and Child's levers from the 1975 Catalogue

providing easy access to brakes from the top of the bar, a useful feature when descending lengthy Alpine passes. These became popular in Britain amongst rough stuff riders, who quickly realised the advantage in being able to control braking from the top of the bars whilst off road. In the 1970s and 80s the company marketed a dual lever – a drop bar lever with an extension to allow braking from the top. Originally produced by Dia-Compe they were manufactured under licence by Weinmann in

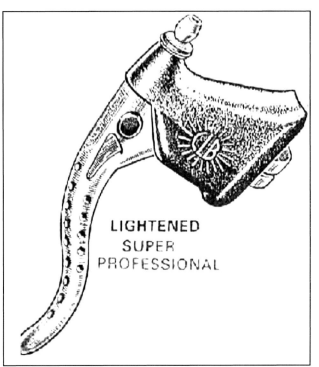

Fig 4a 1970's Professional lever: drilled showing CLB 'sun' logo (Rebour drawing)[5]

huge quantities, especially for the safety conscious American market. Ironically the dual lever was less effective than the standard lever, a fact not understood by non-cyclists. CLB's version was superior to that of Weinmann with far less flexing of the lever upon application.

1960s and 1970s

During the 1960s CLB brakes were imported by Ron Kitching.[2] At this time British manufacturers and riders began to favour Weinmann as the brake of choice and CLB-equipped British bikes were extremely unusual.

At the end of the 1960s the range included (Fig. 5):

- centre pull 'Racer' (like MAFAC); not the most attractive brake, looking rather heavy and clumsy compared to MAFAC, Weinmann or Universal models.[3] However, it provided extremely solid and effective stopping.
- cantilever, called 'Cantil-racer'.
- a full range of sidepulls, an updated version of the Competition plus cheaper brakes for lower priced bikes.
- a range of levers, the ones for drop bars being made in four different sizes.
- an alloy chain guard.

CLB brakes were fitted as original equipment by many of the larger volume French manufacturers, such as Peugeot and Motobecane. The writing was on the wall for CLB when these companies switched to using Japanese brakes (principally Dia-Compe), a process which started at the end of the 1970s. Throughout the 70s CLB's main focus was on reducing weight. Lighter and lighter alloys were trialled, levers were drilled and even titanium was used for some very expensive brakes. They had some success in breaking into the US market during the mid 1970s. It is interesting to note that despite the change of material and design, the distinctive quick release was retained (Fig. 6). They even tried to lighten the brake cables, marketing a lighter cable (model Duralinox) for the true lightweight obsessive – someone who would put weight saving above safety. CLB offered a number of other innovations during this period:[4]

- wedge shaped brake blocks designed to enhance braking (Fig. 7).

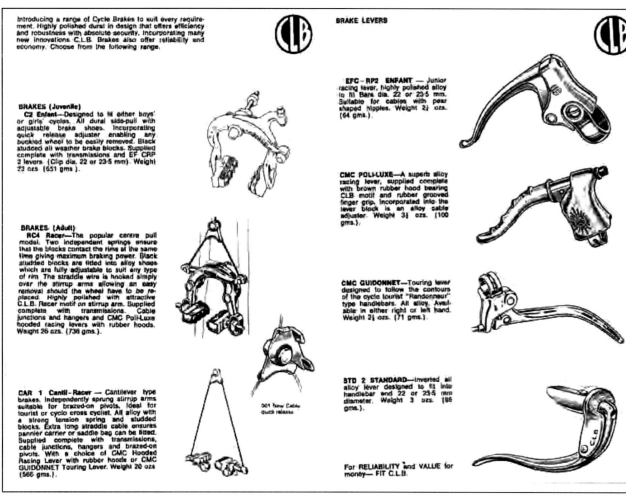

Fig. 5 1970 CLB range as marketed by Ron Kitching

Fig. 6 1980 Advertisement – with 450 employees a sizeable company

- quick release for a cantilever located on the straddle cable bridge.
- plastic bushing for smooth operation.
- an aerodynamic seat pin.

Demise

In 1984 CLB was taken over by Sachs, which had bought Huret and Maillard three years earlier. Around this time they took part in a joint venture with Vitus, which marketed aluminium frames. The 1975 brakes continued for a few more years under the CLB name and then disappeared. Sachs found that CLB, and other French companies with their outdated factories, outdated management and union practices were simply unable to compete in the modern world. With the exception of some top quality cantilevers for the Sachs New Success ATB group set, the new owner ceased brake production. A nice touch is that these final products have a brake shoe that is actually shoe shaped![6]

References

[1] Tony Oliver *Touring Bikes* 1990 p139 (the title is a bit misleading as this book is a guide to frame design and component selection).

[2] Ron Kitching: *Everything Cycling* catalogue 1970.

[3] Evian catalogues. 1970s.

[4] 1983 Freewheel catalogue.

[5] *The World of Daniel Rebour:* Vol 4 2005 (Japanese reprint of Rebour drawings).

[6] For the history of CLB's principal rivals – MAFAC TB171/4 and Weinmann TB182/37. See relevant chapters in this book

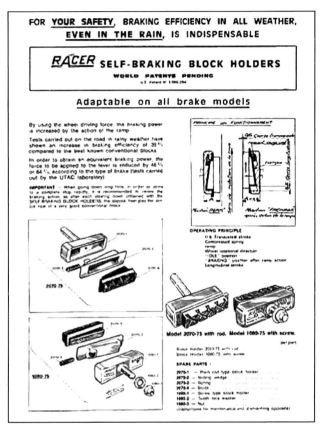

Fig. 7 Self-braking block holders

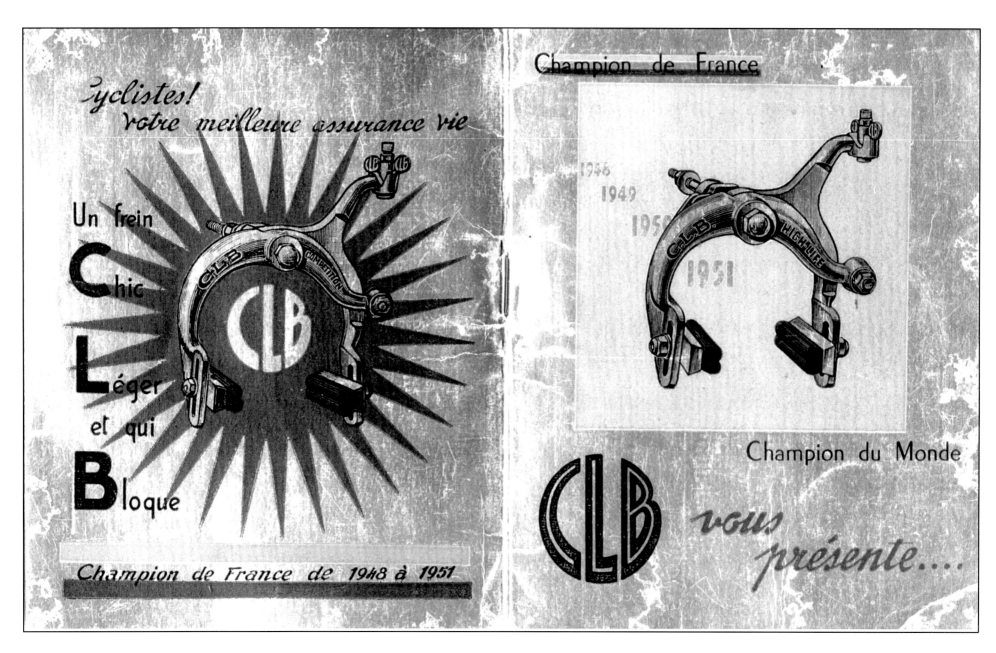

FREINS EN ALLIAGE LEGER
haute résistance
(modèles brevetés déposés)

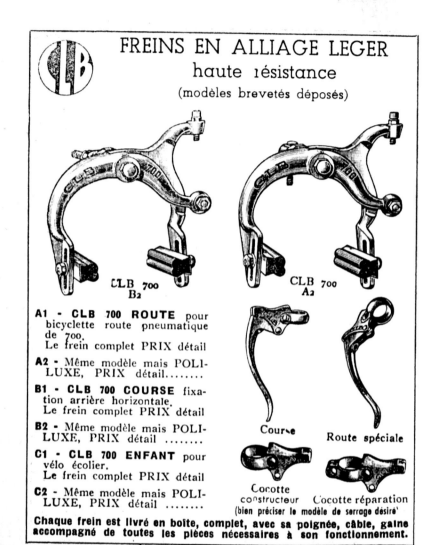

CLB 700 B2

CLB 700 A2

Course

Route spéciale

Cocotte constructeur

Cocotte réparation

(bien préciser le modèle de serrage désiré)

A1 - CLB 700 ROUTE pour bicyclette route pneumatique de 700.
Le frein complet PRIX détail........

A2 - Même modèle mais POLI-LUXE, PRIX détail........

B1 - CLB 700 COURSE fixation arrière horizontale.
Le frein complet PRIX détail

B2 - Même modèle mais POLI-LUXE, PRIX détail ....

C1 - CLB 700 ENFANT pour vélo écolier.
Le frein complet PRIX détail

C2 - Même modèle mais POLI-LUXE, PRIX détail ....

Chaque frein est livré en boîte, complet, avec sa poignée, câble, gaine accompagné de toutes les pièces nécessaires à son fonctionnement.

— 2 —

UNE FABRICATION CE LÈBRE
6 FOIS CHAMPION DE FRANCE
CHAMPION DU MONDE

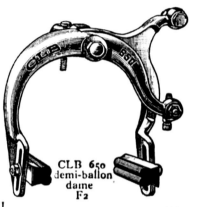

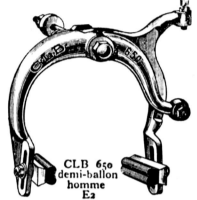

CLB 650 demi-ballon dame F2

CLB 650 demi-ballon homme E2

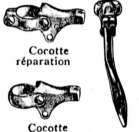

Cocotte réparation

Cocotte constructeur

Route spéciale

E1 - CLB 650 DEMI-BALLON HOMME pour bicyclette demi-ballon.
Le frein complet, PRIX détail.....

E2 - Même modèle mais POLI-LUXE PRIX détail . ...

F1 - CLB 650 DEMI-BALLON DAME tirage inversé pour bicyclette dame.
Le frein complet, PRIX détail.....

F2 - Même modèle mais POLI-LUXE PRIX détail . ...

Nos divers modèles sont livrés avec n'importe quel type de poignée route, route spéciale, course - cocotte constructeur ou réparation (au choix) sans supplément de prix (voir page 8).

Chaque paire de freins comporte une poignée gauche, une poignée droite permettant d'obtenir toute la visserie à l'extérieur - ainsi, un montage et une présentation de choix.

— 3 —

FREINS EN ALLIAGE LÉGER
haute résistance
(modèles brevetés déposés)

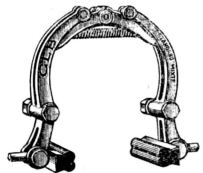

Route

Cocotte
réparation

Cocotte
constructeur

G2 - STANDARD MIXTE NM
Poli-luxe type réparation fixation à collier.
Le frein complet PRIX détail

G 202 - Même modèle mais livré avec tasseaux à braser.
Le frein complet PRIX détail

G 302 - Même modèle mais avec tasseaux non joints.
Le frein complet PRIX détail

Chaque frein est livré en boîte, complet avec sa poignée, câble, gaine, accompagné de toutes les pièces nécessaires à son fonctionnement.

Nos divers modèles sont livrés avec n'importe quel type de poignée route, route spéciale, course : cocotte constructeur ou réparation (au choix), sans supplément de prix (voir page 8).

Pour les différents modèles de supports, se reporter page 6.

Chaque paire de freins comporte une poignée gauche, une poignée droite, permettant d'obtenir toute la visserie à l'extérieur et ainsi un montage et une présentation de choix.

UNE FABRICATION CÉLÈBRE
6 FOIS CHAMPION DE FRANCE
CHAMPION DU MONDE

Pour les anciens modèles de bicyclettes à tubes gros diamètre ou tête de fourche non percée.

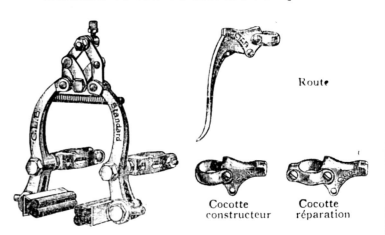

Route

Cocotte
constructeur

Cocotte
réparation

D 2 - CLB STANDARD poli luxe, breveté S.G.D.G. type réparation, fixation à collier. Le frein complet, PRIX détail..

D 202 - Même modèle mais livré avec tasseaux à braser.
Le frein complet, PRIX détail..............

D 302 - Même modèle mais avec tasseaux non joints.
Le frein complet, PRIX détail..............

Nos divers modèles sont livrés avec n'importe quel modèle de poignée route, route spéciale, course : cocotte constructeur ou réparation (au choix) sans supplément de prix (voir page 8).

Chaque paire de freins comporte une poignée gauche, une poignée droite permettant d'obtenir toute la visserie à l'extérieur et ainsi un montage et une présentation de choix.

CANTILEVER SPORT 1951

Gagnant du 1ᵉʳ Tour de France Cyclotouriste

(catégorie cyclosportifs)

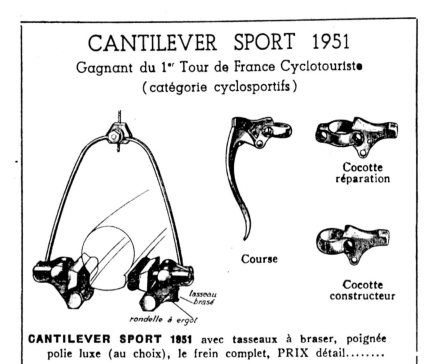

Cocotte
réparation

Course

Cocotte
constructeur

tasseau
brasé

rondelle à ergot

CANTILEVER SPORT 1951 avec tasseaux à braser, poignée polie luxe (au choix), le frein complet, PRIX détail.......

Nos modèles « STANDARD MIXTE NM » et « CLB CANTILEVER » sont livrés avec les supports ci-dessous, au choix

| AR à braser | AV tête de fourche | AV cranté | AV uni | AR tige de selle | AR entretoise |

— 6 —

INSTRUCTIONS POUR LE MONTAGE

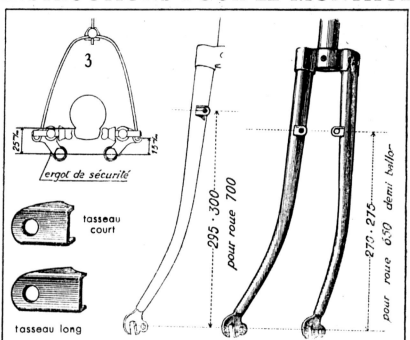

3

ergot de sécurité

tasseau
court

tasseau long

295 - 300
pour roue 700

270 - 275
pour roue 650 demi ballon

Le centre de l'œil des tasseaux brasés doit se trouver à 25 mm. en-dessous de la partie supérieure de la jante. Les tasseaux doivent être rapprochés le plus possible, laissant seulement le libre passage du pneu gonflé.

Pour vélos normaux homme et dame, on utilisera donc des tasseaux courts à l'avant et à l'arrière.

Le tasseau long sera utilisé **exclusivement à l'arrière des cadres mixtes.**

Le CANTILEVER SPORT CLB 1951 comporte une rondelle à ergot qui double la sécurité en cas de rupture du câble ; à ce moment un cantilever mal étudié pénètre dans les rayons, occasionnant une chute grave. Avec le CANTILEVER SPORT CLB 1951, en cas de rupture de câble, le frein est retenu par le ressort ; il faudrait que le ressort casse pour que les ergots entrent en action.

Les ergots doivent être placés dans la ligne des deux axes (voir croquis 3) pour ne pas gêner le nettoyage des patins de freins.

Entre la rondelle à ergot et le bras du frein, bien placer la rondelle acier en 2/10ᵉ d'épaisseur, supprimant bruit et jeu axial.

— 7 —

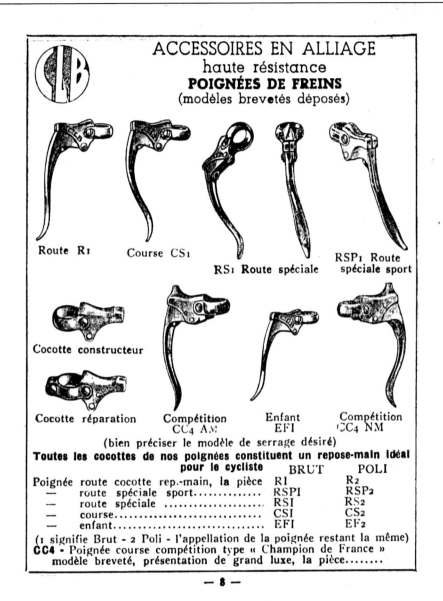

ACCESSOIRES EN ALLIAGE
haute résistance
POIGNÉES DE FREINS
(modèles brevetés déposés)

Route R1

Course CS1

RS1 Route spéciale

RSP1 Route spéciale sport

Cocotte constructeur

Cocotte réparation

Compétition CC4 A.M.

Enfant EFI

Compétition CC4 NM

(bien préciser le modèle de serrage désiré)

Toutes les cocottes de nos poignées constituent un repose-main idéal pour le cycliste

	BRUT	POLI
Poignée route cocotte rep.-main, la pièce	RI	R2
— route spéciale sport..............	RSPI	RSP2
— route spéciale	RSI	RS2
— course...........................	CSI	CS2
— enfant...........................	EFI	EF2

(1 signifie Brut - 2 Poli - l'appellation de la poignée restant la même)
CC4 - Poignée course compétition type « Champion de France » modèle breveté, présentation de grand luxe, la pièce........

— 8 —

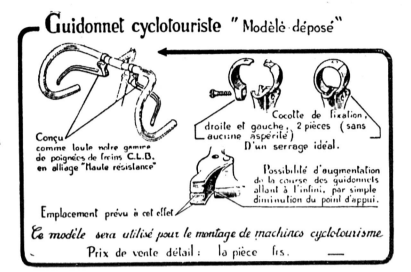

Guidonnet cyclotouriste "Modèle déposé"

Conçu comme toute notre gamme de poignées de freins C.L.B. en alliage "Haute résistance"

Cocotte de fixation, droite et gauche, 2 pièces (sans aucune aspérité) D'un serrage idéal.

Possibilité d'augmentation de la course des guidonnets allant à l'infini, par simple diminution du point d'appui.

Emplacement prévu à cet effet

Ce modèle sera utilisé pour le montage de machines cyclotourisme

Prix de vente détail : la pièce frs.   —

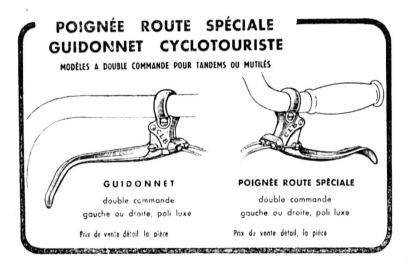

POIGNÉE ROUTE SPÉCIALE
GUIDONNET CYCLOTOURISTE

MODÈLES A DOUBLE COMMANDE POUR TANDEMS OU MUTILÉS

GUIDONNET
double commande
gauche ou droite, poli luxe
Prix de vente détail, la pièce

POIGNÉE ROUTE SPÉCIALE
double commande
gauche ou droite, poli luxe
Prix de vente détail, la pièce

— 9 —

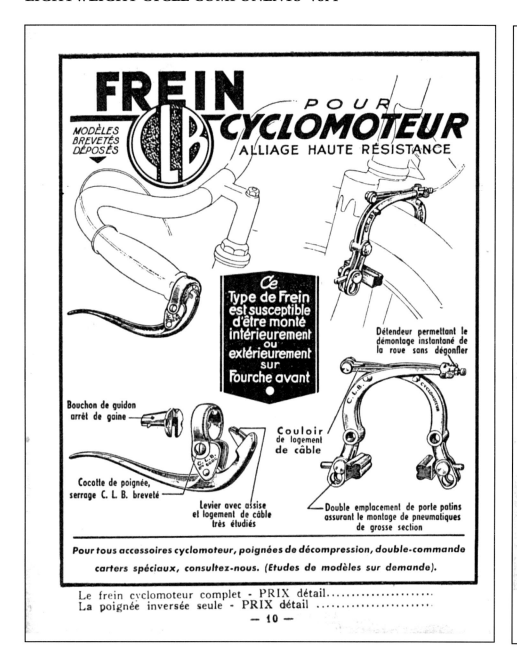

FREIN POUR CYCLOMOTEUR

MODÈLES BREVETÉS DÉPOSÉS

ALLIAGE HAUTE RÉSISTANCE

Ce Type de Frein est susceptible d'être monté intérieurement ou extérieurement sur Fourche avant

Détendeur permettant le démontage instantané de la roue sans dégonfler

Bouchon de guidon arrêt de gaine

Couloir de logement de câble

Cocotte de poignée, serrage C. L. B. breveté

Levier avec assise et logement de câble très étudiés

Double emplacement de porte patins assurant le montage de pneumatiques de grosse section

Pour tous accessoires cyclomoteur, poignées de décompression, double-commande carters spéciaux, consultez-nous. (Etudes de modèles sur demande).

Le frein cyclomoteur complet - PRIX détail.....................
La poignée inversée seule - PRIX détail ....

— 10 —

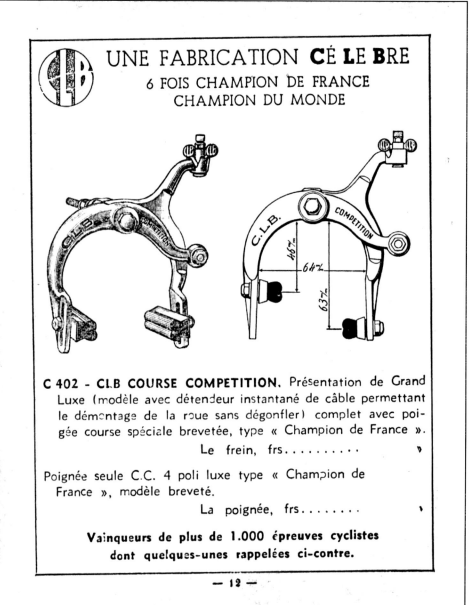

UNE FABRICATION CÉLÈBRE

6 FOIS CHAMPION DE FRANCE
CHAMPION DU MONDE

C 402 - CLB COURSE COMPETITION. Présentation de Grand Luxe (modèle avec détendeur instantané de câble permettant le démontage de la roue sans dégonfler) complet avec poignée course spéciale brevetée, type « Champion de France ».

Le frein, frs.......... ,

Poignée seule C.C. 4 poli luxe type « Champion de France », modèle breveté.

La poignée, frs........ ,

Vainqueurs de plus de 1.000 épreuves cyclistes dont quelques-unes rappelées ci-contre.

— 12 —

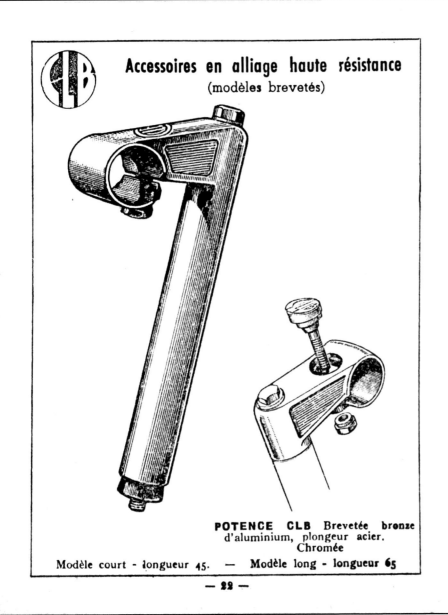

Accessoires en alliage haute résistance
(modèles brevetés)

POTENCE CLB Brevetée bronze
d'aluminium, plongeur acier.
Chromée

Modèle court - longueur 45. — Modèle long - longueur 65

— 22 —

UNE FABRICATION CE LÈ BRE

PAPILLON CLB. Alliage haute résistance.
Modèle très étudié, ailettes dégagées convenant pour tous modèles de bicyclettes.
Existe en 8 - 9 - 9 mm. 5.
PRIX de vente détail, la pièce....

PIECES DÉTACHÉES DIVERSES

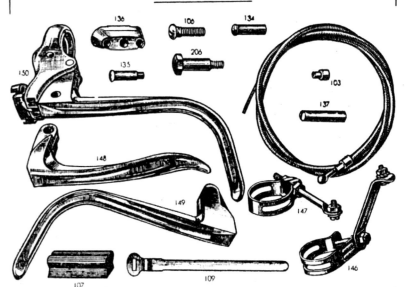

101 **Barillet** de réglage 4 pièces ....
102 **Serre-câble** 3 pièces de frein route ....
103 **Arrêt** de gaine ordinaire, le cent ....
106 **Vis** de poignée ....

— 23 —

139

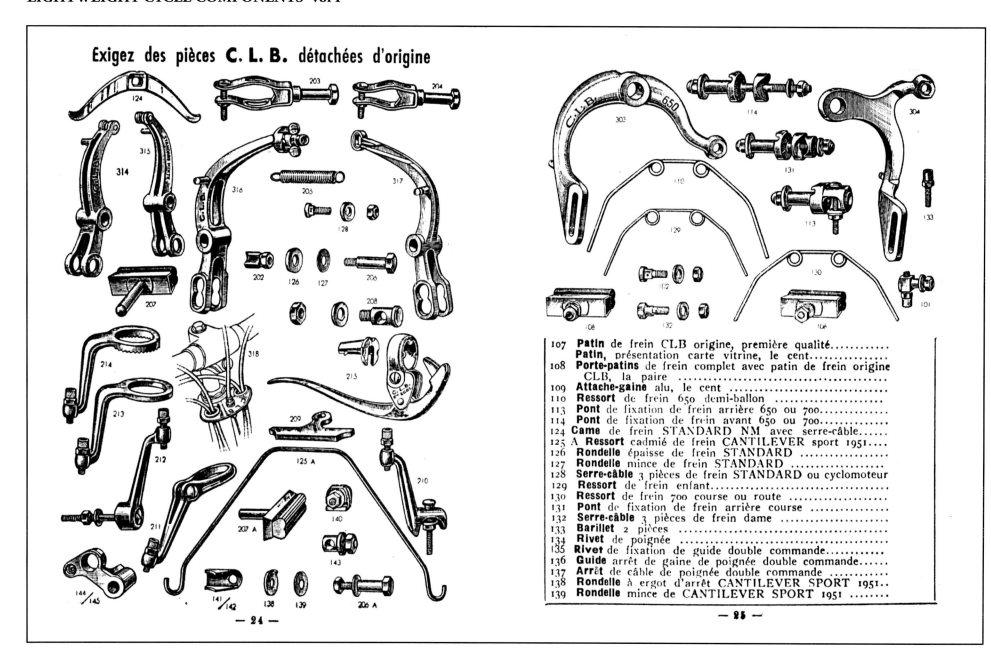

Exigez des pièces **C. L. B.** détachées d'origine

107 **Patin** de frein CLB origine, première qualité............
   Patin, présentation carte vitrine, le cent...............
108 **Porte-patins** de frein complet avec patin de frein origine
   CLB, la paire ....
109 **Attache-gaine** alu, le cent ....
110 **Ressort** de frein 650 demi-ballon ....
113 **Pont** de fixation de frein arrière 650 ou 700.............
114 **Pont** de fixation de frein avant 650 ou 700..............
124 **Came** de frein STANDARD NM avec serre-câble......
125 A **Ressort** cadmié de frein CANTILEVER sport 1951....
126 **Rondelle** épaisse de frein STANDARD ....
127 **Rondelle** mince de frein STANDARD ....
128 **Serre-câble** 3 pièces de frein STANDARD ou cyclomoteur
129 **Ressort** de frein enfant...................................
130 **Ressort** de frein 700 course ou route ....
131 **Pont** de fixation de frein arrière course ....
132 **Serre-câble** 3 pièces de frein dame ....
133 **Barillet** 2 pièces ....
134 **Rivet** de poignée ....
135 **Rivet** de fixation de guide double commande...........
136 **Guide** arrêt de gaine de poignée double commande......
137 **Arrêt** de câble de poignée double commande ....
138 **Rondelle** à ergot d'arrêt CANTILEVER SPORT 1951..
139 **Rondelle** mince de CANTILEVER SPORT 1951 ....

— 24 —

— 25 —

140	**Niche** avec serre-câble 3 pièces de frein CANTILEVER SPORT 1951	.....
141	**Tasseau** court de frein CANTILEVER SPORT 1951...	
142	**Tasseau** long de frein CANTILEVER SPORT 1951....	
143	**Tourillon** 3 pièces de frein CANTILEVER SPORT 1951	
144	**Sabot** côté droit de frein CANTILEVER SPORT 1951..	
145	**Sabot** côté gauche de frein CANTILEVER SPORT 1951	
146	**Collier** de carter complet	
147	**Collier** de carter dérailleur avant complet	
	Jeu de trois colliers de carters (deux gros diamètre, un petit diamètre), pour carters 3 attaches, le jeu.......	
148	**Levier** seul de poignée, brut	
149	**Levier** de guidonnet seul, brut	
150	**Guidonnet** complet double commande, poli luxe........	
202	**Tasseau** décolleté de frein STANDARD, la paire	
203	**Collier** avant complet de frein STANDARD	
204	**Collier** arrière complet de frein STANDARD	
205	**Ressort** de frein STANDARD	
206	**Vis** tête 6 pans de frein STANDARD NM	
206 A	**Vis** tête six pans avec rondelle et écrou de fixation pour CANTILVER SPORT 1951	
207	**Porte-patin** de frein STANDARD avec patin de frein CLB origine, la paire	
207 A	**Porte-patin** long pour cyclomoteur avec patin origine CLB, la paire ..	
	Patin long seul pour cyclomoteur origine CLB	
208	Tourillon 3 pièces de frein STANDARD ou cyclomoteur	
209	**Support** de frein STANDARD fixation arrière à braser sur haubans	
210	**Support** de frein STANDARD fixation arrière entretoise	
211	**Support** de frein STANDARD fixation arrière à la tige de selle .	
212	**Support** de frein STANDARD fixation avant à la tête de fourche	
213	**Support** de frein STANDARD fixation avant au jeu de direction uni ..	
	de direction cranté	
214	**Support** de frein STANDARD fixation avant au jeu	
215	**Embout** de poignée inversée cyclomoteur	
301	**Branche** ronde de frein 650 demi-ballon homme.......	
302	— Y de frein 650 demi-ballon homme	
303	— ronde de frein 650 demi-ballon dame........	
304	— Y de frein 650 demi-ballon dame tirage inversé	
305	— ronde de frein 700	
306 A	— Y de frein 700 route ou course...........	
306 B	— Y de frein enfant garçonnet	
307	— ronde de frein enfant garçonnet	
308	— ronde de frein enfant fillette	

Exigez des pièces **C.L.B.** détachées d'origine

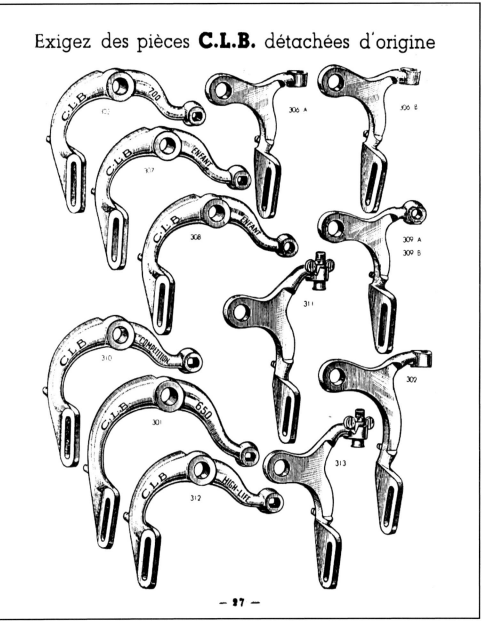

309 A **Branche** Y de frein 700 dame tirage inversé...........
309 B — Y de frein fillette tirage inversé.............
310 — ronde de frein compétition ....
311 — Y de frein compétition avec détendeur ....
312 — ronde de frein High Life ....
313 — Y de frein High Life avec détendeur .. ..
314 — de frein STANDARD NM gauche...........
315 — de frein STANDARD NM droite ....
316 — gauche avec détendeur, de frein cyclomoteur..
317 — droite de frein cyclomoteur ....
318 **Guide** de direction pour cyclomoteur (permet de canaliser toutes les gaines - sert d'arrêt de gaine pour frein avant) existe pour jeux de direction diamètre 25 mm. et 28 mm. - Préciser le modèle désiré
Transmission complète de frein avant long. o m. 6o......
— complète de frein arrière, long. 1 m. 25....
— complète de frein arr. dame, long. 1 m. 6o
Câble de frein CLB o m. 6o.........................
— — — 1 m. 25.........................
— — — 1 m. 6o.........................

Carters C.-L.B. (voir gravures pages 17 et 18)

C.L.B. enfant . . ..
— enfant mixte . . ..
— Sport . . ..
— Sport ajouré . . ..
— 3 attaches . . ..
— 3 attaches large ....
— 3 attaches S.T. ....
— max 3 attaches ....
— max B demi-ajouré, 3 attaches ....
— MIX 3 attaches ....
— P 21 3 attaches ....
— SPORT pour dérailleur avant avec collier (Réf. C.H. ou S) ....
— SPORT pour dérailleur avant sans collier (Réf. C.H. ou S.) ....

EXIGEZ ⟨CLB⟩ **LA MARQUE**

SPÉCIALITÉS VÉLOCIPÉDIQUES C L B - SAINT-ÉTIENNE (Loire) FRANCE

— 28 —

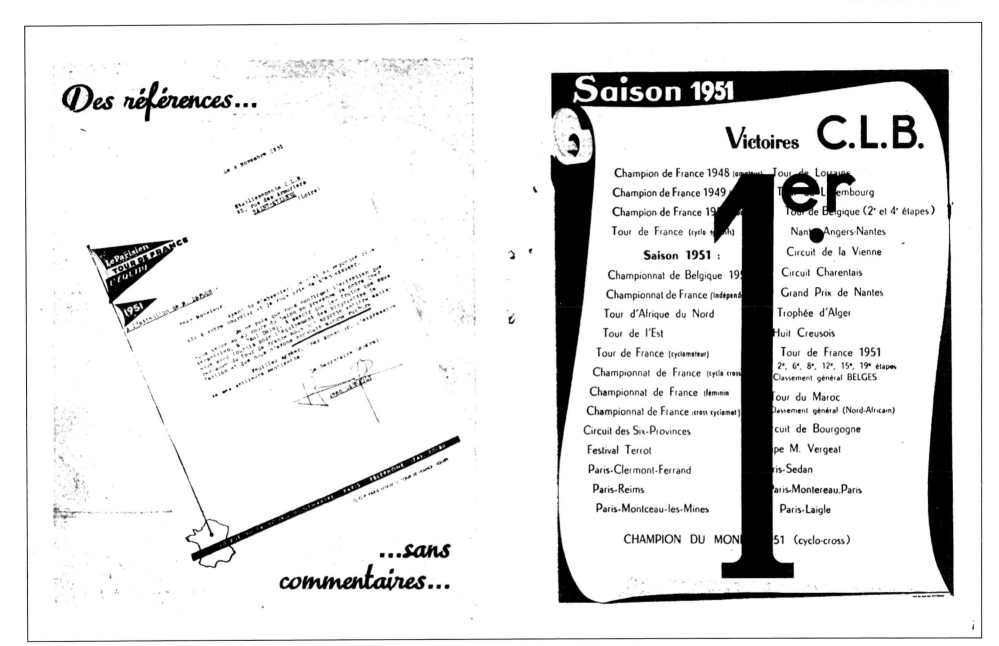

Des références...

...sans commentaires...

Saison 1951

Victoires **C.L.B.**

Champion de France 1948 (amateur) — Tour de Lorraine
Champion de France 1949 — Tour du Luxembourg
Champion de France 19 — Tour de Belgique (2ᵉ et 4ᵉ étapes)
Tour de France (cyclo sports) — Nantes-Angers-Nantes

Saison 1951 : — Circuit de la Vienne
Championnat de Belgique 195 — Circuit Charentais
Championnat de France (Indépend — Grand Prix de Nantes
Tour d'Afrique du Nord — Trophée d'Alger
Tour de l'Est — Huit Creusois
Tour de France (cyclomoteur) — Tour de France 1951
Championnat de France (cyclo cross) — 2ᵉ, 6ᵉ, 8ᵉ, 12ᵉ, 15ᵉ, 19ᵉ étapes Classement général BELGES
Championnat de France (féminin — Tour du Maroc
Championnat de France (cross cyclomot.) — Classement général (Nord-Africain)
Circuit des Six-Provinces — cuit de Bourgogne
Festival Terrot — pe M. Vergeat
Paris-Clermont-Ferrand — ris-Sedan
Paris-Reims — aris-Montereau-Paris
Paris-Montceau-les-Mines — Paris-Laigle

CHAMPION DU MON 51 (cyclo-cross)

1er.

6 fois champion de France

Champion du Monde

C.L.B. HIGH-LIFE

35% 64% 53%

Modèle HIGH LIFE PROFESSIONNEL avec détendeur de câble instantané permettant le démontage de roue sans dégonfler.

Complet avec poignée-course repose-mains brevetée « Champion de France. » Présentation de grand luxe.

Le frein, PRIX DETAIL, frs. »

— 14 —

Détendeur permettant un dégagement *breveté* *instantané de la roue*

tension normale du câble

le détendeur a pivoté dans son logement

dégagement de la roue

Poignée cocotte repose main Champion de France

Ces modèles sont prévus pour serrage sur guidon, diamètre 23 ᵐ/ᵐ 5 La poignée seule : PRIX DETAIL, frs :

CC4 AM   CC4 NM

Pour serrage sur guidon d'un diamètre inférieur et notamment guidon de 22 ᵐ/ᵐ, utilisez **notre bague référence** 220.

PRIX DETAIL......

— 15 —

M.A.F.A.C. Manufacture Auvergnoise de Freins et Assessoires pour Cycle

(Manufacturer in the Auvergne of Brakes and Cycle Components)

'Ah Mafac' one senior V-CC member remarked when I took on this role 'that steady arrestor of laden bikes and the first brakes that really worked.'

I am firmly of the view that Mafac occupy a crucial place in the development of braking. They developed the first of the modern generation of centre-pull brakes and their design of cantilever provided the foundation for braking on all Mountain Bikes. Mafac brakes are amongst that select band of components that were used by a wide range of cyclists from Tour de France riders, time-trialists to tourists and riders of tandems/trikes. Thus pretty much any lightweight from early 50s to mid 80s could be appropriately retro fitted with Mafacs.

ORIGINS

Established after WWII they were originally known as Securité (the 'r' elongated to underline the word as the first 'a' later in Mafac). It was founded by Auguste Bourdel who also invented the original cantilever and centre pull. Under their original name they marketed three out of four of their core products: the cantilever, the brake lever (at this stage without a rubber hood and the blade of solid construction) and the tool kit (in either a

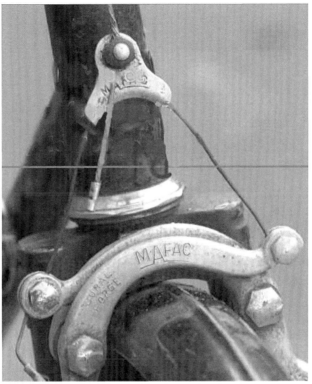

A Mafac Racer of the earlier type simply stamped Dural Forge – callipers of this type date from between 1955 and 1969 approx

metal tin[1] or leather pouch). The name changed in the autumn of 1947 (ref ad in Le Cycliste 11/47).

The rubber lever hoods originated in the late

---

1   The *Data Book Joto Ringyo* 1998 reprint p112 shows a 1949 metal box 10 piece tool kit. Although labelled Mafac it also says 'Securité du Cycliste'

1940s first as a half hood and later as a full hood. Typically the hoods were black or tan but also came in other colours including white, blue and green. They also offered a Guidonnet lever[2] which was popular with tourists, offering access to the brakes from the top of the bars. These were best used with randonneur bars, which swept up from the centre, as with ordinary Maes type bars there was very little distance between lever and bar. The first use of these in Britain that I am aware of was in the late 50s when the owner of Major Brothers (a small builder in Thornton Heath, SE London) brought them back from France as he found he could not use a conventional lever with his arthritis.

Mafac studded brake blocks (four, or for tandems, five stud) were an excellent balance between being durable, effective and not too wearing on rims. Short three studded block were made for the S type centre pull and their models for childrens bikes the Jacky and Kathy(both cantilevers with very short arms)

CANTILEVERS

The cantilever was the first Mafac brake, the earliest reference I can find is 1946[3] it remained in production almost unchanged for nearly 40 years, extremely powerful yet simple and lightweight. The cantilever was the first Mafac brake made

---

2   Ibid 1950 p119
3   Ibid 1946 p74

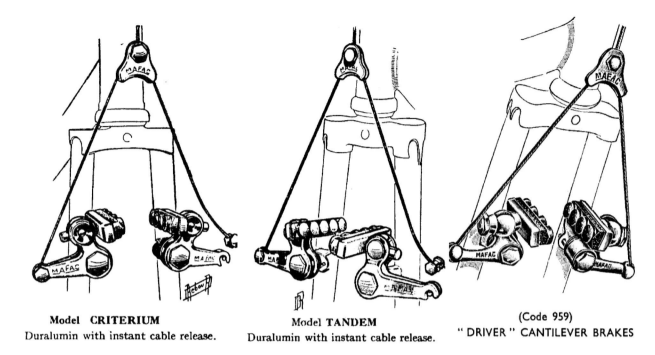

Model CRITERIUM
Duralumin with instant cable release.

Model TANDEM
Duralumin with instant cable release.

(Code 959)
" DRIVER " CANTILEVER BRAKES

Fig 1 Above left, the standard cantilever brake (named the Criterium for most of its life). Above centre, the Tandem version also used on cyclemotors and sometimes named Cyclemoteur. Right is the Driver cantilever from the 1960s with cast arms and Tiger/ Top-63 type brake shoes

from 1946; it remained in production almost unchanged for nearly 40 years. The cantilever design evolved during the 30's with a number of French makers producing a brake we would recognise as a cantilever eg Barra and Lewis, essentially Bourdel refined the design. Extremely powerful yet simple and lightweight. Their effectiveness is based upon the closeness of the pivot to the brake block which eliminates any flex (some of the most inefficient brakes are side pulls with a large gap from pivot to brake block). Also with the wide profile design (arms in line with the pivots) the mechanical efficiency improves as the lever is applied. To use these

brakes you needed braze-ons. These braze-ons had three spring positions, which was not just useful for increasing leverage but also could compensate if the brazing position was less than optimum. Several different models were offered, the standard one being the Criterium. A longer arm version was marketed and advertised as being suitable for tandems (sometimes known as model Cyclomoteur). These two are shown in fig 1.

Mafac offered a lever, drilled to take two cables, so that a third brake could be used primarily for tandem use. The Driver was a shorter arm cast aluminium model available in the late 50s and 60s,

which had the same brake shoe mounting as the Top- 63 (see below). A 70s short arm model, the Jacky was advertised as suitable for children's bikes.

Cantilevers were extremely popular with cyclo-cross riders (the distinctive profile of the arms at 90° to the forks can been seen in most cyclocross photos), tandems and tourists. To avoid the rear brake arms fouling pannier bags some builders fitted the braze-on facing forward on the seat stays. Most of the specialist builders fitted these on their touring bikes, examples being Jack Taylor and Wester Ross.

The importance of this designed cannot be overstated. Copied by Japanese manufacturers and it lead to the development of the V-type brake so ubiquitous on modern mountain and hybrid bikes.

RACER

In 1952 the Racer centre pulls were introduced (fig 2). These were a huge advance being efficient and easy to set up. The first version featured oil holes on the arms for lubricating the springs.(fig 9) A further difference was that the lower end of the spring instead of fitting round the brake pad holder nut hooked around the top end of the vertical brake shoe adjustment. Also the dural forged stamping was smaller. The advantages were many:

a   Quick release straddle cable enabled easy wheel removal

b   Blocks were multi-adjustable in both the vertical and horizontal plane. They could also be angled, a great advantage when using a rim such as the Constrictor Asp whose braking surfaces were not parallel

c   Wide range of drop (50 to 75mm) which could accommodate most frames. In the late 50s also a

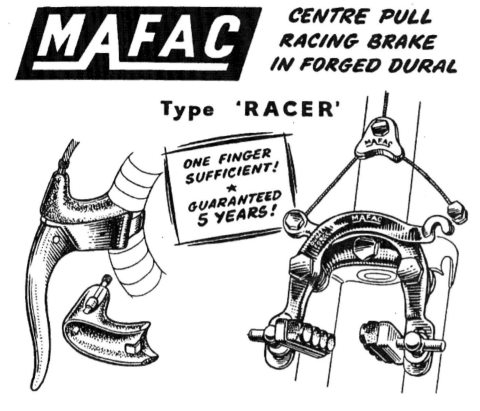

Fig 2 The classic Mafac Racer

shallow drop version was offered (45 to 68mm)

d As the length of the straddle cable could easily be altered so could the mechanical advantage of the brake. Also the straddle cable length could be altered to avoid fouling a rack/bag support. Furthermore, a length of gear cable could be used rather than as with other manufacturers only a purpose made cable

e A consequence of the design of the lever clamp was that the lever body could be removed without untaping the bars.

f Cable tension could be altered when riding thanks to the adjusters on the lever hoods

g Easy to disassemble and service, the advertising slogan was 'one finger sufficient!'

The only design weakness was the front brake hanger, which was rather flexible and worked best when wedged against the top headset race. This was easy to do with a headset such as the Stronglight P4, which had a wide circumference.

One disadvantage was the poor resistance to rust of the chromed parts eg cable clamp bolts and brake shoe holders.

The first type of brake levers in the 1950s were the open back style (these were known as the Professional), but by 1955 a closed back style lever named the Racer had been introduced. For a period both were available, ref Ron Kitching 1960 *Everything Cycling.*

The profile of these brakes is very distinctive and even a cursory glance at photos of Tour riders in the 50s and 60s will reveal many to be stopping on Mafacs. I remember buying a set of Mafac and upon asking which model, the seller said 'you know the ones Anquetil won the Tour

on'. Once they became available in Britain in 1953 many club riders switched en mass. None of Mafac's competitors eg GB, Weinmann or Universal marketed centre pulls until the late 1950s.

TA offered a front bag support, which fitted on to the brake's pivot bolts and under the fork crown.

A number of specialist French builders used cut down cantilever pivot bolts to create a brazed-on brake.[4] The advantage was more efficient operation with less flexing; the top ends of the springs fitted straight on to the frame rather than on to a back plate. The only disadvantage was that it required very exact workmanship otherwise he brake would not centre.

In the early 60s plastic pivot bushings replaced the bronze ones and in the late 1960s 'Racer' replaced the stamping 'dural forge'. In the early 1970s a longer arm version was introduced, the Raid, (drop 60 to 85 mm with wheel guides built into the brake shoe fitting). This was aimed at 650B balloon tyred machines for which the Racer did not provide a big enough drop. This was originally designed by Bourdel (he died in 1957) but for some reason was not marketed until much later

DEVELOPMENT: THE TIGER & TOP-63

Mafac's major innovation was the introduction of the Tiger brake (fig. 3) in the late 1950s (first available in Britain in 1960). The arms were set further apart to provide increased leverage giving a squarer profile and the straddle cable was redesigned. This became double ended with a tiny nipple at one end and a tab at the other for

4   Touring Bikes: Tony Oliver p 138 1990 Crowood Press

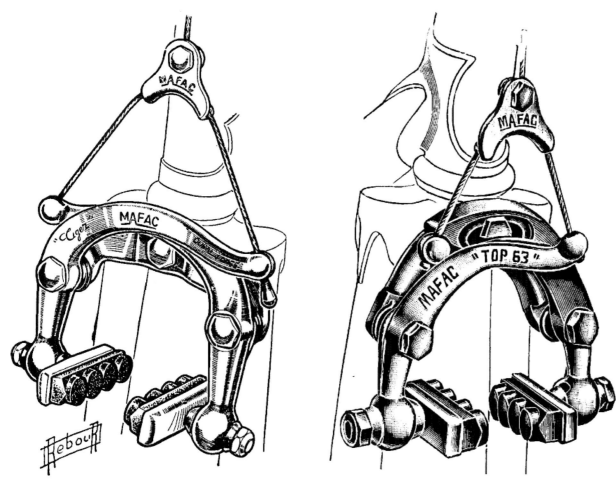

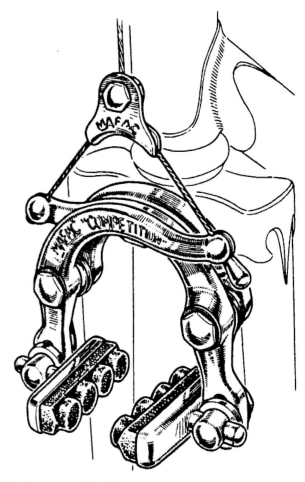

Figs 3 & 4 Left the first development the Mafac Tiger from c1960, right the much collected Mafac Top-63

Fig 5 An early 70s Mafac Competition

release. This now meant the straddle wire length was fixed. A great step backwards because the mechanical advantage could not be altered and also if not lubricated carefully the nipple would corrode into the brake arm holder. The lower end of the spring now fitted in the stirrup arms rather than as before against the brake shoe holder. The brake shoes could not be moved up or down, only angled

which dramatically reduced the drop range. Mafac compensated for this by elongating the frame clamp bolt hole to give 10mm adjustment of drop.

This brake was further developed into the Top-63 (fig 4) introduced in 1963. In the 1964 *Holdworthy Aids* catalogue described the brake as :

'developed from the earlier Tiger this has the main carrying arm formed by two mouldings which are

bolted together and to the frame via a curved slot. One arm slides into the other allowing the stirrups to be opened and supplies the vertical adjustment needed to align blocks to the rim. There is no up or down movement of blocks.'

This was not a commercial success, partly because it was quite complex to set up and it did not offer better braking than the Racer. In 1964 at

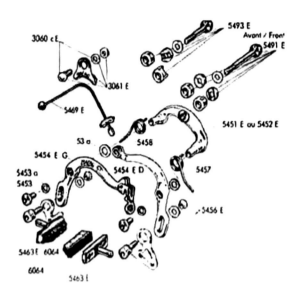

Fig 6 The ultimate development, the Mafac GT

Fig 7 An early example of a Mafac toolkit – this one supplied in a tin which is embossed both with Mafac and Securite names

75/- it was significantly more expensive than the Racer at 59/9. The Top-63 is the most sought after of Mafac brakes amongst collectors, solely because of its rarity. It remained in production for only a few years. An interesting example of a manufacturer having to abandon innovation and revert to the original product. A parallel example that comes to mind is Sturmey Archer when they gave up on the SW and reverted to the AW.

MAFAC in the 1970s and 1980s

The core Mafac products remained unchanged until their demise in the mid-1980s Plastic was introduced into the lever bodies but not successfully as it distorted over time and the cable adjusters would break off. This variant in either black or white plastic was called the Promotion. There was even a version of the Guidonnet lever with a white plastic blade. Any force exerted caused the lever to flex, not something to fill the rider with confidence. A shorter arm version of the Guidonnet know as the VDA or Ville was introduced. Black, white or coloured plastic lever blade covers were also offered, as was an inverted lever which fitted on the bars in place of a bar end stop.

Around 1973, the centre pulls were updated with a short arm version, the Competition (47 to 60mm) and a longer arm, the 2000 (same reach as the Racer). This I interpret as a bid to develop separate brakes for tourists and racers. However the Racer continued to be made and was about 20% cheaper. The main differences were the arms were, more rounded and wheel guides were introduced. The first versions of both these brakes had the model names in the same engraved script as the racer. Later versions were anodised with the name on a transfer in gold on black background and used a doubled ended ball type straddle cable rather like that used by GB. An example of an early version of the Competition is illustrated in fig 5.

The levers became shorter in reach and were drilled. The adjusters became larger in diameter. Some were marketed under the Spidel name (the late 1970s French failed attempt to create a groupset to compete with Campag and Shimano). A cheaper centre pull, the S, which looked and worked like a poor quality Weinmann copy, features in the 1977 catalogue. The final centre pull

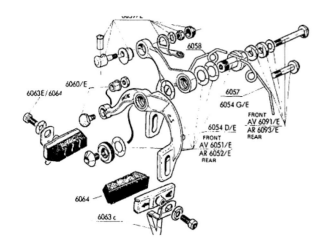

Fig 8 Mafac LS side-pull brake

model was the GT, (fig 6 early 1980s which was a centre pull with allen key fittings and quick release on the straddle cable.

TOOLKITS

A Mafac tool kit was ideal for fitting their brakes. For example the cable clamps required two 9mm spanners to adjust, which all toolkits came with.

According to the Ron Kitching 1960 *Everything Cycling* there were three versions of the tool kit all in a grey plastic fold out wallet:
– The Constructor 6 tools
– Touriste 7 tools
– Randonneur 10 tools

All came with puncture repair kit and the three single ended spanners doubled as tyre levers. The three double ended spanners (8/9mm 10/11mm and 12/14mm) are some of the most useful tools ever invented. Less successful are the large tools eg cone spanners, screwdrivers. The set covered pretty much all fittings on a lightweight bike. Later versions introduced Allen keys. An early example supplied in a tin is shown in fig 7. Both Reg and Milremo copied the tools kits that latter being marketed as the 'Riparo'.[5]

DECLINE

Mafac experienced a short revival in the early 1980s when their cantilevers became popular on first generation mountain bikes. Cantilevers had always been the favoured means of stopping for cyclocross and rough stuff riders[6] (less metal to clog up with mud). However the writing was on the wall, caused primarily by the move to side pulls, a process started by Campag in 1969. Centre pulls

5   Ron Kitching *Everything Cycling* 1970
6   Correspondence in the Rough Stuff Journal especially 1981 from Chater Willis and Bill Hill (the latter the inventor of the Trivelox gear)

had simply become unfashionable. Mafac lost out on the mountain bike market when the Japanese started developing cantilever brakes specifically designed to work with flat bars. The Mafac cantilever stuck out at 90° this could be a problem for some riders (eg catching on panniers) and the Japanese models that were angled at 45° soon found favour.

The Mafac brake lever has a high leverage and consequently it works very poorly with a modern cantilever where the standard brake levers used have a lower leverage. With a combination of

Fig. 9: Oil hole in very early Mafac Racer calliper from c1953–55

Mafac levers and modern cantilever brakes, the grip is very spongy and unless adjusted very close to the rim you end up with the lever touching the bar. In terms of development another example of a European company being left behind by the Japanese.

Mafac were slightly more expensive than Weinmann and thus lost out in the OEM market. Also for a manufacturer, fitting a sidepull was always going to be far quicker.

Mafac introduced a range of side pulls in the late 1970s of which the LS was the top model (fig 8). These were essentially copies of existing side pulls and took a tiny market share. The problem for Mafac was that their name was very much synonymous with centre pulls and cantilevers. If you wanted sidepulls you did not buy Mafac.

Mafac ceased trading in 1983. Writing in the October 1983 CTC magazine review of that years Harrogate show Chris Juden reported:

"I can confirm that Mafac that steadfast arrestor of laden bicycles has gone out of business." p 284

There was short lived management buy out reference being made to this in the CTC magazine October 1984:

"The old company who sold their products too cheaply have been revived by a management buyout"

However I have been unable to find any further reference so this may not have lasted beyond 1985. So a sad end to the company who created the first of the modern centre pulls and developed what for many years was the most powerful braking option the cantilever. Weinmann bought the tooling making a copy of the cantilever however their demise was not long afterwards[7].

With the exception of the Tiger and the Top 63 there was very little product development. The cantilevers were essentially unchanged throughout their production lifespan of nearly 40 years. If a product is to be judged by the number of copies it sired then Mafac rates very high; I have seen copies by Galli, Shimano, Olimpic, Zeus, Favourit, Weinmann, Dia Compe and several other un-branded far Eastern copies.

Finally I always liked the story of two riders out in the Alps . Whenever they started a descent the one would mumble something under his breathe. Finally the other one asked what he was saying. The reply:

"a prayer to St Mafac the patron saint of braking"

I shall leave the last word to H. H. Willis (known as Chater) a frequent writer to the cycling press in the 60's and 70's and a former VCC librarian. He wrote in the December 1975 CTC magazine:

"For steep descents you need either iron nerves or first class brakes. The Mafac with brazed pivots appear best and also collect less mud".

APPENDICES

Dating

– There are versions of the Competition marked Peugeot and Spidel (the late 1970's French failed attempt by Maillard, Mafac, Stronglight and Simplex to create groupsets to compete with Campagnolo and Shimano). Mafac drilled levers stamped Spidel date from this time. – Any component with Securité alone is pre-autumn 1947

– Early levers had solid blades

– The hollow (both open and close back) brake lever blades were stamped M.A.F.A.C. (as were most of the parts such as straddle wire bridges). Some time in the 1960s they became simply MAFAC.

– At the end of the 1960s the stamping on stirrups altered from Dural Forge to Racer.

– At the same time levers were stamped Mafac, France.

– Early centre pulls had a tiny oil hole above the pivots

– There are versions of the Competition marked Peugeot and Spidel (the late 1970's French failed attempt by Maillard, Mafac, Stronglight and Simplex to create groupsets to compete with Campagnolo and Shimano). Mafac drilled levers stamped Spidel date from this time.

– The later versions of the 2000 and Competition had the month and date of manufacture stamped on the inside of the left arm (the earliest example I have seen is dated 1975). This was altered around 1978 to two letters, one for year the other for month

Logos

there are three versions :

– Mafac underlined by the A elongated

– As above but with punctuation after each letter

– Mafac without punctuation on the front but on the rear the name within an oblong

Design Weaknesses

---

7   *Cycletouring*. (magazine of the CTC) Oct 1986 review of the York Rally

- Cable adjusters on lever can break off especially if the adjuster is unscrewed   and when worn they can unwind. The brass part of the cable adjuster which fits into the top of the brake lever can bend preventing the cable from operating effectively
- Bronze bushing on the dural forge once worn cannot be replaced. One advantage of the plastic bushing on the 'Racer' is that they can be replaced.
- Chroming is poor on the metal parts eg pivot bolts and cable clamps.
- Driver straddle cables can foul arms if not correct length.
- Top 63 & Driver straddle cable nipples being very small can corrode into the body making them very difficult to remove. Recommend they are regularly re greased

- The smaller tools (7 to 11mm) although well designed are not durable and will round. The larger tools lack the leverage for some jobs eg wheel removal, seat pin adjustment. The serrated cone spanner designed to fit different size cones is not effective as it can slip.

Using Mafacs today

I would recommend the dural forge for almost any lightweight from 1950 to the late 60s. From that date to the mid 80's the 'Racer' is the ideal. If you have cantilever braze ons then the longer arm Criterium is the one to have for powerful braking. Sometimes on the short arm models the straddle cable can foul the end of the brake block shoe arm. Drivers are fiddly to set up and don't offer any improved braking.

Additional cable adjustment: normally the Mafac hanger will not take a barrel adjuster, as the hole is too small. You can use the screwed adjuster from a plastic Simplex down tube gear lever for this.

Sources

From 1955 to 1972 Mafac were featured in *Holdsworthy Aids* catalogues. Evian and Ron Kitching also imported them until the late 1960s and his *Everything Cycling* catalogues are a useful source. All the importers used Daniel Rebour drawing to illustrate their adverts, which were a regular feature in *Cycling* in the early 1970s. The earliest importer was Fonteyn. The only Mafac catalogue I have see is the one in the V-CC library from 1977 and is reproduced on the following pages.

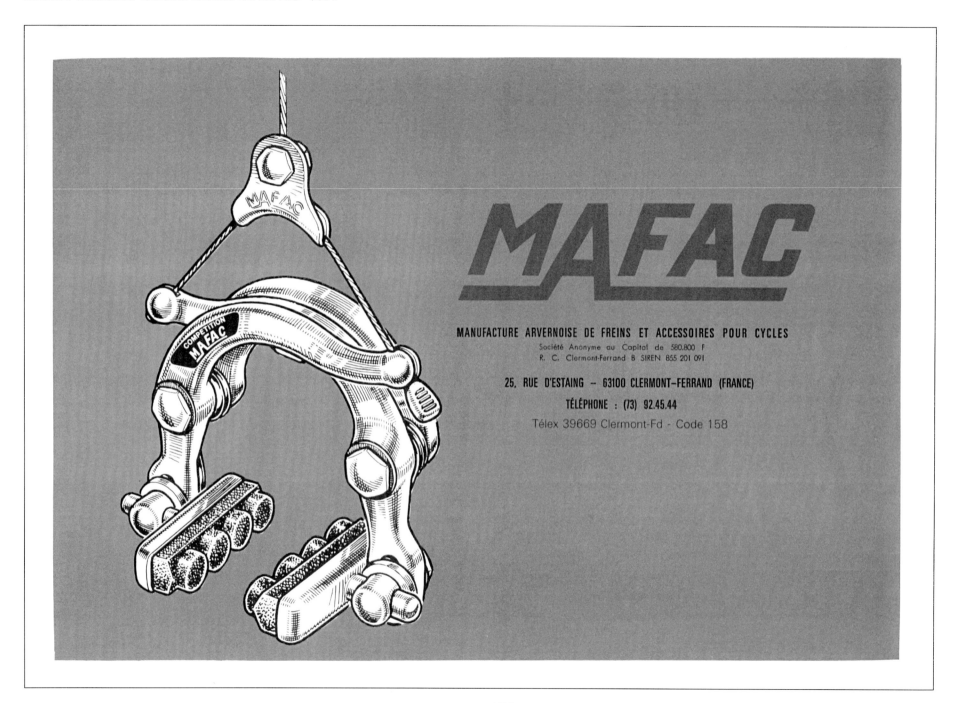

MANUFACTURE ARVERNOISE DE FREINS ET ACCESSOIRES POUR CYCLES

Société Anonyme au Capital de 580.800 F
R. C. Clermont-Ferrand B SIREN 855 201 091

25, RUE D'ESTAING — 63100 CLERMONT—FERRAND (FRANCE)

TÉLÉPHONE : (73) 92.45.44

Télex 39669 Clermont-Fd - Code 158

Poignée course ‹dural›

Racing lever « dural »

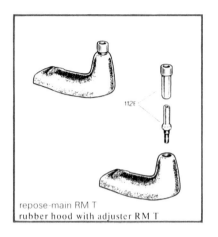

repose-main RM - GT
rubber hood with large adjuster RM - GT
1412E

repose-main RM T
rubber hood with adjuster RM T
112E

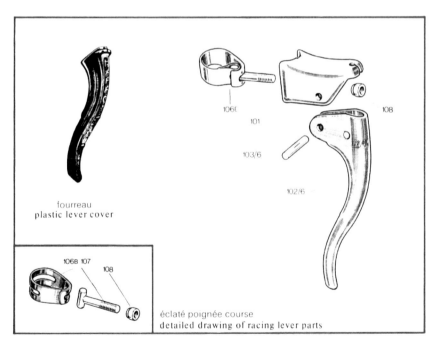

fourreau
plastic lever cover

106E
101
103/6
102/6
108

106B 107
108

éclaté poignée course
detailed drawing of racing lever parts

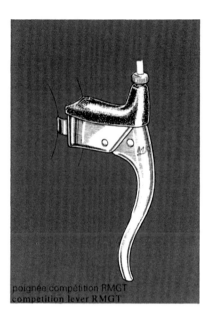

poignée compétition RMGT
competition lever RMGT

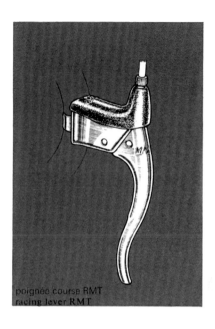

poignée course RMT
racing lever RMT

CB	poignée course - collier breveté inox
	racing lever - patented stainless clip
CS	poignée course - collier simplifié inox
	racing lever - simplified stainless clip
PM	retouche du levier pour petite main, sur demande
	on demand, shorter lever for small hands
RMT	repose-main tendeur (blanc, rouge, bleu, vert, noir)
	rubber hood with adjuster (white, red, blue, green, black)
RMGT	repose-main gros tendeur (blanc, rouge, bleu, vert, noir)
	rubber hood with large adjuster (white, red, blue, green, black)
F	fourreau plastique
	plastic lever cover

2

Frein _MAFAC_ ‹ compétition ›

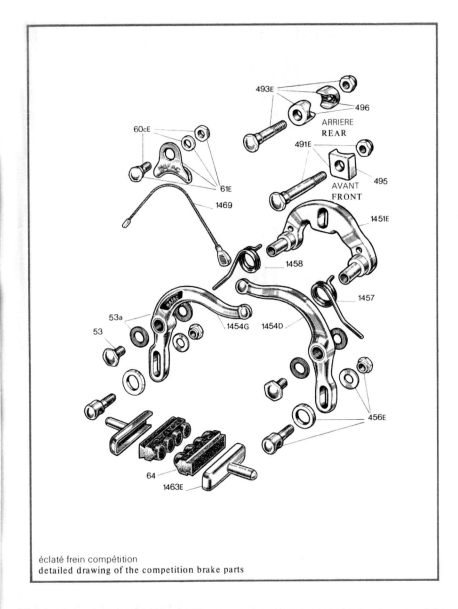

493E
496
ARRIERE
REAR
60cE
491E
61E
495
AVANT
FRONT
1469
1451E
1458
1457
53a
1454G 1454D
53
456E
64
1463E

éclaté frein compétition
detailed drawing of the competition brake parts

MAFAC « competition » Brake

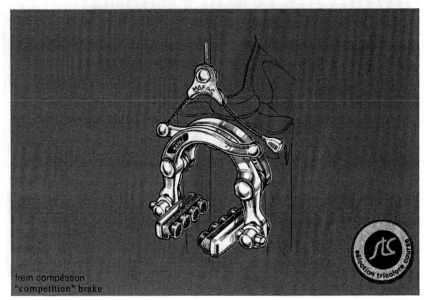

frein compétition
"competition" brake

Présentation grand luxe :
Super de luxe finish

Cn 1	étrier 451 - petit modèle	
	451 center stirrup-small size	
Cn 2	étrier 452 - grand modèle	
	452 center stirrup-large size	
Cn 3	étrier 1451 - réglable	
	1451 center stirrup-adjustable	

(peuvent être livrés avec guide-roue)
(can be delivered with wheel-guides)

Présentation anodisée :
Anodized finish

Argent	Cn 1 A - Cn 2 A - Cn 3 A
Silver	Cn 1 A - Cn 2 A - Cn 3 A
Or	Cn 1 D - Cn 2 D - Cn 3 D
Gold	Cn 1 D - Cn 2 D - Cn 3 D

(toujours livrés avec guide-roue)
(always delivered with wheel-guides)

3

Poignée course ‹2000›   Racing lever «2000»

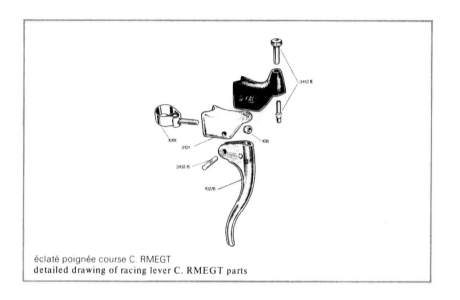

éclaté poignée course C. RMEGT
detailed drawing of racing lever C. RMEGT parts

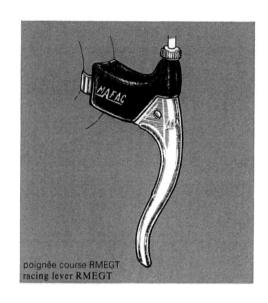

poignée course RMEGT
racing lever RMEGT

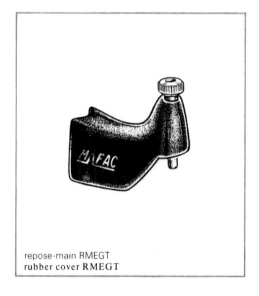

repose-main RMEGT
rubber cover RMEGT

Présentation grand luxe :
Super de luxe finish

C RMEGT   poignée course - collier breveté inox - repose-main enveloppant gros tendeur.
racing lever-patented stainless clip-rubber cover for lever bracket-large adjuster.

Présentation anodisé Argent :
Anodized silver finish

CA RMEGT   poignée course - collier breveté inox - repose-main enveloppant gros tendeur
racing lever-patented stainless clip-rubber cover for lever bracket-large adjuster.

Présentation anodisé Or :
Anodized gold finish

CD RMEGT   poignée course - collier breveté inox - repose-main enveloppant gros tendeur.
racing lever-patented stainlers clip-rubber cover for lever bracket-large adjuster.

RMEGT   repose-main enveloppant gros tendeur
rubber cover for lever bracket-large adjuster.

4

Frein *MAFAC* ‹2000›

MAFAC «2000» Brake

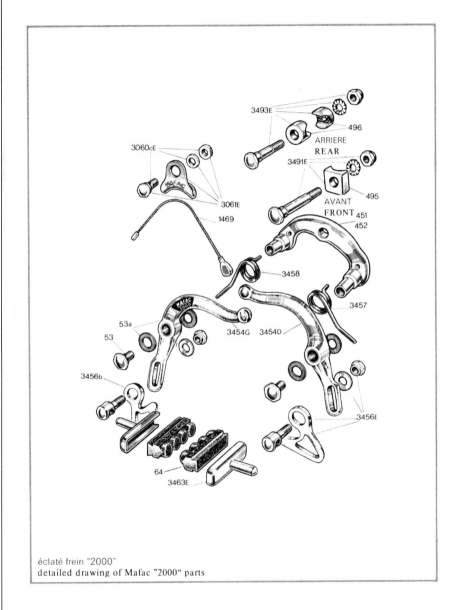

3493E
496
ARRIERE
REAR
3060cE
3491E
3061E
495
AVANT
FRONT 451
452
1469
1448
3458
3457
53a
3454G 3454D
53
3456b
3456E
64
3463E

éclaté frein "2000"
detailed drawing of Mafac "2000" parts

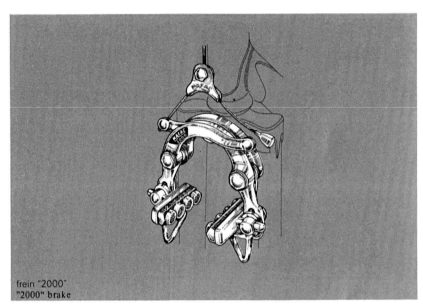

frein "2000"
"2000" brake

Présentation anodisé Argent :
Anodized silver finish

M 1 A	étrier 451 - petit modéle	
	451 center stirrup-small size	
M 2 A	étrier 452 - grand modèle	
	452 center stirrup-large size	
M 3 A	étrier 1451 - réglable	
	1451 center stirrup-adjustable	

Présentation anodisé Or :
Anodized gold finish

M 1 D	étrier 451 - petit modèle	
	451 center stirrup-small size	
M 2 D	étrier 452 - grand modèle	
	452 center stirrup-large size	
M 3 D	étrier 1451 - réglable	
	1451 center stirrup-adjustable	

5

Poignée promotion

modèle breveté déposé - LEVIER DETENTION

Promotion lever

patented-registered trade-mark - QUICK RELEASE LEVER

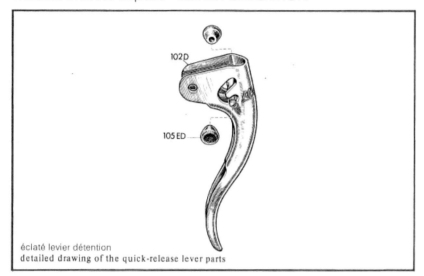

102D

105 ED

éclaté levier détention
detailed drawing of the quick-release lever parts

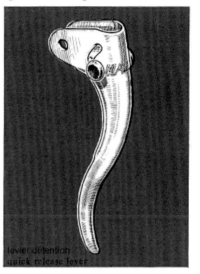

levier détention
quick release lever

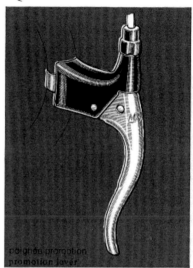

poignée promotion
promotion lever

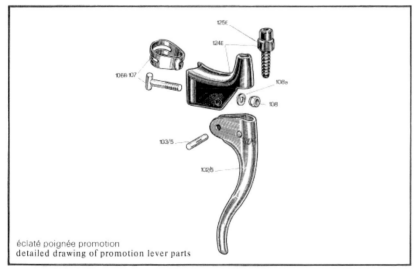

125E

124E

106B 107

108a

108

103/5

102/5

éclaté poignée promotion
detailed drawing of promotion lever parts

6

PB   poignée promotion - collier breveté inox
        promotion lever-patented stainless clip

PS   poignée promotion - collier simplifié inox
        promotion lever-simplified stainless clip
        (livrable avec cocotte blanche ou noire)
        (can be delivered with white or black lever brackets)

Détention :
Quick-release system

Le levier peut se monter sur toutes nos cocottes course ou
promotion.

Our quick-release lever can be fitted on all our racing or
promotion lever brackets.

Frein *MAFAC* ‹Racer›

MAFAC «Racer» Brake

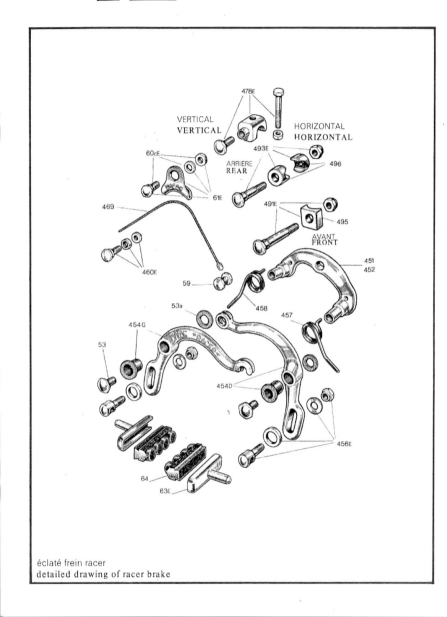

éclaté frein racer
detailed drawing of racer brake

frein racer
racer brake

Présentation grand luxe :
Super de luxe finish

Rb GL étrier 451 - petit modèle
451 center stirrup-small size

RGL étrier 452 - grand modèle
452 center stirrup-large size

Présentation luxe :
De luxe finish

Rb L étrier 451 - petit modèle
451 center stirrup-small size

RL étrier 452 - grand modèle
452 center stirrup-large size

7

Poignées ville et guidonnet dural forgé

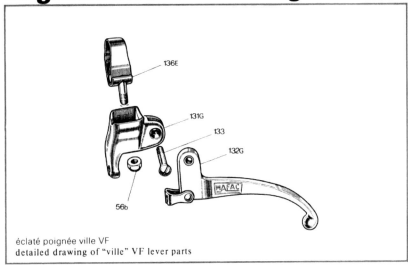

136E
131G
133
132G
56b

éclaté poignée ville VF
detailed drawing of "ville" VF lever parts

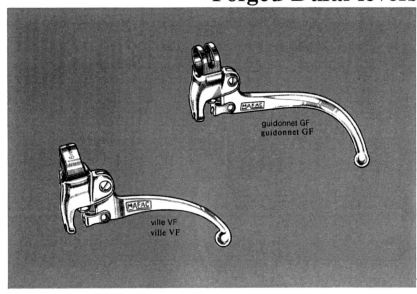

guidonnet GF
guidonnet GF

ville VF
ville VF

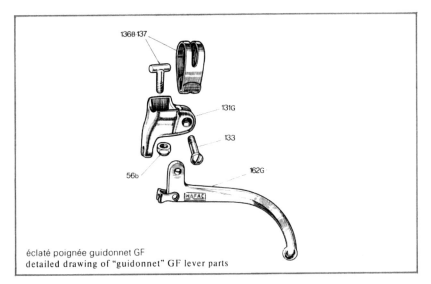

136B-137
131G
133
56b
162G

éclaté poignée guidonnet GF
detailed drawing of "guidonnet" GF lever parts

VF B	poignée ville - collier breveté inox "ville" lever-patented stainless clip
VF S	poignée ville - collier simplifié inox "ville" lever-simplified stainless clip
GF B	poignée guidonnet - collier breveté inox "guidonnet" lever-patented stainless clip
GF S	poignée guidonnet - collier simplifié inox "guidonnet" lever-simplified stainless clip

8

Frein *MAFAC* ‹ Raid ›

MAFAC « Raid » Brake

60cE

478E

491E

61E

ARRIERE
REAR

AVANT
FRONT

495

469

59

53a

2451E

2454G

2458

2457

53

2454D

456E

64

63E

éclaté frein Raid
detailed drawing of the Raid brake parts

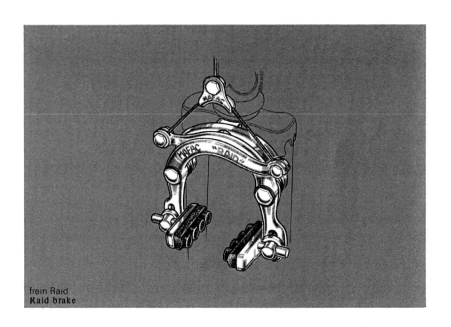

frein Raid
Raid brake

Présentation grand luxe	**Rd GL**
Super de luxe finish	Rd GL
Présentation luxe	**Rd L**
De luxe finish	Rd L

9

Poignées ville ‹VDA›
et guidonnet ‹GDA›

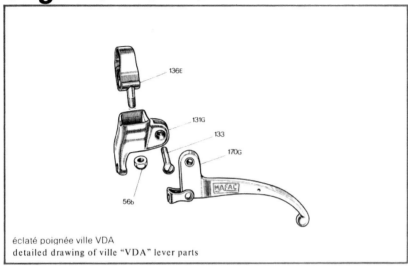

éclaté poignée ville VDA
detailed drawing of ville "VDA" lever parts

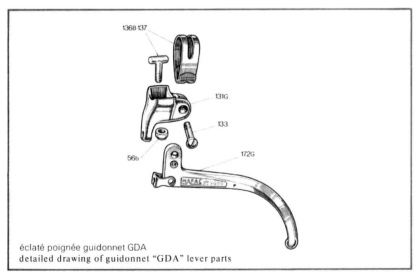

éclaté poignée guidonnet GDA
detailed drawing of guidonnet "GDA" lever parts

10

Ville «VDA» levers
and guidonnet «GDA» levers

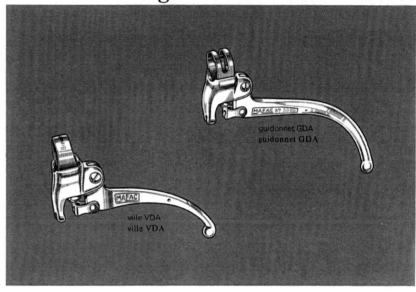

guidonnet GDA
guidonnet GDA

ville VDA
ville VDA

VDA B   poignée ville - collier breveté inox
ville lever-patented stainless clip

VDA S   poignée ville - collier simplifié inox
ville lever-simplified stainless clip

GDA B   poignée guidpnnet - collier breveté inox
guidonnet lever-patented stainless clip

GDA S   poignée guidonnet - collier simplifié inox
guidonnet lever-simplified stainless clip

Frein *MAFAC* ‹ S ›

A late 70's /80's Weinmann copy

MAFAC « S » Brake

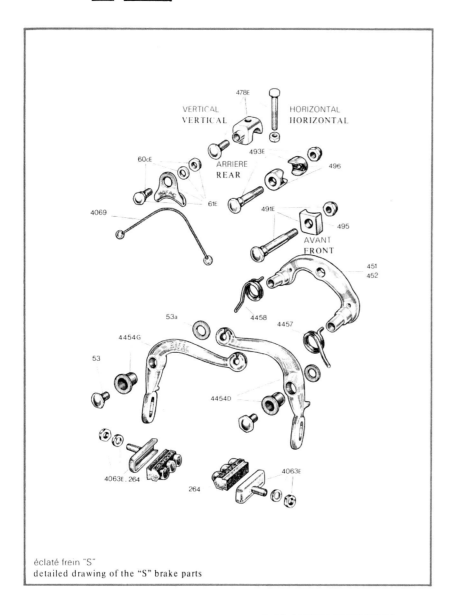

478E

VERTICAL
VERTICAL

HORIZONTAL
HORIZONTAL

493E

60cE

ARRIERE
REAR

496

61E

4069

491E

495

AVANT
FRONT

451
452

53a

4458   4457

4454G

53

4454D

4063E . 264

264

4063E

éclaté frein "S"
detailed drawing of the "S" brake parts

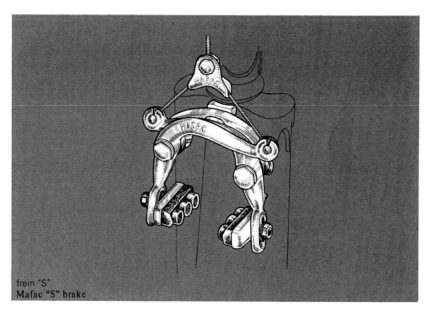

frein "S"
Mafac "S" brake

Présentation luxe :
De luxe finish

Sb L étrier 451 - petit modèle
451 center stirrup-small size

SL étrier 452 - grand modèle
452 center stirrup-large size

11

Brasage des tasseaux

Brake pivots brazing

Modèles / Types	Roues / Wheels	AV / Front	AR / Rear	E / Clearance between pivots
Critérium	600 B	246	241	63 à 68
	650 B	270	265	63 à 68
	700 C	290	285	63 à 68
Cyclo-tandem	600 B	246	241	67 à 72
	650 B	268	263	65 à 70
Jacky	450 A	177	172	54 à 62
	500 A	205	200	54 à 62
	550 A	230	225	54 à 62
	600 A	255	250	54 à 62
Racer et 2000	700 C	350 + 3	346 + 3	60 à 64
Compétition	700 C	345 + 2	341 + 2	62 à 68
Raid	650 B	333 + 3	330 + 3	70 à 76

Ces cotes sont données à titre indicatif et il serait utile, selon le type de cadre et dans le cas de montage avec garde-boue, de présenter sur la carcasse un ensemble de frein avec étrier.

Nota : les tasseaux Critérium 51 ER et 52 ER sont livrés **rivés non brasés.**

These dimensions are given for guidance and it would be useful (considering the type of the frame and if a mudguard is fitted or not) to position the whole assembly (brake and stirrup) on the frame, as a trial.

Nota : Criterium pivots 51 ER and 52 ER are rivetted, **not brazed on.**

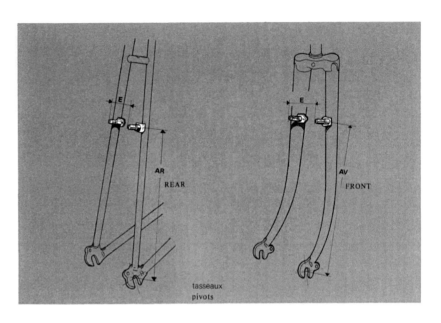

tasseaux
pivots

Tasseau T1 pour	T1 pivot for :
Compétition AV	Front Competition brake
2000 AV	Front "2000" "
Racer AV	Front Racer "
Raid AV	Front Raid "
Raid AR	Rear Raid "
"S" AV	Front "S" "

Tasseau T2 pour	T2 pivot for :
Compétition AR	Rear Competition brake
2000 AR	Rear "2000"
Racer AR	Rear racer "
"S" AR	Rear "S" "

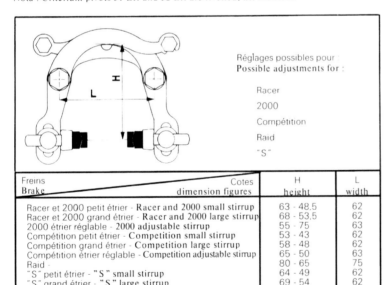

Réglages possibles pour :
Possible adjustments for :

Racer

2000

Compétition

Raid

"S"

Freins / Brake — Cotes / dimension figures	H / height	L / width
Racer et 2000 petit étrier - Racer and 2000 small stirrup	63 - 48.5	62
Racer et 2000 grand étrier - Racer and 2000 large stirrup	68 - 53.5	62
2000 étrier réglable - 2000 adjustable stirrup	55 - 75	63
Compétition petit étrier - Competition small stirrup	53 - 43	62
Compétition grand étrier - Competition large stirrup	58 - 48	62
Compétition étrier réglable - Competition adjustable stirrup	65 - 50	63
Raid -	80 - 65	75
"S" petit étrier - "S" small stirrup	64 - 49	62
"S" grand étrier - "S" large stirrup	69 - 54	62

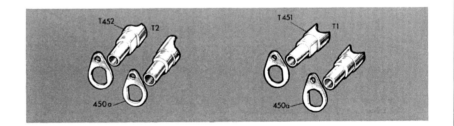

Frein _MAFAC_ ‹ Critérium ›

MAFAC « Criterium » brake

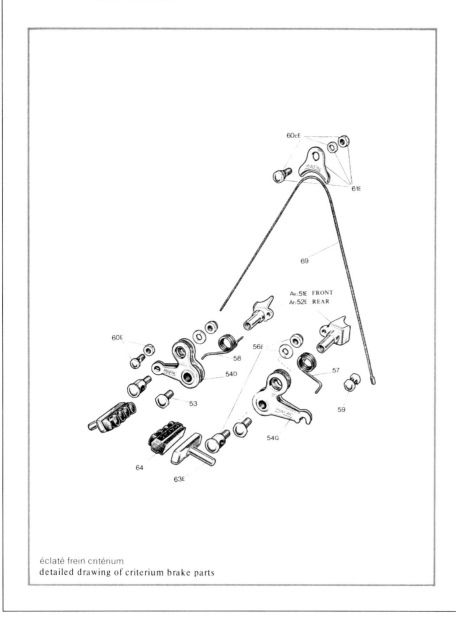

éclaté frein critérium
detailed drawing of criterium brake parts

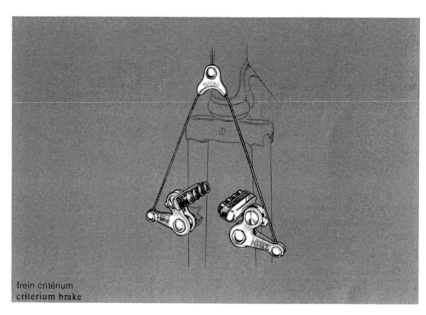

frein critérium
criterium brake

Présentation grand luxe	**KGL**
Super de luxe finish	KGL
Présentation luxe	**KL**
De luxe finish	KL

13

Frein _MAFAC_ ‹Jacky›

MAFAC «Jacky» brake

60cE

61E

269

Av:251E FRONT
Ar:252E REAR

260E

256E

258

255b

254D

250

257

254G

264

263E

éclaté frein Jacky
detailed drawing of Jacky brake parts

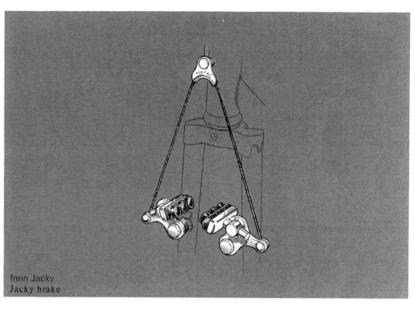

frein Jacky
Jacky brake

réf. J

For fitting on childrens' bikes. NB the braze on is different to all other Mafac brakes

15

Poignée inversée

Inverted lever

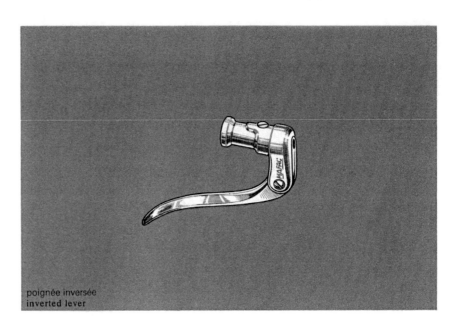

poignée inversée
inverted lever

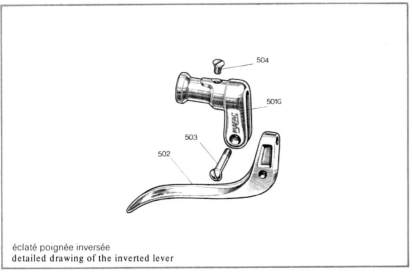

éclaté poignée inversée
detailed drawing of the inverted lever

réf. I/19,3 pour cintre Ø 22 acier
for steel handlebars bends of Ø 22 millimeters

réf. I/20,8 pour cintre Ø 23,5 acier
for steel handlebars bends of Ø 23,5 millimeters

réf. I/19,8 pour cintre Ø 23,5 dural
for dural handlebars bends of Ø 23,5 millimeters

16

Frein *MAFAC* ‹Cyclo-Tandem›
Pour cyclomoteurs et tandems

MAFAC «Cyclo-Tandem» brake
For mopeds and tandems

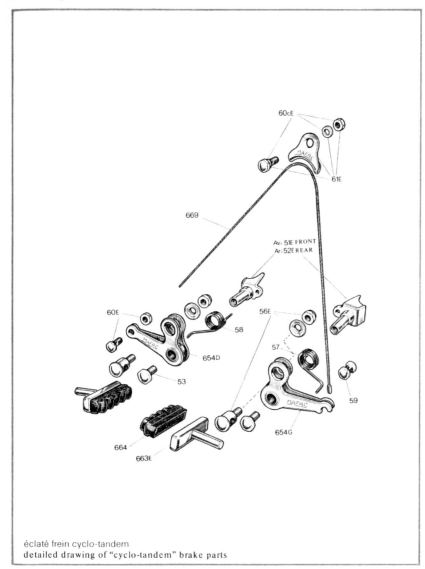

éclaté frein cyclo-tandem
detailed drawing of "cyclo-tandem" brake parts

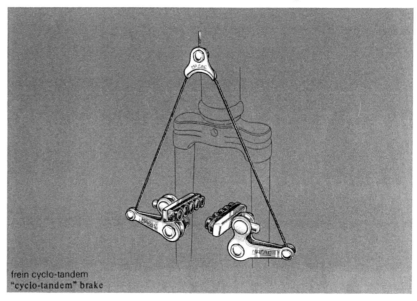

frein cyclo-tandem
"cyclo-tandem" brake

frein cyclo-tandem
"cyclo-tandem" brake

HC 4	avec patin 4 ventouses	with 4 studs blocks
HC 5	avec patin 5 ventouses	with 5 studs blocks

Présentation luxe :
De luxe finish

HZ 4	avec patin 4 ventouses	with 4 studs blocks
HZ 5	avec patin 5 ventouses	with 5 studs blocks

17

Supports

Holders

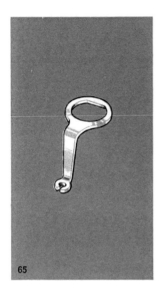

65

65 p

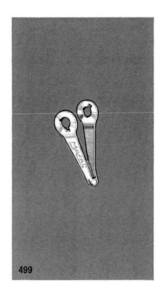

499

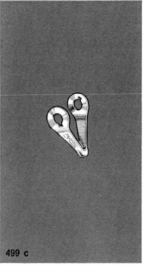

499 c

499 p

499 cp

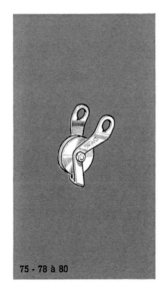

75 - 78 à 80

77 à 80

Présentation grand luxe :
Super de luxe finish

65	à méplat (alésage 25 ou 25,4)
	with flat part (internal diameter 25 or 25,4 millimeters)
65 P	à ergot
	with stop pin
499	pour boulon de selle à ergot
	for saddle bolt with stop pin
499 c	court, pour boulon de selle à ergot
	short, for saddle bolt with stop pin
499 P	pour boulon de selle à méplat
	for saddle bolt with flat part
499 cP	court, pour boulon de selle à méplat
	short, for saddle bolt with flat part

Présentation luxe :
De luxe finish

65 Z	à méplat (alésage 25 ou 25,4)
	with flat part (internal diameter 25 or 25,4 millimeters)
65 PZ	à ergot
	with stop pin
499 Z	pour boulon de selle à ergot
	for saddle bolt with stop pin
499 cZ	court, pour boulon de selle à ergot
	short, for saddle bolt with stop pin
499 PZ	pour boulon de selle à méplat
	for saddle bolt with flat part

18

Trousses

Tool-kits

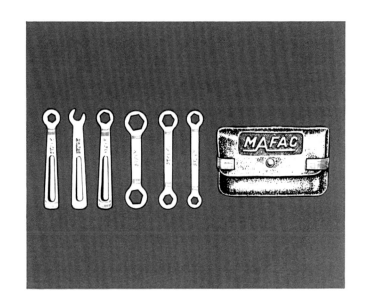

Trousse 45			Tool-kit 45		
1 démonte-pneu	**H 7**		1 tyre-lever	H 7	
1 démonte-pneu	**F 8**		1 tyre-lever	F 8	
1 démonte-pneu	**H 9**		1 tyre-lever	H 9	
1 clé double-œil	**12 x 14**		1 double-eyed spanner	12 x 14	
1 clé double-œil	**10 x 11**		1 double-eyed spanner	10 x 11	
1 clé double-œil	**8 x 9**		1 double-eyed spanner	8 x 9	

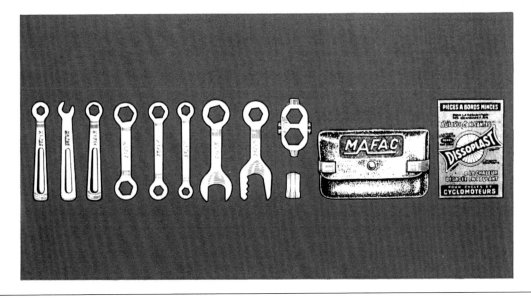

Trousse 48			Tool-kit 48		
1 démonte-pneu	**H 7**		1 tyre-lever	H 7	
1 démonte-pneu	**F 8**		1 tyre-lever	F 8	
1 démonte-pneu	**H 9**		1 tyre-lever	H 9	
1 clé double-œil	**12 x 14**		1 double-eyed spanner	12 x 24	
1 clé double-œil	**10 x 11**		1 double-eyed spanner	10 x 11	
1 clé double-œil	**8 x 9**		1 double-eyed spanner	8 x 9	
1 clé à pédale			1 pedal spanner		
1 clé à cône			1 cone spanner		
1 clé à rayon			1 spoke spanner		
1 clé tube	**8 x 9**		1 box spanner	8 x 9	
1 sachet réparation			1 repair kit		

MAFAC TOOL KITS

ALL MAFAC Tool Kits, CYCLEMOTOR, MOTORCYCLE or SCOOTER are supplied either in CLOTH TOOL ROLL or in solid, washable PLASTIC POUCH self fixing to any machine.

PLASTIC POUCH

CLOTH ROLL

From 1958 Ron Kitching *Everything Cycling* Catalogue

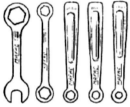

Model CYCLEMOTOR, M51.

5 items in treated steel forming 7 tools and 3 tyre levers.

Model CYCLEMOTOR, M61.

6 items in treated steel forming 9 tools and 3 tyre levers, screw driver and plug spanner.

Model M.18 for all models CYCLEMOTORS and MOBYLETTE. 8 items in treated steel forming 13 tools, 3 tyre levers, screw driver and plug spanner, complete with tube of solution and packet of patches.

Model 101—VELOMOTOR—MOTORCYCLE, 10 items in treated steel forming 17 tools, 3 tyre levers, screw driver, and plug spanner, complete with tube of solution and packet of patches.

MAFAC have carefully studied the requirements of users of CYCLE-MOTORS, VELOMOTORS and SCOOTERS and these tool kits although

MAFAC TOOL KITS

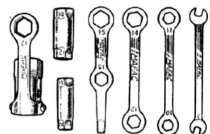

Model 71. Special VESPA

7 items in treated steel forming 14 tools and screw driver, complete with tube of solution and packet of patches

Model 91. Special LAMBRETTA

9 items in treated steel forming 16 tools and screw driver, complete with tube of solution and packet of patches

SUPER MAFAC Plug Spanner for CYCLEMOTOR — MOTORCYCLE

Length of tube : 100m/m — 75m/m — 50m/m
Box — 6 sides of 15 — 16 — 17 — 18 or 19.

SUPER-MAFAC Plug Spanner for MOTOR CAR.

Length of tube : 120m/m. Box : 120m/m —6 sides of 17.

See separate List for Prices

WEINMANN
Swiss Precision and Reliability

The best known Swiss maker of cycle parts, Weinmann were a large volume supplier of brakes and rims, especially in the 1970s when most British 'sports bikes' featured Weinmann as original equipment.

This was true for Raleigh, Carlton, Dawes and Falcon. Weinmann were most successful with their brakes and achieved a near dominance of the UK market, with only top end cycles featuring Mafac, Universal or Campagnolo. GB experienced a gradual decline throughout the 1960s and 70s with no real innovation after the end of the 1950s. Other makes, such as CLB (French), were rarely found on cycles outside their country of origin.

The company, based in Schaffhausen, northern Switzerland, was founded by Otto Weinmann, whose side pull brake was popular during the 1930s[1]. Weinmann brakes started appearing in the British market around 1949[2]. Originally made in steel, by the late 40s forged alloy parts were used. Prior to 1946 brakes did not have a model number.

In the mid 1950s the product range was as follows:

1. Side pull brakes: 730 standard and 500 close clearance models (Fig. 1). These were made until the late 1980s, and for over thirty years were the competitively priced core product. The 500 was always the cheapest option for equipping a close clearance frame and the design had a great influence on the emergent Far Eastern

The Choice of the Champions

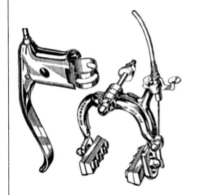

Swiss Light Metal Brakes can NOW be supplied: No. 730/730/144/66 Q.R. or 500/730/144/66 Q.R. with Stirrups and Levers in RED, BLUE or SILVER anodised finish with cables to match at 45/- pair.

No. 144 Levers only in all SILVER or HOOD Silver Lever RED or BLUE anodised 16/6d. pair.

In Standard highly polished 41/9d. and 15/- respectively.

Without No. 66 Quick Release 38/- pair.

No. 730/810 (slightly deeper rear stirrup) with No. 136 TOURIST Lever 35/- pair. WEINMANN Beige Rubber Hoods for No. 144 Levers, 5/6d. pair.

No. 66: Weinmann quick-release fitment allows instantaneous release of brake cable tension for speedy wheel removal. Can be fitted to any pattern Weinmann brake. 5/- pair.

Weinmann studded brake blocks, 1¼in. or 1½in.—10d. pair. Complete with brake shoes—2/3d. pair.

No. 136: TOURIST Lever. 12/- pair.

High pressure rim from the Weinmann range with depressed nipple holes and serrated braking surface. 40/- pair.

Fig. 1 Walter Flory advertisement *Coureur, Sporting Cyclist* February 1958.

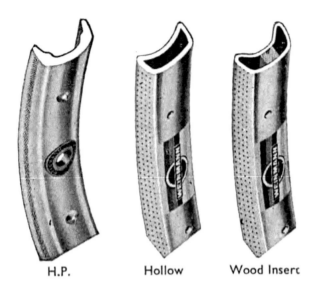

Fig. 2 A section of a Flory advertisement in *Coureur, Sporting Cyclist* January 1959.

manufacturers. There were longer reach versions, the 810, 890 and 1020, originally for balloon tyred bikes. There was also a cheaper version for children's bikes, the 'Junior.' The 730 was also made in the 1950s under another model name, 'Capella', and these are extremely rare. 730 brakes fitted to Dawes cycles in the 50s and 60s carried the trade name 'Talon'.

The numeric model number refers to the mid-point reach in mm, with another zero added. Thus the 500 model has between 43mm and 56mm reach.

2. Rims (Fig. 2): Wood insert sprint rim model 'Scherens' weighing 11½ oz. Hollow sprint rim, the 'Criterium', weighing 10⅕ oz. High pressure rim, model name 'Alesa' (box section), weighing 18oz. Endrick rim weighing 22oz.

Sizes available in Britain were 27 x 1¼, 26 x 1³/₈ and 26 x 1¼, and later, 700c.

3. Alloy wing nuts, larger than normal, with a circular cut out on the two wings, stamped Weinmann. Anodised blue and gold versions were also made, but only in the 1960s.

Weinmann products were initially imported by Walter Flory, a Swiss national who also imported components from Lucifer, Lapize, Huret, Pletscher and Maillard. He advertised regularly in the cycling press, especially *in Coureur, Sporting Cyclist*. On Flory's retirement the agency was transferred to R J Chicken, a relationship that lasted until the 1990s.

In 1957 Weinmann introduced centre pull brakes, the longer reach 750, and the shorter 610. The model name given to these was 'Vainqueur' (Victor) 999.

Fig. 3 Weinmann brakes from a *Coureur, Sporting Cyclist* advertisement 1959

They were first imported to Britain in 1959[3] (Fig. 3), and mainly used by racing cyclists for the first few years. Mafac and Universal were the major competitors. From the late 1960s most racers used side pulls, a change accelerated by the introduction of the Campagnolo sidepull in 1969. The 610 and 750 became popular amongst tourists and were fitted to all Dawes Galaxies (the most successful 'off the peg' tourer) until the mid 80s, when there was a move to cantilevers.

OTHER PRODUCTS:

While the foregoing were the core Weinmann products the company also made:

1. A dual pivot brake, the 'Dynamic', in the late 60s. It was similar to the better known GB dual pivot, the 'Synchron', itself the result of a joint venture between GB and Altenburger in the early 1960s. For some reason the 'Dynamic' was not successful in the UK. It was claimed these brakes offered the advantages of a side pull (easy to set up) without the disadvantages (hard to centre) and were simpler than a centre pull in that they did not require straddle cables and hangers. The bushing was made from Delrin© as were Mafac 'Racers' from this date. In the 1980s this was redesigned and became known as the 'Symmetric'. Later in the 1980s it was referred to by the initials PBS, but by this time had become a very down market product.

2. A two piece handlebar stem (late 60s to mid 70s), the vertical part being steel, the extension alloy (Fig. 4).

3. Alloy chainsets and chainrings (five pin).were made in the 1950s and were not successful, hence are very rare.

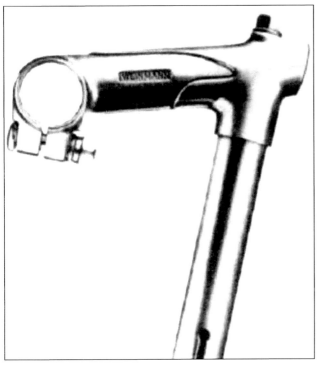

Fig. 4 Weinmann stem. the vertical part steel the horizontal alloy

4. Cantilever brakes. Two versions both made in the mid 80s:
   - A Mafac copy produced after Mafac went out of business around 1984, when apparently Weinmann bought the tooling.
   - A model aimed specifically at the ATB market.
5. Superior quality side pull brakes:
   - 605 with quick release on the stirrup.
   - 'Carrera', a high priced Campagnolo copy in the mid 70s
   - the top model (Fig. 5).
   - 400, black anodised, close clearance.

BRAKES

WEINMANN

CARRERA

A really up-to-date anodised sidepull brake incorporating the refinements and attention to detail for which the Swiss are famous. Every bearing is plastic bushed, rattle-free and non-binding. Butterfly quick-release with twist off action gives ½cm rim clearance. Black X-pattern patented blocks in sealed shoes with wheel guides. Depth adjustable 45-60mm. Levers are drilled with translucent rubber hoods. Complete with graphite lubricated cables.

Boxed set £55.20

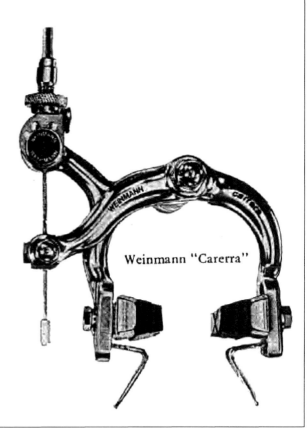

Weinmann "Carerra"

Fig. 5 Top of the range Carrera sidepull from *Holdsworthy Aids* 1981

6. Polished alloy mudguards, stays fitted in French style. Also short 'racer ' mudguards which were popular in the 70s and fitted to many 'sports' racing bikes. Needless to say they offered no protection against the elements.
7. Brake tools: allen keys, brake clamp bolt spanner, inverse allen key, third hand brake tool.
8. Late 70s concave rims. These were extremely strong but could lead to corrosion of the spoke nipples due to the shape of the rim retaining road salt.
9. Valve inserts: model Alligaro (1950s). According to Weinmann: 'makes pumping almost a pleasure….'
10. 730 and 500 brakes in gold, red and blue anodised. These were stamped 'De Luxe'.
11. Lever sleeves, white plastic, which covered three quarters of the lever blade. Hooked to improve finger grip

MODEL CHANGES

1. Early versions of the centre pulls have arms with a different curve. The last version of these brakes has the name and model on a black background as opposed to the earlier red. There is a version of this brake with solid flat metal instead of a straddle cable (model 737), produced in the early 1980s.
2. Original versions of the side pulls have the name stamped in large letters on the brake arm without any border – until the late 60s, and the larger the lettering, the earlier the brake.

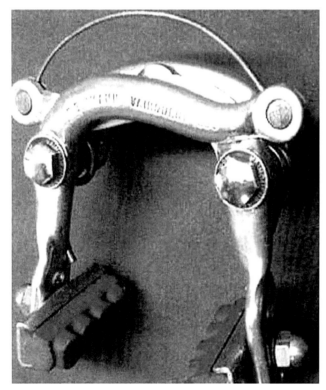

Fig. 6 An earlier Vainqueur 1957 – early 1960s.

Fig. 7 Later version of Vainqueur – 1970s/80s. Final version had the model number on a black background rather than red

3. Final versions of the side pulls have the forward centre bolt replaced with a black plastic reverse Allen key fitting. I think this was designed to make centring easier although to me it looks very cheap.
4. Earlier wheel rims had a smooth surface; later ones have a recessed channel running near the edge on either side.
5. Later Weinmann rims are marked 'Made in Belgium' and were made in the Alesa factory in Antwerp. This company was established in 1946 as a joint venture between Otto Weinmann and Belgian Tom Beyltjens[4]. Now owned by Rigida, rims are still made to this day under the Alesa trademark (and very good touring rims they are too).

DATING

– Some brakes have the month and year of manufacture on the rear of the arms, eg 0576 = May 1976.
– Levers up to about 1964 have 'Made in Switzerland' stamped on one side of the upper lever blade (visible when lever is open).
– Progressively the writing on the brake arms became smaller and finally was enclosed in a rectangle.
– Later products are stamped 'Made in Belgium'.

PERCEPTIONS AND PERFORMANCE

Weinmann brakes and rims are not generally highly regarded by club cyclists, nor by V-CC members. They rarely sell at cycle jumbles, lacking the period appeal of GB and CLB, or the stylish appeal of Mafac and Universal. I think this is because they were used widely in Britain as original equipment on many 'starter' cycles. In terms of performance my view is as follows:

1. Rims – Are generally excellent, hard wearing and trouble free and liked by wheel builders. However, on some 1970s high pressure rims the braking surface is very narrow.
2. Brakes – I find the side pulls always seem to need centring but provide smooth and effective braking. The longer reach 810 and 890 models suffer from flex due to the length of the arms and are best avoided. Apart from the first generation, the centre pulls are too spongy for my liking, and not surprisingly, as the Marque Enthusiast, I prefer Mafac.
3. Levers – I personally don't find the levers comfortable. I think this is because the top of the

blade by the pivot is flat, not curved. I find cable replacement can be fiddly as the nipple tends to pop out of the lever end when setting up. A further problem is the lever pivots become loose due to wear and there is no easy way to tighten them.

4. Lever Hoods –Are hard wearing; maybe its just personal preference, but I find the ribbed design uncomfortable.

With the move of manufacturing to Belgium (starting in the late 1960s, but a gradual process) there was a definite drop in the quality of products.

DEMISE

After the mid 1960s there was very little innovation, and Weinmann essentially produced the core products of rim and brakes for the next 25 years. Their popular 1970s 'Safety Levers' (an extra arm from the lever running parallel with the flat of the drop bar) were in fact a Dia-Compe patent licensed by Weinmann. I am of the view that the presence of these levers automatically relegates a bike to low price/ quality. That they became a requirement for bikes imported into the USA shows just how little cycle braking is understood by non-cycling regulators.

In the 1980s the company relied increasingly on licensing products from Dia-Compe, which at that time was the world's largest volume cycle brake producer. Thus Weinmann Aero brakes are in fact badged Dia-Compe products. Interestingly Weinmann first worked with this Japanese firm on technical development as far back as 1963.

Weinmann ceased trading in 1988. Like many other companies it failed to make the transition to mountain bikes, pricing their MTB brakes too high for the market[5]. Mavic cornered the rim market and Shimano moved into brakes. Alesa still survives as a maker of rims, based in Belgium and a subsidiary of Rigida.

Brake Reach

MODEL	Min. (mm)	Max (mm
400	40	54
500	43	56
730 Junior/Capella	56	75
810	60	79
890	68	85
605 & Carrera	45	58
610 centre pull	50	65
750 & 737 centre pulls	53	80
Dynamic Model 712	54	68
Dynamic Model 812	62	79

.

References

[1] Graeme Fife, Bob Chicken *A Passion for the Bike*, (London 2005) p192. This book gives much information on the business relationship between Bob Chicken and Otto Weinmann.

[2] *Cycling* 25 August 1949 p213 refers to the importation of Lucifer, Huret and Weinmann by Walter Flory.

[3] *Sporting Cyclist* Jan 1959.

[4] Graeme Fife, Bob Chicken *A Passion for the Bike*, (London 2005) p 196. 5 Ibid p 268.

[5] Ibid p 268

Sources

Holdsworth Aids from 1958 to 1981.
Sporting Cyclist, late 50s and early 60s.
Walter Flory's advertisements in *Sporting Cyclist* 1956 to 1963.

My thanks to Hansjurg Albrecht, a Swiss V-CC member, for first hand information, and Ray Miller for information from the V-CC library.

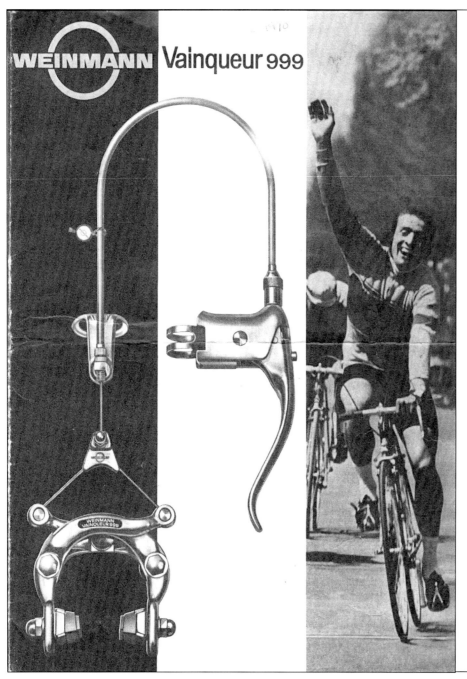

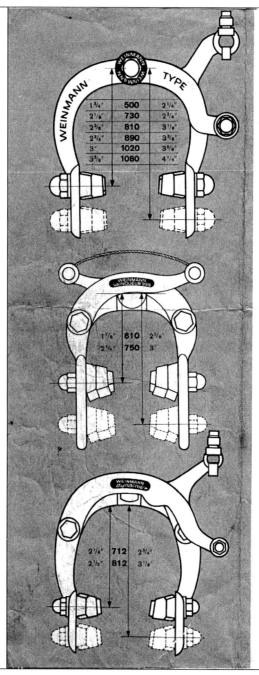

Complete WEINMANN Brakes

The most popular Side Pull Brakes

Ref. No.	Front	Rear	Lever	Price	
	500	500	161	42/–	pair
	500	730	161	42/–	pair
	730	730	161	42/–	pair
	730	730	144	39/–	pair
	810	810	144	39/–	pair
	890	890	144	39/–	pair
	730	810	136	34/6	pair
	730	730	133	30/–	pair
	730	730	131	30/–	pair

The New

WEINMANN VAINQUEUR

symetric action Centre Pull Brake

999 (610/750)

Ref. No.	Front	Rear	Lever	Price	
	610	750	144	57/6	pair
	610	750	161	60/–	pair
*	610	610	161	60/–	pair
	750	750	161	60/–	pair
	610	750	162	67/6	pair

* with translucent R/Hoods.

DYNAMIC Side Pull with CENTRE

Pull action braking .

Ref. No.	Front	Rear	Lever	Price	
	712	712	144	50/–	pair
	712	712	161	52/6	pair
	712	712	136	47/6	pair

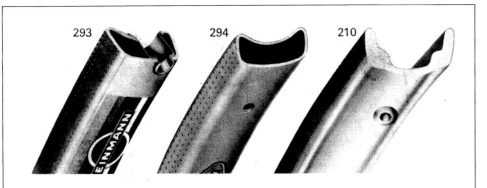

WEINMANN Precision Light Metal Rims

Ref. No.		Price
210	26″ and 27 × 1¼″ 32/40 or 36/36 H	
	High Pressure	40/– pair
293	27″ New hollow sprint rim with built-in	
	spoke ferrules 36/36 H only (12 ozs.)	80/– pair
294	27″ Hollow 32/40 or 36/36 with	
	N/washers (13 ozs.)	65/– pair

WEINMANN Cables Guaranteed breaking strength over 500 lbs.

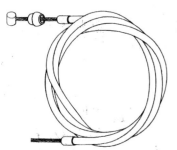

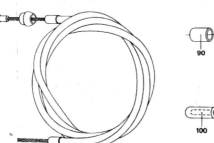

90

100

For TOURIST Levers
131, 133, 135, 136, 151 & 154
(with Barrel Nipples)

Ref. No.		Price
80.741	Front inner cable only 29″	1/– each
80.1321	Rear inner cable only 52″	1/6 each
80.1591	L/Rear inner cable only 63″	1/9 each
84.74	Front inner and outer cables	2/6 each
84.132	Rear inner and outer cables	3/9 each
84.159	L/Rear inner and outer cables	4/6 each
90	Ferrules for outer cable	–/2 each
100	Inner cable end ferrule	–/2 each

For Racing Levers
144, 160, 161 & 162
(with Pear shaped Nipples)

Ref. No.		Price
86.741	Front inner cable only 29″	1/– each
86.1321	Rear inner cable only 52″	1/6 each
86.1591	L/Rear inner cable only 63″	1/9 each
86.74	Front inner and outer cables	2/6 each
86.132	Rear inner and outer cables	3/9 each
86.159	L/Rear inner and outer cables	4/6 each

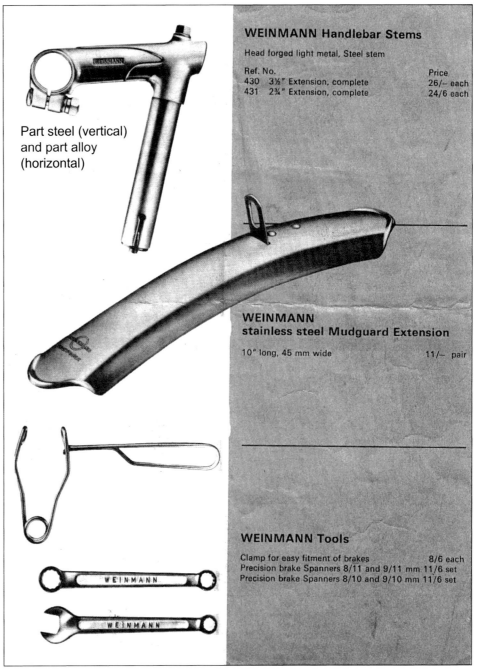

WEINMANN Handlebar Stems

Head forged light metal, Steel stem

Ref. No.		Price
430	3½″ Extension, complete	26/– each
431	2¾″ Extension, complete	24/6 each

Part steel (vertical)
and part alloy
(horizontal)

WEINMANN
stainless steel Mudguard Extension

10″ long, 45 mm wide   11/– pair

WEINMANN Tools

Clamp for easy fitment of brakes   8/6 each
Precision brake Spanners 8/11 and 9/11 mm 11/6 set
Precision brake Spanners 8/10 and 9/10 mm 11/6 set

179

Retail Prices for **WEINMANN** Replacement Parts

WEINMANN Side pull brake

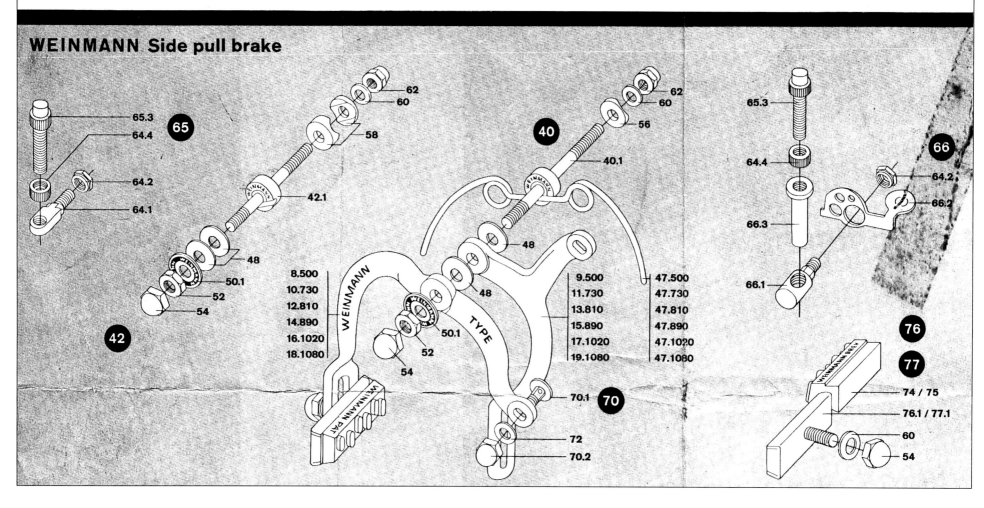

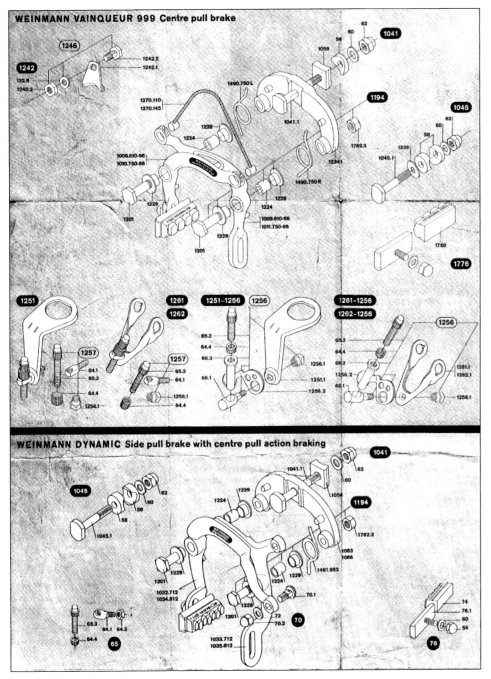

WEINMANN VAINQUEUR 999 Centre pull brake

WEINMANN DYNAMIC Side pull brake with centre pull action braking

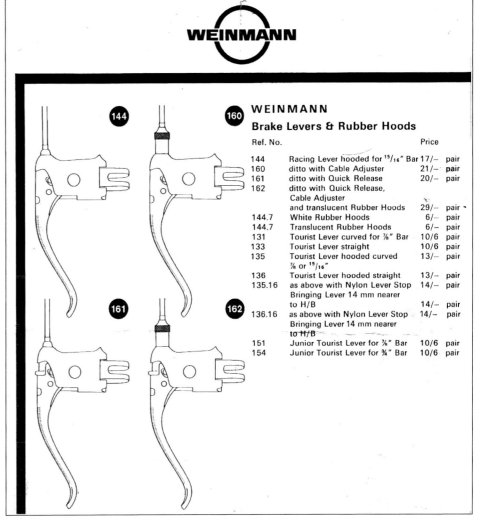

WEINMANN
Brake Levers & Rubber Hoods

Ref. No.		Price	
144	Racing Lever hooded for $^{15}/_{16}$" Bar	17/–	pair
160	ditto with Cable Adjuster	21/–	pair
161	ditto with Quick Release	20/–	pair
162	ditto with Quick Release, Cable Adjuster and translucent Rubber Hoods	29/–	pair
144.7	White Rubber Hoods	6/–	pair
144.7	Translucent Rubber Hoods	6/–	pair
131	Tourist Lever curved for $^{7}/_{8}$" Bar	10/6	pair
133	Tourist Lever straight	10/6	pair
135	Tourist Lever hooded curved $^{7}/_{8}$ or $^{15}/_{16}$"	13/–	pair
136	Tourist Lever hooded straight	13/–	pair
135.16	as above with Nylon Lever Stop Bringing Lever 14 mm nearer to H/B	14/–	pair
136.16	as above with Nylon Lever Stop Bringing Lever 14 mm nearer to H/B	14/–	pair
151	Junior Tourist Lever for $^{7}/_{8}$" Bar	10/6	pair
154	Junior Tourist Lever for $^{3}/_{4}$" Bar	10/6	pair

What would now be called a dual pivot brake.

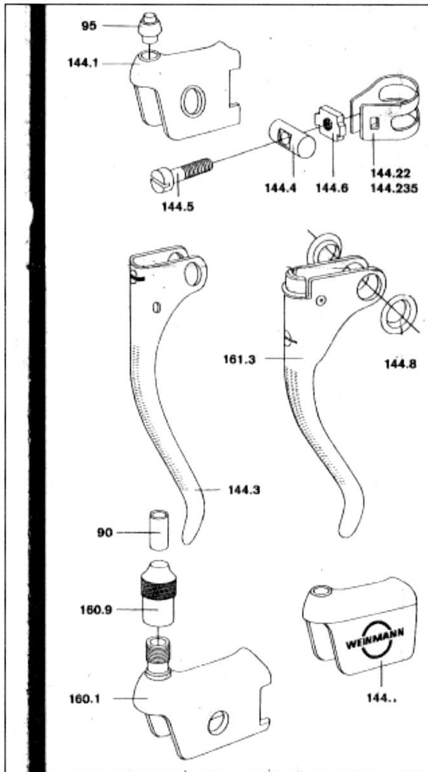

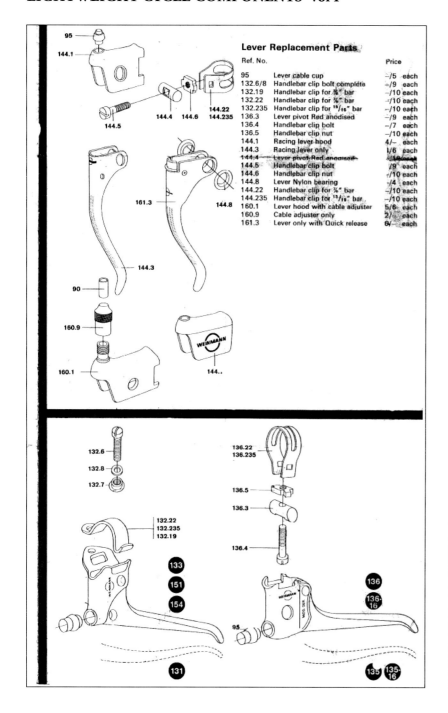

Lever Replacement Parts

Ref. No.		Price	
95	Lever cable cup	–/5	each
132.6/8	Handlebar clip bolt complete	–/9	each
132.19	Handlebar clip for ⅝" bar	–/10	each
132.22	Handlebar clip for ⅞" bar	–/10	each
132.235	Handlebar clip for ¹⁵/₁₆" bar	–/10	each
136.3	Lever pivot Red anodised	–/9	each
136.4	Handlebar clip bolt	–/7	each
136.5	Handlebar clip nut	–/10	each
144.1	Racing lever hood	4/–	each
144.3	Racing lever only	1/6	each
~~144.4~~	~~Lever pivot Red anodised~~	[illegible]	~~each~~
144.5	Handlebar clip bolt	–/9	each
144.6	Handlebar clip nut	–/10	each
144.8	Lever Nylon bearing	–/4	each
144.22	Handlebar clip for ⅞" bar	–/10	each
144.235	Handlebar clip for ¹⁵/₁₆" bar	–/10	each
160.1	Lever hood with cable adjuster	5/6	each
160.9	Cable adjuster only	2/–	each
161.3	Lever only with Quick release	6/–	each

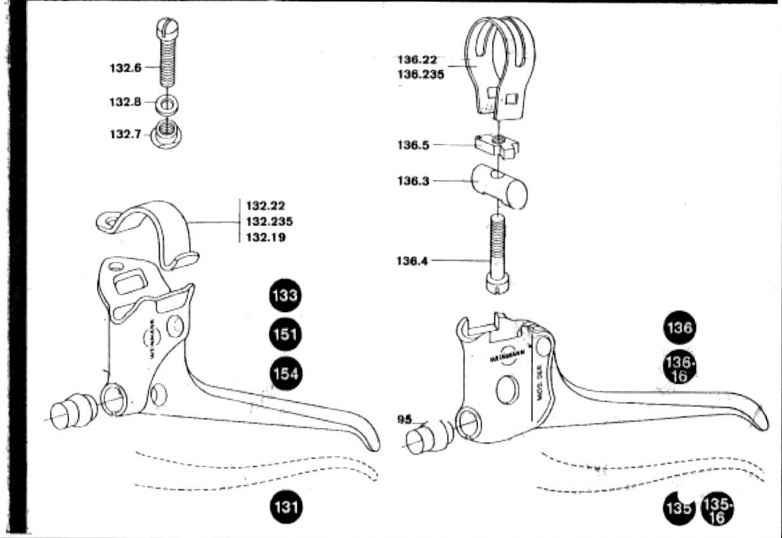

Replacement Parts for:

WEINMANN, VAINQUEUR & DYNAMIC Brakes

Ref. No.		Price	
8.500	Left Stirrup for No. 500	5/6	each
9.500	Right Stirrup for No. 500	5/6	each
10.730	Left Stirrup for No. 730	5/6	each
11.730	Right Stirrup for No. 730	5/6	each
12.810	Left Stirrup for No. 810	5/6	each
13.810	Right Stirrup for No. 810	5/6	each
14.890	Left Stirrup for No. 890	5/6	each
15.890	Right Stirrup for No. 890	5/6	each
16.1020	Left Stirrup for No. 1020	7/–	each
17.1020	Right Stirrup for No. 1020	7/–	each
18.1080	Left Stirrup for No. 1080	10/–	each
19.1080	Right Stirrup for No. 1080	10/–	each
40	Front pivot bolt complete	4/6	each
40.1	Front pivot bolt only	2/9	each
42	Rear pivot bolt complete	4/6	each
42.1	Rear pivot bolt only	2/9	each
47.500	Caliper spring for No. 500	–/10	each
47.730	Caliper spring for No. 730	–/10	each
47.810	Caliper spring for No. 810	–/10	each
47.890	Caliper spring for No. 890	–/10	each
47.1020	Caliper spring for No. 1020	1/–	each
47.1080	Caliper spring for No. 1080	1/6	each
48	Pivot washer for No. 40/42	–/2	each
50.1	Weinmann anodised disc	–/4	each
52	Pivot lock nut	–/4	each
54	Pivot and B/shoe nut, domed	–/7	each
56	Pivot seating pad for No. 40	–/4	each
58	Pivot seating pad for No. 42	–/10	each
60	Pivot and Brake shoe washer	–/2	each
62	Brake fixing nut	–/7	each
64.1	Eye bolt for adjuster sleeve	–/7	each
64.2	Eye bolt nut	–/3	each
64.4	Adjuster lock nut	–/5	each
65	Cable adjuster complete	1/9	each
65.3	Cable adjuster	–/7	each
66	Quick release complete	4/6	each
66.1	Adjuster eye bolt	1/3	each
66.2	Quick release Cam	1/–	each
66.3	Cable adjuster socket	1/2	each
70	Cable clamp bolt complete	1/–	each
70.2	Cable clamp domed nut	–/4	each
72	Clamp bolt washer	–/2	each
74	Brake blocks 1⅜" long	1/–	pair
75	Brake blocks 1⅝" long	1/–	pair
76	Brake blocks and shoes 1⅜"	2/6	pair
77	Brake blocks and shoes 1⅝"	2/6	pair

1008.610.66	Left studded stirrup arm	6/6	each
1009.610.66	Right grooved stirrup arm	6/–	each
1010.750.66	Left studded stirrup arm	6/6	each
1011.750.66	Right grooved stirrup arm	6/–	each
1032.712	Left stirrup arm	7/–	each
~~1033.712~~	~~Right stirrup arm~~	~~6/–~~	~~each~~
1034.812	Left stirrup arm	7/–	each
1035.812	Right stirrup arm	6/–	each
1041	Front pivot bolt complete	4/–	each
1041.1	Front pivot bolt only	2/6	each
1045	Rear pivot bolt complete	4/–	each
1045.1	Rear pivot bolt only	2/6	each
1056	Square seating pad	–/10	each
1083	Back stirrup for 812	6/6	each
1086	Back stirrup for 712	6/6	each
1194	Stirrup pivot complete (1201, 1229, 1224 and 1782.3)	3/6	each
1201	Pivot bolt only	1/6	each
1224	Stirrup bush	–/8	each
1229	DELRIN bearing	–/4	each
1234.1	Back Plate for 610 and 750	6/6	each
1235	Pivot washer for 1045	–/3	each
1242	Straddle cable bridge complete	2/6	each
1246	Cable clamp bolt complete	1/6	each
1250	Front hanger complete (dogged)	6/9	each
1250/1256	with Quick release (dogged)	9/6	each
1251	Front hanger complete (flatted)	6/9	each
1251/1256	with Quick release (flatted)	9/6	each
1256	Quick release only	5/–	each
1256.1	Quick release bolt nut	–/6	each
1256.2	Quick release cam	1/–	each
1257	Cable adjuster complete	2/–	each
1261	Rear hanger complete	6/–	each
1261/1256	with Quick release	9/–	each
1262	Extra short rear hanger 22 mm wide	6/–	each
1262	Extra short rear hanger 30 mm wide	6/–	each
1270.110	Straddle cable 4¾" long	2/6	each
1270.145	Straddle cable 5¾" long	2/6	each
1461.952	Return spring for 712/812	1/3	each
1490.750	Left and Right spring for 610/750	2/–	pair
1750	1⅝" long extra deep brake blocks	1/2	pair
1776	1⅝" long extra deep Blocks and Shoes	2/9	pair
1782.3	Pivot nut for 1194	–/4	each

WEINMANN Brakes and Rims are universally known for their superior finish and precision workmanship and have long been the first choice of the World's Leading Riders.

Stirrups are forged from special light alloy, rustproof and highly polished and are available in various depths to suit all types of cycles and wheels.

The maximum and minimum stirrup range to which brake shoes can effectively be adjusted is shown against each Number, measured from the middle of the centre bolt.

Brake sets listed are made up by pairing the most suitable Front and Rear stirrup to fit all popular frames.

Levers are forged special alloy of modern design with Nylon bearings to ensure smooth operation. The large choice of Levers should meet all requirements for Racing and Touring viz No. 144 hooded Standard, 160 incorporating cable adjuster, 161 Quick Release, 162 Quick Release and cable adjuster. Hooded Tourist 135 and 136, apart from popular 131, 133 and Junior 151 and 154, the latter for ¾" bars.

Central Pivot Bolts are of High Tensile Steel, Nuts and bolts are precision made and rustproof.

Brake Cables have a guaranteed breaking strength of over 500 lbs., are well greased before leaving the factory ensuring long life and smooth braking.

Brake Blocks of exclusive studded pattern provide the most effective and safe braking in all weather conditions.

No. 75 1⅝" long and No. 74 1⅜" in red or grey are fitted to all brakes except VAINQUEUR 999 Centre Pull which are supplied with very deep 1⅝" long No. 1750 brake blocks specially suitable for Sprint Rims and for hilly country.

WEINMANN Rims made of special alloy are rigid, seamless, durable and extremely light in weight. They are manufactured to precision limit, their accuracy and perfect static balance not only ensuring easy wheel building, but providing wheels that will remain true almost indefinitely.

For Racing: No. 294 27" hollow with nipple washers 32/40 or 36/36 H
293 27" hollow with inserted spoke ferrules 36/36 H only
For Touring: 210 26 or 27" High Pressure 32/40 or 36/36 H

When fitting WEINMANN you may rest assured that you could have made no wiser choice.
The Trade name WEINMANN is your GUARANTEE.

WEINMANN Ltd. Schaffhausen (Switzerland)

Printed in Switzerland

Sole U.K. Distributor: Stockist:
WALTER FLORY
20/21, Duncan Terrace. London N.1
OBTAINABLE through all Leading Dealers

T.A. CHAINRINGS & CRANKS

I really rate T.A., the chainrings have an incredibly long life and are still useable even when the teeth have been worn and sharpen to needle like points!

Also they made odd size rings rather than most makers who just do even or popular sizes. The cranks were made in increments of 2.5mm from 150 to 185mm. No other manufacturer ever made such a range!

However I have only recently come to understand the different versions which this article attempts to clarify.

Chainrings

T.A. started making rings in 1948 up to the early 60's the cut outs were done by hand (look for the saw marks). The earliest rings have on the outside the French aluminium trade mark: 'forge duralinium cedegur' within an oval and the early T.A. logo, a chainwheel with T above and A below. Sometime in the 1950's the two were incorporated into one logo. On the inside of the ring is the size between: 'Made in' and 'France'. At some point, I think in the 70's the cedegur trade mark was dropped Due to lack of space many smaller rings are only marked with the size and 'Made in

France' on the inside . More recent rings have the size on the outside and are the marked 'Specialities T.A.'. None of the adapters are stamped at all

T.A. made the following models with the inner(s) ring attaching by six arms to the outer:

1. Cycletourist 5 pin the most common for double or triple range 26 to 56 , although large rings could be made to special order. Inner 80 PCD. Aimed at tourists but widely used by other riders.

2. Randonneur: 5 pin and 3 arm the standard continental size (Inner 116 PCD) for double or

triple, range 36 to 43 inner and 44 to 68 outer.. Described as being for club riders. These are the rarest rings to find. The 3 arm outers were initially made with six bolt holes so they could be used with 3 or 6 arm inners.

3. Criterium : 5 pin and 3 arms (Inner 152 PCD) for double or triple range inner 43 upwards and 47 to 68 outer.   Described as for amateurs of all categories.

Extremely unusual in the triple version as few riders would bother with a triple with an inner ring of 43 or above

In the 50's T.A. developed the adaptor system aimed at Professional & Independent riders which enabled rings to be changed without the need to remove the crank from the bottom bracket as is the case with the above rings. All adaptors are designed for 6 arm rings the same as the Criterium inner ring PCD (152mm). The range of rings was also the same 43 to 68. These were called Professional rings Adaptors were made from about 1953 as follows:

5 pin: single or double/triple

3 arm: single or double/triple

For all the above types the outer rings are countersunk on the outside, inner on the inside.

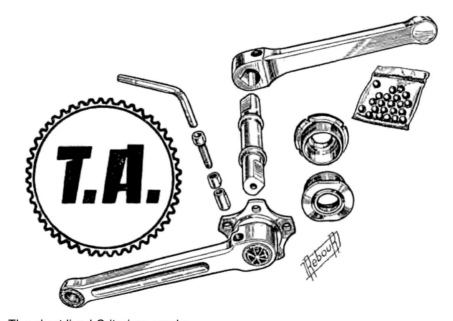

The short lived Criterium cranks

Left: 1st generation ring stamping (40s early 50s)
Right: 2nd generation stamping late 50s

T.A. Single Rings:

5 pin 26 to 68, 3/32 and 1/8. NB all T.A. 1/8 rings are stamped on the inside with a '3'. Also inch pitch 20 to 34.

All single rings are only drilled for the crank attachment.

There was also a Cyclo Cross model which was a standard single 5 pin ring but with a protector disc bolted on either side at 6 points at 152mm PCD.

The larger size rings are useful for small wheel bikes eg Moultons.

3 arm 36 to 68 3/32 and 1/8 and inch pitch 20 to 34

Cranks

T.A. only started to making cranks in the late 50's. Initially they offered a 5 pin with a kite shaped cotter fitted with an allen key. This is sometimes called the Criterium This required a special

bottom bracket and had the benefit of offering some lateral movement to get the perfect chainline. However they do not seem to have been successful, some users complained the alloy cotter pin wore out quickly.

From 1963 they made the classic 5 pin cotterless cranks, correctly known as the Pro 5 Viz. The 50.4mm PCD are the same as cranks produced in the 1920s by Cyclo. Albert Raimond , the founder of Cyclo. He used the same system as T.A. i.e. inner rings bolting on to the outer but he used a smaller PCD which meant with Cyclo you could have a 24 inner compared to 26 for T.A..

T.A. also made the elegant Rene Herses cranks and a version of the Pro 5 for Alex Singer with a slighter greater ring crank clearance for front mechs.

At the end of the 1960s T.A. produced a 3 arm crank. This was based on the defacto European standard 116 PCD . This was favoured by Beryl Burton who judging from pictures was using at least a 54 outer. NB the left hand cranks are exactly the same for both models.

Many riders find T.A. cranks extremely comfortable to pedal a consequence perhaps of their very low Q factor (a narrow distance between the pedals as the cranks are straight)

A major disadvantage is that it is necessary to remove the crank to change the rings. Also the gap between ring inner crank surface is only 11mm which is quite tight for some front mechs, hence the number of cranks you see marked by the front mech outer cage.

There is only one correct position to fit the outer/single ring to the 5 pin cranks so that the

crank is equi-distant between ring cut outs.

T.A. bottom brackets: single ref 314, double ref 344 and triple ref 373 or wider ref 374

Crank identification:

1. Early cranks have the cedegur trade mark on the front and the rear of the pedal thread is blanked out except for a tiny oil hole There is no T.A. black and white transfer, the fluting is left bank.
2. Cranks marked W are British thread
3. Cranks marked   G are tandem so check the pedal threads on these as all bar one right hand crank will be reverse threaded
4. Later cranks (90's) are marked BSC and a letter number eg F2 or M7. I think this is a year / month code but I am unable to confirm this.
5. The most recent cranks have T.A. laser etched on the front rather than the transfer. T.A. last made a batch of these cranks in 2007 for their 60th anniversary.

In 1976 T.A. made a Campagnolo copy (144 PCD) marketed under the Tevano trademark, both cranks and rings. The name was derived from T.A.'s founder Georges Navet's name spelt backwards with an 'o' added.

Chainring bolts

These were originally acorn headed on the crank side but was changed to a flat 8mm bolt. The various types:

- Ref 25 crank to outer/single ring
- Ref 43 3 arm crank to single ring
- Ref 64 inner to outer ring for Cycletourists, Randonneur and Criterium doubles
- Ref 85 inner and middle to outer ring for

Randonneur and Criterium triples
- Ref 87   ditto for Cycletourist triple
- Ref 62 for Professional doubles i.e. with Adaptor
- Ref 84 for Professional triples

There was also a pair of extended bolts which fitted either side of the crank to prevent the chain jamming in the event of it derailing.

T.A. rings can be used with the Stronglight 49D cranks (indeed for many years this was the classic combination) although the T.A. bottom brackets are not always the right length. Many other makers produced cranks in this PCD eg Milremo & Gnutti. Zeus made a copy but annoying with slightly different PCD so the rings are not interchangeable.

T.A. was very closely associated with Ron Kitching in the UK, who to his credit imported the entire range. My 1970 *Everything Cycling* has a picture of Ron holding the smallest ring, a 26 and the largest a 100 made for a world record attempt on rollers. In fact the relationship was so close that Ron was able to register the T.A. trademark in the UK.

Other T.A. products include: shoe plates, bottles and cages, front handlebar bags and carriers, headsets, pedals, brake cable guides and tools. The vast majority were very high products and in many cases set the benchmark for quality and innovation.

Finally T.A. stands for Traction Avant an ill fated attempt at a front wheel drive system in the late 1940s.

References

Ron Kitching: Everything Cycling is the best references. I have used 1963, 1970 and 1983 in researching this article.

Vintage Bicycle Quarterly has two excellent articles on TA:
Vol 5 no 4: review of T.A. and Stronglight49D
Vol 6 no.1   interview with the current owners of T.A. and review of products

There is some very useful information on the following website:
www.classiclightweights.co.uk

Useful summary of TA rings and cranks and numerous illustrations www.blackbird.com
Illustrations of practically every T.A. product

CHAINWHEELS OF THE CHAMPIONS

RON KITCHEN
EVERYTHING CYCLING
1960

Tested by the World's best riders, proving that they are the World's best chainwheels, TA fitments have been the automatic choice of :—

FAUSTO COPPI
Twice winner Tour de France
Winner Tour of Italy
World's Road Champion
Hour Record, etc.

JACQUES ANQUETIL
Winner Grand Prix des Nations
1953-58
Tour de France
Hour Record, etc.

LOUISON BOBET
Three times winner Tour de France
World's Road Champion
Bordeaux Paris, etc.

ROGER RIVIERE
World's Pursuit Champion
Hour Record, etc.

MICHEL ROUSSEAU
World's Sprint Champion

For 10 years every leading Continental star including KUBLER, KOBLET, WALKOWIAK, OCKERS, GEMINIANI, ANGLADE, HASSENFORDER, DARRIGADE in addition to the WORLD CHAMPIONS above, and our own British star ROBINSON and the teams of ELSWICK-HOPPER, VIKING, LANGSETT, WILSON, ELLIS-BRIGGS, OVALTINE-ALP, GEMINIANI - St. RAPHAEL, MOTTRAM, RORY O'BRIEN, ILSLEY-MAITLAND, etc., etc., have proved by their choice that TA chainwheels are a must in every racing cyclist's equipment.

Remember only TA can give you these exclusive features :—

* Made in CEDEGUR forged duralumin - unrivalled in the World for lightness and long-life. Beware of imitations - no dural is equal to CEDEGUR in any respect.

* Adaptor sets have a continuous double flanged rim giving incomparable rigidity. Obviously rings mounted in any other way cannot remain as true.

* Adaptor chainrings are easily obtainable throughout the world at reasonable prices and have the advantage of fitting either 3 or 5-pin crank adaptors.

* TA single, double, triple chainwheels and adaptor sets fit ALL POPULAR cranks, both steel or dural, cottered or cotterless types. No need to buy special cranks for TA chainwheels.

* There is a range of chainwheels to suit every purpose, touring, clubriding or racing, in sizes from 26 to 68 teeth, single, double or triple pattern.

* Assembly of all double and triple chainwheels is by standard 6 sided round headed bolts and slotted flush fitting nuts. No need for special assembly tools.

TA employ no professional riders — their products are used entirely on merit.

15

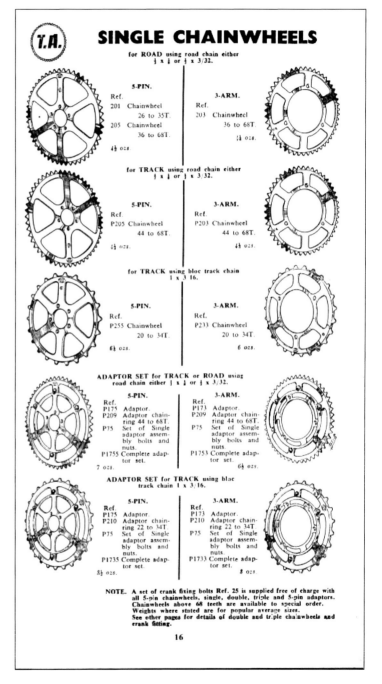

16

DOUBLE & TRIPLE CHAINWHEELS
FOR RACING

Type PROFESSIONEL

as used by Professional, Independant and 1st Category amateurs.

Assembly on adaptor.

RANGE :— Minimum 44 T.
Maximum 68 T.

Note :—There is a difference in inner and outer chainrings. Always specify exact requirements and quote reference

8½ ozs.

8 ozs.

5-PIN

Ref.
2175 Double adaptor set complete.
3175 Triple adaptor set complete.
175 Adaptor only.
104 Outer adaptor chainring.
106 Inner adaptor chainring.
62 Set assembly bolts etc. (Doubles)
84 Set assembly bolts etc. (Triples)
25 Set of fixing bolts to crank.

3-ARM.

Ref.
2173 Double adaptor set complete.
3173 Triple adaptor set complete.
173 Adaptor only.
104 Outer adaptor chainring.
106 Inner adaptor chainring.
62 Set assembly bolts etc. (Doubles)
84 Set assembly bolts etc. (Triples)

Ref. 104
Outer chainring crank side

Ref. 106
Inner chainring

Type CRITERIUM

as used by amateurs of all categories.

RANGE :— Inner 44 T upwards.
Outer 47 to 68 T.

8 ozs.

7½ ozs.

5-PIN.

Ref.
2205 Double chainwheel complete.
3205 Triple chainwheel complete.
CR 205 Outer chainring only.
204 Inner chainring only.
64 Set assembly bolts etc. (Double)
85 Set assembly bolts etc. (Triple)
25 Set of fixing bolts to crank.

3-ARM.

Ref.
2203 Double chainwheel complete.
3203 Triple chainwheel complete.
CR 203 Outer chainring only.
204 Inner chainring only.
64 Set assembly bolts etc. (Double)
85 Set assembly bolts etc. (Triple)

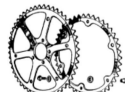

NOTE. A set of crank fixing bolts Ref. 25 is supplied free of charge with all 5-pin chainwheels, single, double, triple and 5-pin adaptors.

Chainwheels above 68 teeth are available to special order.

Weights where stated are for popular average sizes.

Only ⅛ x 3/32 chains are recommended for double and triple chainwheels and therefore doubles and triples are only stocked in this fitting. (See other page for details of single chainwheels.)

See next page for details of crank fitting.

17

DOUBLE & TRIPLE CHAINWHEELS
FOR CLUBRIDING & TOURING

Type RANDONNEUR.

as used by clubriders.

RANGE :— Inner 36 to 43 T.
Outer 44 to 68 T.

7½ ozs.

7½ ozs.

5 - PIN	**3 - ARM**
Ref. 2215 Double chainwheel complete.	Ref. 2213 Double chainwheel complete.

3215 Triple chainwheel complete.
RA 205 Outer chainring only.
206 Inner chainring only.
64 Set assembly bolts etc. (Double)
85 Set assembly bolts etc. (Triple)
25 Set fixing bolts to crank.

3213 Triple chainwheel complete.
RA 203 Outer chainring only.
206 Inner chainring only.
64 Set assembly bolts etc. (Double).
85 Set assembly bolts etc. (Triple).

Type CYCLOTOURISTE

for all home and overseas touring.

5 - PIN ONLY

RANGE :— Doubles. Inner 26 to 35 T.
Outer 40 to 56 T.
Triples. Outer 40 to 56 T.
1st Inner 30 to 42 T.
2nd Inner 26 to 35 T.

7½ ozs.

8½ ozs.

5 - PIN DOUBLE

Ref.
2235 Double chainwheel complete.
CY 205 Outer chainring only.
207 Inner chainring only.
64 Set assembly bolts etc.
25 Set fixing bolts to crank.

TCY Outer chainring only.
208 2nd Inner chainring only.
208 1st Inner chainring only.

5 - PIN TRIPLE

Ref.
3235 Triple chainwheel complete.
TCY 205 Outer chainring only.
208 1st Inner chainring only.
208 2nd Inner chainring only.
87 Set assembly bolts etc.
25 Set fixing bolts to crank.

208 1st Inner and 208 2nd Inner chainrings are identical but there is a price increase over 35 T.

NOTE :—A set of crank fixing bolts Ref. 25 is supplied free of charge with all 5-pin chainwheels, single, double, triple and 5-pin adaptors.

Chainwheels above 68 teeth are available to special order.

Weights where stated are for popular average sizes.

Only ⅛ x 3/32 chains are recommended for double and triple chainwheels and therefore doubles and triples are only stocked in this fitting. (See other page for details of single chainwheels).

CRANK FITTING.

TA chainwheels and adaptors will fit the following popular makes of cranks.

3-Arm Pattern.

MILREMO - DUPRAT - DURAX - STRONGLIGHT - CINELLI GNUTTI - MAGISTRONI etc.

5-Pin Pattern.

MILREMO - DUPRAT - DURAX - STRONGLIGHT (type 45 cottered and 49D cotterless) - T.A. - GNUTTI - WILLIAMS.

NOTE :—TA Rings will not fit CAMPAGNOLO or STRONGLIGHT 57 cranks.

18

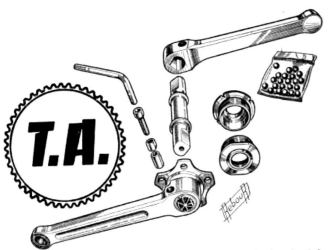

The T.A. Crank Set — offering the first original ideas to be introduced in crank design for 25 years.

No other crank set can offer you all these superb 12 star features.

* Constructed in the famous **T.A.** French duralumin, respected throughout the world for it's unique qualities.
* Right hand crank is designed to take **any** 5-pin fixing chainwheel — no need to buy special rings.
* Axle and cranks are accurately matched together on a right-angled spline, thus ensuring at all times a correct solid drive.
* Cranks are pinned to the axle by a neat securing bolt, collar and threaded bush inserted in the usual cotter pin hole, locating against a small flat on the axle opposite the right angle. (See small inset illustration.)
* A half turn, anti-clockwise of the securing bolt, so easing the tension, allows the crank to slide laterally on the axle enabling exact chainline to be obtained. This movement is 4 mm. Subsequent tightening of the securing bolt locks the crank into the desired position.
* No extractor or elaborate tool set required. The small Allen key provided unscrews the securing bolt and allows the crank to be easily removed.
* No axle end bolts requiring constant attention.
* A permanent attractive coloured **T.A.** badge is fixed over the usual crank axle hole — no detachable dust cap is necessary.
* Replaceable washer set in a recess protects the crank dural. from damage by the pedal spindle.
* The back of the pedal spindle hole is neatly blanked off for protection.
* All bearing surfaces are highly polished and coated with special hard chrome. A set of balls is included.
* All exterior parts are completely rustless and in a highly polished finish.

T.A. cranks are available in the following lengths :—
 160, 165, 170, 175 and 180 mm.

Crank set Ref. 755 TRACK has clearance for single chainwheel.

Crank set Ref. 1500 ROAD has clearance for double and triple chainwheels.

Bracket axles are available in 3 lengths :—
 Ref. P315 TRACK — 345 ROAD — 375 TRIPLE.

Weight :— Pair of cranks only 12½ ozs. — Complete crank set including bracket set, balls and Allen key 27½ ozs.

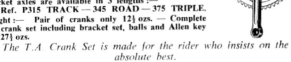

The T.A. Crank Set is made for the rider who insists on the absolute best.

19

BRITISH IS NO LONGER BEST

The response of the British cycle components industry to the increasing preference for continental products starting at the end of the 1940s

Introduction

The scope of this article is to look at the response of the British components industry to the increasing popularity of continental lightweight parts. Towards the end of the 1940s/early '50s the British components industry began to lose its dominant position as club cyclists began to prefer European equipment. In an attempt to counter this some companies copied continental designs or used the magic word continental in their marketing.

Background

Prior to WW2 imported equipment was a rarity. Import tax was high, making prices much higher, and the volumes were small. It was extremely unusual for cycles to be equipped with non-British parts. It was only the smaller more innovative companies who offered continental equipment as an option, examples being Rensch, Hobbs, Claud Butler and Hetchins. In 1935 BSA considered offering a model with the Italian Vittoria Margherita gear but this was never marketed.

There was prevailing view that British was best, this was particularly true with respect to gearing; the British cyclist had no need of the crude chain shifting devises of the French. Cliff Pratt, founder of the CTC York Rally and Hull cycle dealer, describes how in November 1929 he was one of the very first British cyclists to fit a variable gear (a French Standard Cyclo) and just how unusual this was with most club riders on fixed, it being unacceptable at the time to turn up for a club ride with a Sturmey. He described the gear as revolutionising his cycling[1]. The contrasting French and British attitudes to gears are extremely well documented in Frank Berto's *The Dancing Chain*[2].

The major change in post-war attitudes began during WW2 and reflected the great level of social change leading to the landslide Labour victory in 1945. Soldiers returning from the war were dissatisfied with the old order and ways and keen for change.

The image of cycling was important in determining attitudes. In Britain it was seen as utilitarian but in Europe as attractive mainly due to the road-racing scene. Post-war import restrictions merely made continental equipment more desirable; 'you want what you can't have'. Ron Kitching autobiography A Wheel in Two Worlds has some now almost hard to believe examples about the draconian customs rules. In the early post-war period he pretty much had to smuggle equipment in. There was probably also an element of the grass is always greener on the other side.

Throughout much of the 1950s the cycling establishment still clung to the view that British were best. A good example can be found in the review of the 1955 Paris Show in the CTC Gazette[3] by the secretary Reg Shaw. The tone of the article is clear from the title; 'On the whole we do things rather better over here'.

Whilst admitting that specialist builders like Rene Herse and Alec Singer produced an excellent product, the reader was left in no doubt that French products were inferior. Even where it was admitted we had copied, the British version was superior. Re-reading these articles it seems very strange that a review of the Paris show would concentrate on British products e.g. Brooks and Raleigh. However this can at least be partly explained by the fact that at the time it was seen as the Press's job to encourage people to buy British.

The CTC had instituted an award pre-war for the great improvement in cycle component design . The only made one award post world war two and that was basically for a pre-war product; Chater Lea pedals. This was despite the huge amount of innovation of the period

Many British companies were slow to innovate, for example:

1. With the resumption in production after the war many companies merely offered their pre-war range, eg Brampton.

2. Before 1955 British Cyclo mainly made gears for 1/8 in. chain/cogs although riders were moving to 3/32 in. The Standard Cyclo was never made in Britain in 3/32 in.

3. Prior to 1954 no Raleigh bike was supplied fitted with a derailleur.

4. Many of the major British companies were behind their continental counterparts in their use of new materials e.g. aluminium alloys.

There was innovation mainly amongst the smaller companies e.g. Harden (hubs and bottom brackets), Strata (brakes, handlebars, stems and toe clips) and GB (brakes and handlebars). However, many of the newer companies did not last long in the cycle trade e.g. Shelwin only made their innovative hubs with the angled flanges in 1948/9. The cycle trade was just not found to be profitable; a classic example being Harden who grossly over estimated the demand for their hubs.

British conservatism comes to the fore in numerous reviews of products especially if they are not steel. During the post-war period one reads comments like:

'I have come to the conclusion that in recent years the use of aluminium has been overdone except for machines the rider is prepared to nurse[4].

It is important to note that not all cyclists had the same attitude. The keenest to embrace continental ideas were the BLRC riders whose whole approach to the sport was derived from Europe. Time trialists were slower but began gradually to appreciate the benefits of lighter and more efficient equipment. It was the touring cyclist who was most resistant. For them durability was more important than any weight saved by using alloy. There was a fear that alloy was simply not strong enough especially for rims and bars. W. Paul the founder of the Rough Stuff Fellowship writing in The Bicycle in 1954 linked the lack of interest in off-road riding to the continental influence:

'I wonder if the modern lightweight with its

Fig. 1 Shelwin hub. Note the unique angled flanges

continental this and super that prompts the rider to keep to the billiard table surfaces of modern tarmac[5].

The British Response

Products

During the late 1940s most components companies were required to concentrate on exports, this starved the home market. Supply only really caught up with demand in 1950. Many adverts of the period stress that export has priority and goods may not be in stock. In an advertisement for Airlite hubs in 1948[6] British Hub Company stressed that although items were in short supply: *'our fair distribution system is strictly adhered to'*.

Sturmey Archer ran an advert from 1946 to 1949, which consisted of a dialogue between a cyclist and a dealer on the benefits of using a Sturmey (often a clubman's model e.g., ASC, AM or FM)

but ending with the punch-line: *'Stocks are difficult to obtain at the moment but I'll put your name on a waiting list.*

Lucas ran an advertisement featuring a picture of some beef steaks explaining that the priority being given to export was enabling the British population to put meat on the table. The clear

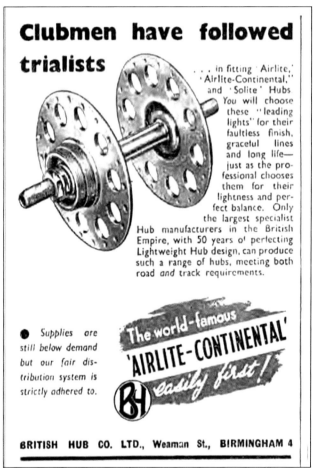

Fig. 2 This BHC advertisement still stresses that supplies remain limited (*Cycling* May 18, 1949)

assumption behind the advertisement was the reader would understand food was more important than cycle parts and would be perfectly content to wait.

With the increasing economic prosperity import restrictions were eased with the result that for the first time continental products became widely available. Gnutti hubs and chainsets and San Georgio rims were amongst the first products to be both available and affordable. I came across a good example of this when clearing out a cycle shop in Leighton Buzzard, HGS which in the immediate post war period was one of the major lightweight shops in the country. Looking through some old ledgers I was struck by the fact until c1948 everything was British. Then suddenly foreign names start appearing in significant quantities. In additional to the Italian names above, French manufacturers appear such as; Exceltoo (hubs), Atom (hubs and freewheels) and Prior (hubs and bottom brackets). Prices are about 20% above domestic products but judging by the volumes of sales plenty of riders were willing to pay this premium.

It was not until a couple of years later that British companies began to offer continental styled products. The reminder of this article discusses some examples:

Bracket Axles

Bayliss Wiley numbers 14 and 23 cottered bottom bracket axles. With the increasing popularity of derailleurs there was a demand for longer bottom bracket axles. The no. 23 was for a 4/5 speed and the no.14 for a double chainwheel. Until 1953 they had offered for lightweights only the

no.15 with ngcc (none gear case clearance). BW also produced a cottered axle, no. 8 for the slightly wider continental bottom brackets shells (70 mm as opposed to 68 mm) and wider on the gear side. This was for the 5 pin Stronglight design used by Gnutti, Duprat, and Durax etc and later by Milremo and TA.

Large Flange Hubs

Since the 1930s large flange hubs were known in Britain as 'the continental'. It is not entirely clear which continental hub this was derived from. It may have been Prior (French) who in the '30s marketed very large riveted flanged hubs. To meet the demands of fashion in the late '30s the British Hub Company (BHC) riveted flanges to the Airlite to create the first version of the Airlite Continental. These are now very sought after by collectors, but have a major flaw in that after prolonged use the rivets work loose. Post-war the Airlite Continental

Fig. 3 Pre-war Airlite Continental with riveted flanges

was a three-piece steel barrel on alloy flanges. In the mid '50s BHC introduced the Racelite a copy of large flange Normandy and other similar French hubs. BHC marketed the Racelite as the first single piece British alloy hub. Other companies like Resilion, Powell, Coventry Ultralite and BW offered large flange hubs marketed as Continental.

Headsets

Brampton Alatet with its knurled screwed race and toothed lock-ring washer, was a direct of copy of the Stronglight which had been made since the late 1930s.[7]

Fig. 4 Bayliss Wiley Continental large flange hub. Slightly smaller flange than Airlite. Similar quality but cheaper

According to the review of its introduction at the London show in the *CTC Gazette* in December 1952[8]:

Fig. 5 Post-war Airlite Continental three-piece, quick release version

'It might be said that the fundamental idea of the new Alatet head fitting that Brampton have introduced is Continental in origin, but nobody over there has ever produced it in better form'.

However most riders viewed it as an inferior product due to the knurled teeth wearing allowing the screwed race to come loose.

TDC, who took over from both Brampton and BW in early '60s, marketed their more expensive headsets with Italian sounding names eg Prima and Italia.

Quick Release hubs

BHC offered a q/r using the Airlite design. These are easily identifiable having BHC on the skewer tip. They used a British thread so the locknut end is not interchangeable with any other make, all of which were continental. According to the 1962 *Holdsworthy Aids*[9] at 80/-, these were 8/- more expensive than the Campagnolo Grand Sport. Both hubs were three pieces with steel barrels so I suspect by this time most cyclists would have opted for the cheaper Italian product. As a consequence of their rarity they have become sought after by some of the 'gen' lightweight collectors. However, in one aspect, the British product was superior; the quality of the chroming.

I have seen Harden hubs with quick release axles and BHC skewers, however these were home modifications.

BSA and Constrictor quick release hubs

In 1953 BSA marketed a front hub, which could be removed leaving the track nuts attached

Fig. 7 Post-war Airlite small flange three-piece, quick release version

to the forks. As a spanner was still needed for wheel removal it was hardly quick! Constrictor never made a quick release hub rather, from 1955, they offered a conversion for the rear hub. This was very similar to a pre-war conversion offered by Chater Lea. According to the 1962 *Holdsworthy Bike Riders Aids*:

'the Q/R skewer is wound out of the hub by means of a short lever and withdrawn. This allows the wheel to drop out, but leaves the fixing nuts in position so the wheel is automatically returned to the same position'.

Gears

With the introduction of the Campagnolo Grand Sport parallelogram rear mechanism in the mid-'50s plunger type gears became obsolete. The major British manufacturer of gears, Cyclo, made a somewhat belated response in 1960 by offering the Super 60 and P2 (the economy version). These were essentially copies of the Grand Sport, but the Super 60 has some additional features notably an angle arm adjustment. By this time club riders had gone over en mass to continental gears; Campagnolo for those who could afford them and Simplex and Huret for those who could not. These were the last British made gears and after this Cyclo concentrated on spares and tools.

Conclusion

Looking back, the decline in the British cycle components industry started in the early '50s and continued at an increasing pace. Partly it could be blamed in the rise of the motor car. Ron Kitching blames the decline on the monopoly position of

Raleigh by the late 1950s, which enabled them to force down supplier prices to such a point they could not remain in business. He illustrates the decline with reference to his *Everything Cycling* catalogues: in 1948 this featured 120 British companies, in 1988 only 13.

The decline also has its roots in the lack of innovation and the failure of British companies to follow market trends often for lighter more stylish products.

Bayliss Wiley ceased to make cycle parts around 1960; BHC ceased at the end of the '60s. Even adding the magic word continental to products was not enough to save them.

References

1. Cliff Pratt, *Sixty Six Years as a Cycle Tourist*, pp 5/6, 1994, Pentland Press.
2. Frank Berto, *The Dancing Chain*, 2005, pp 91–94 and 103–5.
3. *CTC Gazette,* November 1955, pp 362– 367.
4. *CTC Gazette,* November 1952, p806.
5. *The Bicycle*, 27 October 1954, p13.
6. *Cycling*, 26 May 1948, p4.
7. *The Data Book*, p77, Cycling Resources. (Japanese published reprint of old catalogues and magazines. The relevant section is from Le Cycle 1947 a Daniel Rebour drawing of a Stronglight headset.)
8. *CTC Gazette*, December 1952, p866.
9. Holdsworthy, *Bike Riders Aids,* 1949 to 1976. (A cursory glance reveals a steady decline in British products both in volume and prominence.)

Acknowledgements

Permission to use images from the Classic Lightweights website: Peter Underwood.

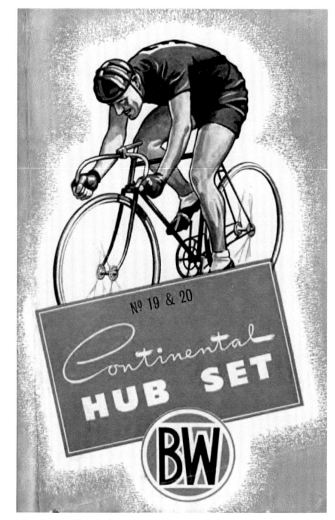

Fig. 7 Bayliss Wiley large flange hubs note the magical word continental as a selling point